Just The Facts 101
Textbook Key Facts

Us National Counter Terrorism Center Handbook

by Cram101
Texbook NOT Included

Table of Contents

Title Page

Copyright

Foundations of Business

Management

Business law

Finance

Human resource management

Information systems

Marketing

Manufacturing

Commerce

Business ethics

Accounting

Index: Answers

Just The Facts101

Exam Prep for

Us National Counter Terrorism Center Handbook

Just The Facts101 Exam Prep is your link from
the textbook and lecture to your exams.

**Just The Facts101 Exam Preps are unauthorized and comprehensive reviews
of your textbooks.**

All material provided by CTI Publications (c) 2019

Textbook publishers and textbook authors do not participate in or contribute to these reviews.

Just The Facts101 Exam Prep

Copyright © 2019 by CTI Publications. All rights reserved.

eAIN 449627

Foundations of Business

A business, also known as an enterprise, agency or a firm, is an entity involved in the provision of goods and/or services to consumers. Businesses are prevalent in capitalist economies, where most of them are privately owned and provide goods and services to customers in exchange for other goods, services, or money.

:: Accounting terminology ::

_____ is a legally enforceable claim for payment held by a business for goods supplied and/or services rendered that customers/clients have ordered but not paid for. These are generally in the form of invoices raised by a business and delivered to the customer for payment within an agreed time frame. _____ is shown in a balance sheet as an asset. It is one of a series of accounting transactions dealing with the billing of a customer for goods and services that the customer has ordered. These may be distinguished from notes receivable, which are debts created through formal legal instruments called promissory notes.

Exam Probability: **Medium**

1. *Answer choices:*

(see index for correct answer)

- a. Fund accounting
- b. Accounts receivable
- c. Enterprise liquidity
- d. Cash flow management

Guidance: level 1

:: Management ::

_____ is the process of thinking about the activities required to achieve a desired goal. It is the first and foremost activity to achieve desired results. It involves the creation and maintenance of a plan, such as psychological aspects that require conceptual skills. There are even a couple of tests to measure someone's capability of _____ well. As such, _____ is a fundamental property of intelligent behavior. An important further meaning, often just called " _____ " is the legal context of permitted building developments.

Exam Probability: **Low**

2. *Answer choices:*

(see index for correct answer)

- a. Statistical process control
- b. Business rule mining
- c. Planning
- d. Communications management

Guidance: level 1

:: Decision theory ::

A _____ is a deliberate system of principles to guide decisions and achieve rational outcomes. A _____ is a statement of intent, and is implemented as a procedure or protocol. Policies are generally adopted by a governance body within an organization. Policies can assist in both subjective and objective decision making. Policies to assist in subjective decision making usually assist senior management with decisions that must be based on the relative merits of a number of factors, and as a result are often hard to test objectively, e.g. work-life balance _____ . In contrast policies to assist in objective decision making are usually operational in nature and can be objectively tested, e.g. password _____ .

Exam Probability: **Medium**

3. *Answer choices:*

(see index for correct answer)

- a. Value of information
- b. Decision-matrix method
- c. Rational planning model
- d. Policy

Guidance: level 1

:: Business ethics ::

_____ is a type of harassment technique that relates to a sexual nature and the unwelcome or inappropriate promise of rewards in exchange for sexual favors. _____ includes a range of actions from mild transgressions to sexual abuse or assault. Harassment can occur in many different social settings such as the workplace, the home, school, churches, etc. Harassers or victims may be of any gender.

Exam Probability: **Low**

4. *Answer choices:*

(see index for correct answer)

- a. Repugnant market
- b. Terror-free investing
- c. Sexual harassment
- d. Corporate sustainability

Guidance: level 1

:: Regression analysis ::

A _____ often refers to a set of documented requirements to be satisfied by a material, design, product, or service. A _____ is often a type of technical standard.

Exam Probability: **Low**

5. *Answer choices:*

(see index for correct answer)

- a. Smoothing spline
- b. Hat matrix
- c. Specification
- d. Residual sum of squares

Guidance: level 1

:: Marketing techniques ::

> _____ is the activity of dividing a broad consumer or business market, normally consisting of existing and potential customers, into sub-groups of consumers based on some type of shared characteristics. In dividing or segmenting markets, researchers typically look for common characteristics such as shared needs, common interests, similar lifestyles or even similar demographic profiles. The overall aim of segmentation is to identify high yield segments – that is, those segments that are likely to be the most profitable or that have growth potential – so that these can be selected for special attention.

Exam Probability: **High**

6. *Answer choices:*

(see index for correct answer)

- a. Social media in the fashion industry
- b. Market segmentation

- c. Enterprise engagement
- d. Product displacement

Guidance: level 1

:: Materials ::

A _____ , also known as a feedstock, unprocessed material, or primary commodity, is a basic material that is used to produce goods, finished products, energy, or intermediate materials which are feedstock for future finished products. As feedstock, the term connotes these materials are bottleneck assets and are highly important with regard to producing other products. An example of this is crude oil, which is a _____ and a feedstock used in the production of industrial chemicals, fuels, plastics, and pharmaceutical goods; lumber is a _____ used to produce a variety of products including all types of furniture. The term " _____ " denotes materials in minimally processed or unprocessed in states; e.g., raw latex, crude oil, cotton, coal, raw biomass, iron ore, air, logs, or water i.e. "...any product of agriculture, forestry, fishing and any other mineral that is in its natural form or which has undergone the transformation required to prepare it for internationally marketing in substantial volumes."

Exam Probability: **Low**

7. *Answer choices:*
(see index for correct answer)

- a. Mesoporous material
- b. Slurry
- c. Whitetopping

- d. Raw material

Guidance: level 1

:: Globalization-related theories ::

> _____ is an economic system based on the private ownership of the means of production and their operation for profit. Characteristics central to _____ include private property, capital accumulation, wage labor, voluntary exchange, a price system, and competitive markets. In a capitalist market economy, decision-making and investment are determined by every owner of wealth, property or production ability in financial and capital markets, whereas prices and the distribution of goods and services are mainly determined by competition in goods and services markets.

Exam Probability: **Low**

8. *Answer choices:*
(see index for correct answer)

- a. post-industrial
- b. postmodernism
- c. Capitalism

Guidance: level 1

:: Social security ::

_____ is "any government system that provides monetary assistance to people with an inadequate or no income." In the United States, this is usually called welfare or a social safety net, especially when talking about Canada and European countries.

Exam Probability: **High**

9. *Answer choices:*
(see index for correct answer)

- a. Child benefit
- b. South African Social Security Agency
- c. Employees%27 State Insurance
- d. Social security

Guidance: level 1

:: Currency ::

A _____ , in the most specific sense is money in any form when in use or circulation as a medium of exchange, especially circulating banknotes and coins. A more general definition is that a _____ is a system of money in common use, especially for people in a nation. Under this definition, US dollars , pounds sterling , Australian dollars , European euros , Russian rubles and Indian Rupees are examples of currencies. These various currencies are recognized as stores of value and are traded between nations in foreign exchange markets, which determine the relative values of the different currencies. Currencies in this sense are defined by governments, and each type has limited boundaries of acceptance.

Exam Probability: **Low**

10. *Answer choices:*

(see index for correct answer)

- a. Monetary sovereignty
- b. De facto currency
- c. Nomisma
- d. Currency

Guidance: level 1

:: Packaging ::

In work place, _____ or job _____ means good ranking with the hypothesized conception of requirements of a role. There are two types of job _____ s: contextual and task. Task _____ is related to cognitive ability while contextual _____ is dependent upon personality. Task _____ are behavioral roles that are recognized in job descriptions and by remuneration systems, they are directly related to organizational _____ ; whereas, contextual _____ are value based and additional behavioral roles that are not recognized in job descriptions and covered by compensation; they are extra roles that are indirectly related to organizational _____ . Citizenship _____ like contextual _____ means a set of individual activity/contribution that supports the organizational culture.

Exam Probability: **High**

11. *Answer choices:*

(see index for correct answer)

- a. Bottle variation
- b. Performance
- c. Hydration pack
- d. Communication design

Guidance: level 1

:: Management occupations ::

_____ is the process of designing, launching and running a new business, which is often initially a small business. The people who create these businesses are called entrepreneurs.

Exam Probability: **Low**

12. *Answer choices:*

(see index for correct answer)

- a. Corporate trainer
- b. Director of nursing
- c. Adjutant general
- d. Entrepreneurship

Guidance: level 1

:: ::

_____ is the production of products for use or sale using labour and machines, tools, chemical and biological processing, or formulation. The term may refer to a range of human activity, from handicraft to high tech, but is most commonly applied to industrial design, in which raw materials are transformed into finished goods on a large scale. Such finished goods may be sold to other manufacturers for the production of other, more complex products, such as aircraft, household appliances, furniture, sports equipment or automobiles, or sold to wholesalers, who in turn sell them to retailers, who then sell them to end users and consumers.

Exam Probability: **Low**

13. *Answer choices:*

(see index for correct answer)

- a. interpersonal communication
- b. Manufacturing
- c. open system
- d. deep-level diversity

Guidance: level 1

:: Commerce ::

_____ relates to "the exchange of goods and services, especially on a large scale". It includes legal, economic, political, social, cultural and technological systems that operate in a country or in international trade.

Exam Probability: **High**

14. *Answer choices:*

(see index for correct answer)

- a. Commerce
- b. Group buying
- c. Too cheap to meter
- d. Oniomania

Guidance: level 1

:: Supply chain management terms ::

In business and finance, _____ is a system of organizations, people, activities, information, and resources involved in moving a product or service from supplier to customer. _____ activities involve the transformation of natural resources, raw materials, and components into a finished product that is delivered to the end customer. In sophisticated _____ systems, used products may re-enter the _____ at any point where residual value is recyclable. _____ s link value chains.

Exam Probability: **Medium**

15. *Answer choices:*

(see index for correct answer)

- a. Widget
- b. Consumable
- c. Last mile
- d. Consumables

Guidance: level 1

:: Elementary arithmetic ::

In mathematics, a _____ is a number or ratio expressed as a fraction of 100. It is often denoted using the percent sign, "%", or the abbreviations "pct.", "pct"; sometimes the abbreviation "pc" is also used. A _____ is a dimensionless number.

Exam Probability: **High**

16. *Answer choices:*

(see index for correct answer)

- a. Square number
- b. Mediant
- c. Percentage
- d. 0

Guidance: level 1

:: Information systems ::

_____ are formal, sociotechnical, organizational systems designed to collect, process, store, and distribute information. In a sociotechnical perspective, _____ are composed by four components: task, people, structure, and technology.

Exam Probability: **Medium**

17. *Answer choices:*

(see index for correct answer)

- a. ISCRAM
- b. Hospital information system
- c. Trust management
- d. Information systems

Guidance: level 1

:: Retailing ::

_____ is the process of selling consumer goods or services to customers through multiple channels of distribution to earn a profit. _____ ers satisfy demand identified through a supply chain. The term "_____ er" is typically applied where a service provider fills the small orders of a large number of individuals, who are end-users, rather than large orders of a small number of wholesale, corporate or government clientele. Shopping generally refers to the act of buying products. Sometimes this is done to obtain final goods, including necessities such as food and clothing; sometimes it takes place as a recreational activity. Recreational shopping often involves window shopping and browsing: it does not always result in a purchase.

Exam Probability: **Low**

18. *Answer choices:*

(see index for correct answer)

- a. Shop in a box
- b. Retail
- c. Tourist trap
- d. Strip mall

Guidance: level 1

:: Private equity ::

_____ is a type of private equity, a form of financing that is provided by firms or funds to small, early-stage, emerging firms that are deemed to have high growth potential, or which have demonstrated high growth. _____ firms or funds invest in these early-stage companies in exchange for equity, or an ownership stake, in the companies they invest in. _____ists take on the risk of financing risky start-ups in the hopes that some of the firms they support will become successful. Because startups face high uncertainty, VC investments do have high rates of failure. The start-ups are usually based on an innovative technology or business model and they are usually from the high technology industries, such as information technology, clean technology or biotechnology.

Exam Probability: **High**

19. *Answer choices:*

(see index for correct answer)

- a. Venture capital
- b. History of private equity and venture capital
- c. Management fee
- d. Public Market Equivalent

Guidance: level 1

:: Project management ::

A _____ is a source or supply from which a benefit is produced and it has some utility. _____ s can broadly be classified upon their availability—they are classified into renewable and non-renewable _____ s. Examples of non renewable _____ s are coal ,crude oil natural gas nuclear energy etc. Examples of renewable _____ s are air,water,wind,solar energy etc. They can also be classified as actual and potential on the basis of level of development and use, on the basis of origin they can be classified as biotic and abiotic, and on the basis of their distribution, as ubiquitous and localized . An item becomes a _____ with time and developing technology. Typically, _____ s are materials, energy, services, staff, knowledge, or other assets that are transformed to produce benefit and in the process may be consumed or made unavailable. Benefits of _____ utilization may include increased wealth, proper functioning of a system, or enhanced well-being. From a human perspective a natural _____ is anything obtained from the environment to satisfy human needs and wants. From a broader biological or ecological perspective a _____ satisfies the needs of a living organism .

Exam Probability: **High**

20. *Answer choices:*

(see index for correct answer)

- a. The Transformation Project
- b. Project cancellation
- c. Resource
- d. Multidisciplinary approach

Guidance: level 1

:: Stock market ::

A _____, equity market or share market is the aggregation of buyers and sellers of stocks, which represent ownership claims on businesses; these may include securities listed on a public stock exchange, as well as stock that is only traded privately. Examples of the latter include shares of private companies which are sold to investors through equity crowdfunding platforms. Stock exchanges list shares of common equity as well as other security types, e.g. corporate bonds and convertible bonds.

Exam Probability: **Low**

21. *Answer choices:*

(see index for correct answer)

- a. Stock market
- b. Control premium
- c. Thinkorswim
- d. Issued shares

Guidance: level 1

:: Classification systems ::

_____ is the practice of comparing business processes and performance metrics to industry bests and best practices from other companies. Dimensions typically measured are quality, time and cost.

Exam Probability: **High**

22. *Answer choices:*

(see index for correct answer)

- a. Galaxy morphological classification
- b. Garside classification
- c. International Standard Classification of Education
- d. British undergraduate degree classification

Guidance: level 1

:: Business ::

The seller, or the provider of the goods or services, completes a sale in response to an acquisition, appropriation, requisition or a direct interaction with the buyer at the point of sale. There is a passing of title of the item, and the settlement of a price, in which agreement is reached on a price for which transfer of ownership of the item will occur. The seller, not the purchaser typically executes the sale and it may be completed prior to the obligation of payment. In the case of indirect interaction, a person who sells goods or service on behalf of the owner is known as a salesman or saleswoman or salesperson, but this often refers to someone _____ goods in a store/shop, in which case other terms are also common, including salesclerk, shop assistant, and retail clerk.

Exam Probability: **Low**

23. *Answer choices:*

(see index for correct answer)

- a. Selling
- b. Joint employment
- c. Les Vergers du Mekong
- d. Kingdomality

Guidance: level 1

:: Consumer theory ::

A _____ is a technical term in psychology, economics and philosophy usually used in relation to choosing between alternatives. For example, someone prefers A over B if they would rather choose A than B.

Exam Probability: **Low**

24. *Answer choices:*

(see index for correct answer)

- a. Preference
- b. Demand set
- c. Income elasticity of demand
- d. Consumption

Guidance: level 1

:: Management ::

The _____ is a strategy performance management tool – a semi-standard structured report, that can be used by managers to keep track of the execution of activities by the staff within their control and to monitor the consequences arising from these actions.

Exam Probability: **High**

25. *Answer choices:*

(see index for correct answer)

- a. Kata
- b. Balanced scorecard
- c. Infrastructure asset management
- d. Business rule mining

Guidance: level 1

:: Corporate crime ::

_____ LLP, based in Chicago, was an American holding company. Formerly one of the "Big Five" accounting firms, the firm had provided auditing, tax, and consulting services to large corporations. By 2001, it had become one of the world's largest multinational companies.

Exam Probability: **Medium**

26. *Answer choices:*

(see index for correct answer)

- a. Arthur Andersen
- b. FirstEnergy
- c. Corporate Manslaughter and Corporate Homicide Act 2007
- d. Walter Forbes

Guidance: level 1

:: Free trade agreements ::

A _____ is a wide-ranging taxes, tariff and trade treaty that often includes investment guarantees. It exists when two or more countries agree on terms that helps them trade with each other. The most common _____ s are of the preferential and free trade types are concluded in order to reduce tariffs, quotas and other trade restrictions on items traded between the signatories.

Exam Probability: **Medium**

27. *Answer choices:*

(see index for correct answer)

- a. Ouchy Convention
- b. Trade, Development and Cooperation Agreement
- c. European Union Central American Association Agreement
- d. Trade agreement

Guidance: level 1

:: Human resource management ::

_____ are the people who make up the workforce of an organization, business sector, or economy. "Human capital" is sometimes used synonymously with " _____ ", although human capital typically refers to a narrower effect. Likewise, other terms sometimes used include manpower, talent, labor, personnel, or simply people.

Exam Probability: **Medium**

28. *Answer choices:*

(see index for correct answer)

- a. Human resources
- b. Employee exit management
- c. Organization chart
- d. Restructuring

Guidance: level 1

:: Marketing ::

The _____ is a foundation model for businesses. The _____ has been defined as the "set of marketing tools that the firm uses to pursue its marketing objectives in the target market". Thus the _____ refers to four broad levels of marketing decision, namely: product, price, place, and promotion. Marketing practice has been occurring for millennia, but marketing theory emerged in the early twentieth century. The contemporary _____ , or the 4 Ps, which has become the dominant framework for marketing management decisions, was first published in 1960. In services marketing, an extended _____ is used, typically comprising 7 Ps, made up of the original 4 Ps extended by process, people, and physical evidence. Occasionally service marketers will refer to 8 Ps, comprising these 7 Ps plus performance.

Exam Probability: **High**

29. *Answer choices:*

(see index for correct answer)

- a. Digital strategy
- b. Counteradvertising
- c. Gold party
- d. Marketing mix

Guidance: level 1

:: Management ::

A _____ is a formal written document containing business goals, the methods on how these goals can be attained, and the time frame within which these goals need to be achieved. It also describes the nature of the business, background information on the organization, the organization's financial projections, and the strategies it intends to implement to achieve the stated targets. In its entirety, this document serves as a road map that provides direction to the business.

Exam Probability: **High**

30. *Answer choices:*

(see index for correct answer)

- a. Business plan
- b. Maryland StateStat
- c. Intopia
- d. Executive compensation

Guidance: level 1

:: ::

An _____ is the production of goods or related services within an economy. The major source of revenue of a group or company is the indicator of its relevant _____ . When a large group has multiple sources of revenue generation, it is considered to be working in different industries. Manufacturing _____ became a key sector of production and labour in European and North American countries during the Industrial Revolution, upsetting previous mercantile and feudal economies. This came through many successive rapid advances in technology, such as the production of steel and coal.

Exam Probability: **Low**

31. *Answer choices:*

(see index for correct answer)

- a. hierarchical perspective
- b. Industry
- c. interpersonal communication
- d. imperative

Guidance: level 1

:: Unemployment ::

In economics, a _____ is a business cycle contraction when there is a general decline in economic activity. Macroeconomic indicators such as GDP, investment spending, capacity utilization, household income, business profits, and inflation fall, while bankruptcies and the unemployment rate rise. In the United Kingdom, it is defined as a negative economic growth for two consecutive quarters.

Exam Probability: **Low**

32. *Answer choices:*

(see index for correct answer)

- a. Reserve army of labour
- b. Employment-to-population ratio
- c. Recession
- d. Mount Street Club

Guidance: level 1

:: Market research ::

_____ is "the process or set of processes that links the producers, customers, and end users to the marketer through information used to identify and define marketing opportunities and problems; generate, refine, and evaluate marketing actions; monitor marketing performance; and improve understanding of marketing as a process. _____ specifies the information required to address these issues, designs the method for collecting information, manages and implements the data collection process, analyzes the results, and communicates the findings and their implications."

Exam Probability: **High**

33. *Answer choices:*

(see index for correct answer)

- a. News ratings in Australia
- b. Sociomapping
- c. Zyfin
- d. Marketing research

Guidance: level 1

:: Management ::

_____ is a process by which entities review the quality of all factors involved in production. ISO 9000 defines _____ as "A part of quality management focused on fulfilling quality requirements".

Exam Probability: **Low**

34. *Answer choices:*

(see index for correct answer)

- a. Business rule mining
- b. Success-oriented management
- c. Critical management studies
- d. Data Item Descriptions

Guidance: level 1

:: Bribery ::

_____ is the act of giving or receiving something of value in exchange for some kind of influence or action in return, that the recipient would otherwise not offer. _____ is defined by Black's Law Dictionary as the offering, giving, receiving, or soliciting of any item of value to influence the actions of an official or other person in charge of a public or legal duty. Essentially, _____ is offering to do something for someone for the expressed purpose of receiving something in exchange. Gifts of money or other items of value which are otherwise available to everyone on an equivalent basis, and not for dishonest purposes, is not _____. Offering a discount or a refund to all purchasers is a legal rebate and is not _____. For example, it is legal for an employee of a Public Utilities Commission involved in electric rate regulation to accept a rebate on electric service that reduces their cost for electricity, when the rebate is available to other residential electric customers. Giving the rebate to influence them to look favorably on the electric utility's rate increase applications, however, would be considered _____ .

Exam Probability: **High**

35. *Answer choices:*

(see index for correct answer)

- a. Bribery
- b. Kickback
- c. Holyland Case
- d. Katta Subramanya Naidu

Guidance: level 1

:: Stock market ::

A _____, securities exchange or bourse, is a facility where stock brokers and traders can buy and sell securities, such as shares of stock and bonds and other financial instruments. _____ s may also provide for facilities the issue and redemption of such securities and instruments and capital events including the payment of income and dividends. Securities traded on a _____ include stock issued by listed companies, unit trusts, derivatives, pooled investment products and bonds. _____ s often function as "continuous auction" markets with buyers and sellers consummating transactions via open outcry at a central location such as the floor of the exchange or by using an electronic trading platform.

Exam Probability: **Low**

36. *Answer choices:*

(see index for correct answer)

- a. Prospectus
- b. Tech Buzz
- c. Stock exchange
- d. PLUS Markets Group

Guidance: level 1

:: Alchemical processes ::

In chemistry, a _____ is a special type of homogeneous mixture composed of two or more substances. In such a mixture, a solute is a substance dissolved in another substance, known as a solvent. The mixing process of a _____ happens at a scale where the effects of chemical polarity are involved, resulting in interactions that are specific to solvation. The _____ assumes the phase of the solvent when the solvent is the larger fraction of the mixture, as is commonly the case. The concentration of a solute in a _____ is the mass of that solute expressed as a percentage of the mass of the whole _____ . The term aqueous _____ is when one of the solvents is water.

Exam Probability: **High**

37. *Answer choices:*

(see index for correct answer)

- a. Congelation
- b. Fixation
- c. Sublimation apparatus
- d. Solution

Guidance: level 1

:: Systems theory ::

A _____ is a set of policies, processes and procedures used by an organization to ensure that it can fulfill the tasks required to achieve its objectives. These objectives cover many aspects of the organization's operations. For instance, an environmental _____ enables organizations to improve their environmental performance and an occupational health and safety _____ enables an organization to control its occupational health and safety risks, etc.

Exam Probability: **Medium**

38. *Answer choices:*

(see index for correct answer)

- a. Black box
- b. subsystem
- c. decentralized system
- d. Management system

Guidance: level 1

:: Debt ::

_____ is when something, usually money, is owed by one party, the borrower or _____ or, to a second party, the lender or creditor. _____ is a deferred payment, or series of payments, that is owed in the future, which is what differentiates it from an immediate purchase. The _____ may be owed by sovereign state or country, local government, company, or an individual. Commercial _____ is generally subject to contractual terms regarding the amount and timing of repayments of principal and interest. Loans, bonds, notes, and mortgages are all types of _____ . The term can also be used metaphorically to cover moral obligations and other interactions not based on economic value. For example, in Western cultures, a person who has been helped by a second person is sometimes said to owe a " _____ of gratitude" to the second person.

Exam Probability: **Medium**

39. *Answer choices:*

(see index for correct answer)

- a. Household debt
- b. Perpetual subordinated debt
- c. Medical debt
- d. Debt

Guidance: level 1

:: Real estate valuation ::

_____ or OMV is the price at which an asset would trade in a competitive auction setting. _____ is often used interchangeably with open _____, fair value or fair _____, although these terms have distinct definitions in different standards, and may or may not differ in some circumstances.

Exam Probability: **Medium**

40. *Answer choices:*

(see index for correct answer)

- a. Rate base
- b. E.surv
- c. cap rate
- d. Market value

Guidance: level 1

:: Actuarial science ::

_____ is the possibility of losing something of value. Values can be gained or lost when taking _____ resulting from a given action or inaction, foreseen or unforeseen. _____ can also be defined as the intentional interaction with uncertainty. Uncertainty is a potential, unpredictable, and uncontrollable outcome; _____ is a consequence of action taken in spite of uncertainty.

Exam Probability: **Low**

41. *Answer choices:*

(see index for correct answer)

- a. Risk
- b. Mortality forecasting
- c. RiskMetrics
- d. Catastrophe modeling

Guidance: level 1

:: Business models ::

A _____, _____ company or daughter company is a company that is owned or controlled by another company, which is called the parent company, parent, or holding company. The _____ can be a company, corporation, or limited liability company. In some cases it is a government or state-owned enterprise. In some cases, particularly in the music and book publishing industries, subsidiaries are referred to as imprints.

Exam Probability: **Low**

42. *Answer choices:*

(see index for correct answer)

- a. Legacy carrier
- b. Subsidiary
- c. Lemonade stand
- d. Data as a service

Guidance: level 1

:: Property ::

The right to property or right to own property is often classified as a human right for natural persons regarding their possessions. A general recognition of a right to private property is found more rarely and is typically heavily constrained insofar as property is owned by legal persons and where it is used for production rather than consumption.

Exam Probability: **Medium**

43. *Answer choices:*

(see index for correct answer)

- a. Right to property
- b. Inalienable possessions
- c. Property rights
- d. Farhud

Guidance: level 1

:: International trade ::

An _____ is a good brought into a jurisdiction, especially across a national border, from an external source. The party bringing in the good is called an _____ er. An _____ in the receiving country is an export from the sending country. _____ ation and exportation are the defining financial transactions of international trade.

Exam Probability: **High**

44. Answer choices:

(see index for correct answer)

- a. Import
- b. Proexport
- c. Ecumenical Advocacy Alliance
- d. Technology gap

Guidance: level 1

:: Business models ::

_____ es are privately owned corporations, partnerships, or sole proprietorships that have fewer employees and/or less annual revenue than a regular-sized business or corporation. Businesses are defined as "small" in terms of being able to apply for government support and qualify for preferential tax policy varies depending on the country and industry. _____ es range from fifteen employees under the Australian Fair Work Act 2009, fifty employees according to the definition used by the European Union, and fewer than five hundred employees to qualify for many U.S. _____ Administration programs. While _____ es can also be classified according to other methods, such as annual revenues, shipments, sales, assets, or by annual gross or net revenue or net profits, the number of employees is one of the most widely used measures.

Exam Probability: **Low**

45. *Answer choices:*

(see index for correct answer)

- a. Volatility, uncertainty, complexity and ambiguity
- b. Small business
- c. Product-service system
- d. Independent business

Guidance: level 1

:: Employment ::

The _____ is an individual's metaphorical "journey" through learning, work and other aspects of life. There are a number of ways to define _____ and the term is used in a variety of ways.

Exam Probability: **High**

46. *Answer choices:*

(see index for correct answer)

- a. Ethical job
- b. Participatory ergonomics
- c. Career
- d. Monster Employment Index

Guidance: level 1

:: Asset ::

In financial accounting, an _____ is any resource owned by the business. Anything tangible or intangible that can be owned or controlled to produce value and that is held by a company to produce positive economic value is an _____. Simply stated, _____ s represent value of ownership that can be converted into cash. The balance sheet of a firm records the monetary value of the _____ s owned by that firm. It covers money and other valuables belonging to an individual or to a business.

Exam Probability: **High**

47. *Answer choices:*

(see index for correct answer)

- a. Asset
- b. Current asset

Guidance: level 1

:: Investment ::

In finance, the benefit from an _____ is called a return. The return may consist of a gain realised from the sale of property or an _____ , unrealised capital appreciation , or _____ income such as dividends, interest, rental income etc., or a combination of capital gain and income. The return may also include currency gains or losses due to changes in foreign currency exchange rates.

Exam Probability: **High**

48. *Answer choices:*

(see index for correct answer)

- a. Investment
- b. Individual Pension Plan
- c. Share Incentive Plan
- d. The Zulu Principle

Guidance: level 1

:: Finance ::

_____ is a field that is concerned with the allocation of assets and liabilities over space and time, often under conditions of risk or uncertainty. _____ can also be defined as the art of money management. Participants in the market aim to price assets based on their risk level, fundamental value, and their expected rate of return. _____ can be split into three sub-categories: public _____, corporate _____ and personal _____ .

Exam Probability: **High**

49. *Answer choices:*

(see index for correct answer)

- a. Finance
- b. Securitization
- c. Performance attribution
- d. Hamilton Community Foundation

Guidance: level 1

:: Association of Southeast Asian Nations ::

The Association of Southeast Asian Nations is a regional intergovernmental organization comprising ten countries in Southeast Asia, which promotes intergovernmental cooperation and facilitates economic, political, security, military, educational, and sociocultural integration among its members and other countries in Asia. It also regularly engages other countries in the Asia-Pacific region and beyond. A major partner of Shanghai Cooperation Organisation, _____ maintains a global network of alliances and dialogue partners and is considered by many as a global powerhouse, the central union for cooperation in Asia-Pacific, and a prominent and influential organization. It is involved in numerous international affairs, and hosts diplomatic missions throughout the world.

Exam Probability: **High**

50. *Answer choices:*

(see index for correct answer)

- a. The ASEAN Way
- b. Hanoi Plan of Action
- c. ASEAN Intergovernmental Commission on Human Rights
- d. ASEAN

Guidance: level 1

:: Macroeconomics ::

A foreign _____ is an investment in the form of a controlling ownership in a business in one country by an entity based in another country. It is thus distinguished from a foreign portfolio investment by a notion of direct control.

Exam Probability: **High**

51. *Answer choices:*

(see index for correct answer)

- a. Domestic liability dollarization
- b. Crowding out
- c. Absolute income hypothesis
- d. Direct investment

Guidance: level 1

:: Management ::

A _____ describes the rationale of how an organization creates, delivers, and captures value, in economic, social, cultural or other contexts. The process of _____ construction and modification is also called _____ innovation and forms a part of business strategy.

Exam Probability: **Medium**

52. *Answer choices:*

(see index for correct answer)

- a. Cross ownership
- b. Project management information system
- c. Business model
- d. Submission management

Guidance: level 1

:: Export and import control ::

" _____ " means the Government Service which is responsible for the administration of _____ law and the collection of duties and taxes and which also has the responsibility for the application of other laws and regulations relating to the importation, exportation, movement or storage of goods.

Exam Probability: **High**

53. *Answer choices:*

(see index for correct answer)

- a. Customs
- b. Neutron scanner
- c. Bureau of Industry and Security
- d. Riding officer

Guidance: level 1

:: Project management ::

_____ is the right to exercise power, which can be formalized by a state and exercised by way of judges, appointed executives of government, or the ecclesiastical or priestly appointed representatives of a God or other deities.

Exam Probability: **High**

54. *Answer choices:*
(see index for correct answer)

- a. Scope creep
- b. Association for Project Management
- c. Authority
- d. Flexible product development

Guidance: level 1

:: Foreign direct investment ::

A _____ is an investment in the form of a controlling ownership in a business in one country by an entity based in another country. It is thus distinguished from a foreign portfolio investment by a notion of direct control.

Exam Probability: **High**

55. *Answer choices:*

(see index for correct answer)

- a. Diamond model
- b. FDi magazine
- c. Foreign direct investment
- d. Immigrant investor programs

Guidance: level 1

:: Payments ::

A _____ is the trade of value from one party to another for goods, or services, or to fulfill a legal obligation.

Exam Probability: **High**

56. *Answer choices:*

(see index for correct answer)

- a. VersaPay
- b. Direct Payments
- c. Payment
- d. Deficiency payments

Guidance: level 1

:: Office administration ::

An _____ is generally a room or other area where an organization's employees perform administrative work in order to support and realize objects and goals of the organization. The word "_____" may also denote a position within an organization with specific duties attached to it ; the latter is in fact an earlier usage, _____ as place originally referring to the location of one's duty. When used as an adjective, the term "_____" may refer to business-related tasks. In law, a company or organization has _____ s in any place where it has an official presence, even if that presence consists of a storage silo rather than an establishment with desk-and-chair. An _____ is also an architectural and design phenomenon: ranging from a small _____ such as a bench in the corner of a small business of extremely small size , through entire floors of buildings, up to and including massive buildings dedicated entirely to one company. In modern terms an _____ is usually the location where white-collar workers carry out their functions. As per James Stephenson, "_____ is that part of business enterprise which is devoted to the direction and co-ordination of its various activities."

Exam Probability: **High**

57. *Answer choices:*

(see index for correct answer)

- a. Office
- b. Office administration
- c. Inter departmental communication
- d. Activity management

Guidance: level 1

:: Organizational theory ::

_____ is the process of groups of organisms working or acting together for common, mutual, or some underlying benefit, as opposed to working in competition for selfish benefit. Many animal and plant species cooperate both with other members of their own species and with members of other species .

Exam Probability: **High**

58. *Answer choices:*

(see index for correct answer)

- a. Cooperation
- b. Organizational performance
- c. Resource dependence theory
- d. Goat rodeo

Guidance: level 1

:: Summary statistics ::

_____ is the number of occurrences of a repeating event per unit of time. It is also referred to as temporal _____ , which emphasizes the contrast to spatial _____ and angular _____ . The period is the duration of time of one cycle in a repeating event, so the period is the reciprocal of the _____ . For example: if a newborn baby's heart beats at a _____ of 120 times a minute, its period—the time interval between beats—is half a second . _____ is an important parameter used in science and engineering to specify the rate of oscillatory and vibratory phenomena, such as mechanical vibrations, audio signals , radio waves, and light.

Exam Probability: **Low**

59. *Answer choices:*

(see index for correct answer)

- a. Mean percentage error
- b. Lorenz asymmetry coefficient
- c. weighted mean
- d. Five-number summary

Guidance: level 1

Management

Management is the administration of an organization, whether it is a business, a not-for-profit organization, or government body. Management includes the activities of setting the strategy of an organization and coordinating the efforts of its employees (or of volunteers) to accomplish its objectives through the application of available resources, such as financial, natural, technological, and human resources.

:: Social psychology ::

In social psychology, _____ is the phenomenon of a person exerting less effort to achieve a goal when he or she works in a group than when working alone. This is seen as one of the main reasons groups are sometimes less productive than the combined performance of their members working as individuals, but should be distinguished from the accidental coordination problems that groups sometimes experience.

Exam Probability: **Medium**

1. *Answer choices:*

(see index for correct answer)

- a. Social character
- b. objectification
- c. Social penetration
- d. Social loafing

Guidance: level 1

:: ::

_____ is the process of collecting, analyzing and/or reporting information regarding the performance of an individual, group, organization, system or component. _____ is not a new concept, some of the earliest records of human activity relate to the counting or recording of activities.

Exam Probability: **Low**

2. *Answer choices:*

(see index for correct answer)

- a. cultural
- b. hierarchical
- c. Performance measurement
- d. functional perspective

Guidance: level 1

:: Systems thinking ::

Systems theory is the interdisciplinary study of systems. A system is a cohesive conglomeration of interrelated and interdependent parts that is either natural or man-made. Every system is delineated by its spatial and temporal boundaries, surrounded and influenced by its environment, described by its structure and purpose or nature and expressed in its functioning. In terms of its effects, a system can be more than the sum of its parts if it expresses synergy or emergent behavior. Changing one part of the system usually affects other parts and the whole system, with predictable patterns of behavior. For systems that are self-learning and self-adapting, the positive growth and adaptation depend upon how well the system is adjusted with its environment. Some systems function mainly to support other systems by aiding in the maintenance of the other system to prevent failure. The goal of systems theory is systematically discovering a system's dynamics, constraints, conditions and elucidating principles that can be discerned and applied to systems at every level of nesting, and in every field for achieving optimized equifinality.

Exam Probability: **Low**

3. *Answer choices:*

(see index for correct answer)

- a. Futuribles International
- b. Ray Hammond
- c. Interdependence
- d. Club of Rome

Guidance: level 1

:: Offshoring ::

A _____ is the temporary suspension or permanent termination of employment of an employee or, more commonly, a group of employees for business reasons, such as personnel management or downsizing an organization. Originally, _____ referred exclusively to a temporary interruption in work, or employment but this has evolved to a permanent elimination of a position in both British and US English, requiring the addition of "temporary" to specify the original meaning of the word. A _____ is not to be confused with wrongful termination. Laid off workers or displaced workers are workers who have lost or left their jobs because their employer has closed or moved, there was insufficient work for them to do, or their position or shift was abolished . Downsizing in a company is defined to involve the reduction of employees in a workforce. Downsizing in companies became a popular practice in the 1980s and early 1990s as it was seen as a way to deliver better shareholder value as it helps to reduce the costs of employers . Indeed, recent research on downsizing in the U.S., UK, and Japan suggests that downsizing is being regarded by management as one of the preferred routes to help declining organizations, cutting unnecessary costs, and improve organizational performance. Usually a _____ occurs as a cost cutting measure.

Exam Probability: **High**

4. *Answer choices:*

(see index for correct answer)

- a. Advanced Contact Solutions
- b. Body shopping
- c. Layoff
- d. Offshore outsourcing

Guidance: level 1

:: ::

_____ is the practice of protecting the natural environment by individuals, organizations and governments. Its objectives are to conserve natural resources and the existing natural environment and, where possible, to repair damage and reverse trends.

Exam Probability: **Medium**

5. *Answer choices:*

(see index for correct answer)

- a. surface-level diversity
- b. information systems assessment
- c. Sarbanes-Oxley act of 2002

- d. Environmental protection

Guidance: level 1

:: Industry ::

_____ describes various measures of the efficiency of production. Often, a _____ measure is expressed as the ratio of an aggregate output to a single input or an aggregate input used in a production process, i.e. output per unit of input. Most common example is the labour _____ measure, e.g., such as GDP per worker. There are many different definitions of _____ and the choice among them depends on the purpose of the _____ measurement and/or data availability. The key source of difference between various _____ measures is also usually related to how the outputs and the inputs are aggregated into scalars to obtain such a ratio-type measure of _____ .

Exam Probability: **Medium**

6. *Answer choices:*
(see index for correct answer)

- a. Tube and clamp scaffold
- b. Tertiary sector of the economy
- c. Prefabrication
- d. Productivity

Guidance: level 1

:: Employment ::

The _____ is an individual's metaphorical "journey" through learning, work and other aspects of life. There are a number of ways to define _____ and the term is used in a variety of ways.

Exam Probability: **Medium**

7. *Answer choices:*

(see index for correct answer)

- a. Career
- b. Performance improvement
- c. Working holiday visa
- d. Legal working age

Guidance: level 1

:: ::

The _____ is a political and economic union of 28 member states that are located primarily in Europe. It has an area of 4,475,757 km2 and an estimated population of about 513 million. The EU has developed an internal single market through a standardised system of laws that apply in all member states in those matters, and only those matters, where members have agreed to act as one. EU policies aim to ensure the free movement of people, goods, services and capital within the internal market, enact legislation in justice and home affairs and maintain common policies on trade, agriculture, fisheries and regional development. For travel within the Schengen Area, passport controls have been abolished. A monetary union was established in 1999 and came into full force in 2002 and is composed of 19 EU member states which use the euro currency.

Exam Probability: **Medium**

8. *Answer choices:*

(see index for correct answer)

- a. interpersonal communication
- b. levels of analysis
- c. surface-level diversity
- d. European Union

Guidance: level 1

:: Stochastic processes ::

_____ in its modern meaning is a "new idea, creative thoughts, new imaginations in form of device or method". _____ is often also viewed as the application of better solutions that meet new requirements, unarticulated needs, or existing market needs. Such _____ takes place through the provision of more-effective products, processes, services, technologies, or business models that are made available to markets, governments and society. An _____ is something original and more effective and, as a consequence, new, that "breaks into" the market or society. _____ is related to, but not the same as, invention, as _____ is more apt to involve the practical implementation of an invention to make a meaningful impact in the market or society, and not all _____ s require an invention. _____ often manifests itself via the engineering process, when the problem being solved is of a technical or scientific nature. The opposite of _____ is exnovation.

Exam Probability: **Medium**

9. *Answer choices:*

(see index for correct answer)

- a. Gamma process
- b. Stopped process
- c. Gaussian free field
- d. Innovation

Guidance: level 1

:: ::

In a supply chain, a _____, or a seller, is an enterprise that contributes goods or services. Generally, a supply chain _____ manufactures inventory/stock items and sells them to the next link in the chain. Today, these terms refer to a supplier of any good or service.

Exam Probability: **Medium**

10. *Answer choices:*

(see index for correct answer)

- a. cultural
- b. Vendor
- c. hierarchical
- d. surface-level diversity

Guidance: level 1

:: ::

_____ is the exchange of capital, goods, and services across international borders or territories.

Exam Probability: **High**

11. *Answer choices:*

(see index for correct answer)

- a. imperative
- b. corporate values
- c. empathy
- d. Character

Guidance: level 1

:: Workplace ::

A _____, also referred to as a performance review, performance evaluation, development discussion, or employee appraisal is a method by which the job performance of an employee is documented and evaluated. _____s are a part of career development and consist of regular reviews of employee performance within organizations.

Exam Probability: **Medium**

12. *Answer choices:*
(see index for correct answer)

- a. Workplace violence
- b. Workplace relationships
- c. Feminisation of the workplace
- d. Performance appraisal

Guidance: level 1

:: Monopoly (economics) ::

_____ is a category of property that includes intangible creations of the human intellect. _____ encompasses two types of rights: industrial property rights and copyright. It was not until the 19th century that the term " _____ " began to be used, and not until the late 20th century that it became commonplace in the majority of the world.

Exam Probability: **High**

13. *Answer choices:*

(see index for correct answer)

- a. Complementary monopoly
- b. Competition Commission
- c. Intellectual property
- d. Monopoly

Guidance: level 1

:: Labor rights ::

A _____ is a wrong or hardship suffered, real or supposed, which forms legitimate grounds of complaint. In the past, the word meant the infliction or cause of hardship.

Exam Probability: **Medium**

14. *Answer choices:*

(see index for correct answer)

- a. China Labor Watch
- b. The Hyatt 100
- c. Swift raids
- d. Grievance

Guidance: level 1

:: Information systems ::

_____ is the process of creating, sharing, using and managing the knowledge and information of an organisation. It refers to a multidisciplinary approach to achieving organisational objectives by making the best use of knowledge.

Exam Probability: **Medium**

15. *Answer choices:*

(see index for correct answer)

- a. Notify NYC
- b. Knowledge management
- c. System for Electronic Document Analysis and Retrieval
- d. CGA

Guidance: level 1

:: ::

The _____ is an agreement signed by Canada, Mexico, and the United States, creating a trilateral trade bloc in North America. The agreement came into force on January 1, 1994, and superseded the 1988 Canada–United States Free Trade Agreement between the United States and Canada. The NAFTA trade bloc is one of the largest trade blocs in the world by gross domestic product.

Exam Probability: **High**

16. *Answer choices:*

(see index for correct answer)

- a. corporate values
- b. North American Free Trade Agreement
- c. surface-level diversity
- d. information systems assessment

Guidance: level 1

:: ::

_____ is the process of making predictions of the future based on past and present data and most commonly by analysis of trends. A commonplace example might be estimation of some variable of interest at some specified future date. Prediction is a similar, but more general term. Both might refer to formal statistical methods employing time series, cross-sectional or longitudinal data, or alternatively to less formal judgmental methods. Usage can differ between areas of application: for example, in hydrology the terms "forecast" and "_____" are sometimes reserved for estimates of values at certain specific future times, while the term "prediction" is used for more general estimates, such as the number of times floods will occur over a long period.

Exam Probability: **High**

17. *Answer choices:*

(see index for correct answer)

- a. functional perspective
- b. Sarbanes-Oxley act of 2002
- c. Forecasting
- d. interpersonal communication

Guidance: level 1

:: Human resource management ::

_____ is a family of procedures to identify the content of a job in terms of activities involved and attributes or job requirements needed to perform the activities. _____ provides information of organizations which helps to determine which employees are best fit for specific jobs. Through _____ , the analyst needs to understand what the important tasks of the job are, how they are carried out, and the necessary human qualities needed to complete the job successfully.

Exam Probability: **High**

18. *Answer choices:*

(see index for correct answer)

- a. Job analysis
- b. Administrative services organization
- c. Joint Personnel Administration
- d. Human resource policies

Guidance: level 1

:: ::

A _____ is a type of job aid used to reduce failure by compensating for potential limits of human memory and attention. It helps to ensure consistency and completeness in carrying out a task. A basic example is the "to do list". A more advanced _____ would be a schedule, which lays out tasks to be done according to time of day or other factors. A primary task in _____ is documentation of the task and auditing against the documentation.

Exam Probability: **High**

19. *Answer choices:*

(see index for correct answer)

- a. Checklist
- b. hierarchical perspective
- c. deep-level diversity
- d. co-culture

Guidance: level 1

:: Training ::

_____ is action or inaction that is regulated to be in accordance with a particular system of governance. _____ is commonly applied to regulating human and animal behavior, and furthermore, it is applied to each activity-branch in all branches of organized activity, knowledge, and other fields of study and observation. _____ can be a set of expectations that are required by any governing entity including the self, groups, classes, fields, industries, or societies.

Exam Probability: **Low**

20. *Answer choices:*

(see index for correct answer)

- a. Teletraining

- b. Screencast
- c. Practicum
- d. Discipline

Guidance: level 1

:: ::

> _____ is a form of development in which a person called a coach supports a learner or client in achieving a specific personal or professional goal by providing training and guidance. The learner is sometimes called a coachee. Occasionally, _____ may mean an informal relationship between two people, of whom one has more experience and expertise than the other and offers advice and guidance as the latter learns; but _____ differs from mentoring in focusing on specific tasks or objectives, as opposed to more general goals or overall development.

Exam Probability: **Medium**

21. *Answer choices:*
(see index for correct answer)

- a. information systems assessment
- b. hierarchical perspective
- c. open system
- d. imperative

Guidance: level 1

:: Project management ::

_____ is the right to exercise power, which can be formalized by a state and exercised by way of judges, appointed executives of government, or the ecclesiastical or priestly appointed representatives of a God or other deities.

Exam Probability: **Low**

22. *Answer choices:*

(see index for correct answer)

- a. Authority
- b. Scope
- c. Trenegy Incorporated
- d. Integrated product team

Guidance: level 1

:: ::

The business environment is a marketing term and refers to factors and forces that affect a firm's ability to build and maintain successful customer relationships. The business environment has been defined as "the totality of physical and social factors that are taken directly into consideration in the decision-making behaviour of individuals in the organisation."

Exam Probability: **Low**

23. *Answer choices:*

(see index for correct answer)

- a. corporate values
- b. interpersonal communication
- c. personal values
- d. Environmental scanning

Guidance: level 1

:: Human resource management ::

_____ involves improving the effectiveness of organizations and the individuals and teams within them. Training may be viewed as related to immediate changes in organizational effectiveness via organized instruction, while development is related to the progress of longer-term organizational and employee goals. While _____ technically have differing definitions, the two are oftentimes used interchangeably and/or together. _____ has historically been a topic within applied psychology but has within the last two decades become closely associated with human resources management, talent management, human resources development, instructional design, human factors, and knowledge management.

Exam Probability: **High**

24. *Answer choices:*

(see index for correct answer)

- a. Mentorship
- b. Job performance
- c. Training and development
- d. Continuing professional development

Guidance: level 1

:: Marketing ::

_____ or stock control can be broadly defined as "the activity of checking a shop's stock." However, a more focused definition takes into account the more science-based, methodical practice of not only verifying a business' inventory but also focusing on the many related facets of inventory management "within an organisation to meet the demand placed upon that business economically." Other facets of _____ include supply chain management, production control, financial flexibility, and customer satisfaction. At the root of _____, however, is the _____ problem, which involves determining when to order, how much to order, and the logistics of those decisions.

Exam Probability: **High**

25. *Answer choices:*

(see index for correct answer)

- a. Negotiation
- b. Impulse purchase
- c. Blind taste test
- d. Porter hypothesis

Guidance: level 1

:: Free trade agreements ::

> A _____ is a wide-ranging taxes, tariff and trade treaty that often includes investment guarantees. It exists when two or more countries agree on terms that helps them trade with each other. The most common _____s are of the preferential and free trade types are concluded in order to reduce tariffs, quotas and other trade restrictions on items traded between the signatories.

Exam Probability: **Medium**

26. *Answer choices:*

(see index for correct answer)

- a. CISFTA
- b. Comprehensive Economic Partnership Agreement
- c. African Free Trade Zone
- d. Trade agreement

Guidance: level 1

:: Human resource management ::

_____ is the strategic approach to the effective management of people in an organization so that they help the business to gain a competitive advantage. It is designed to maximize employee performance in service of an employer's strategic objectives. HR is primarily concerned with the management of people within organizations, focusing on policies and on systems. HR departments are responsible for overseeing employee-benefits design, employee recruitment, training and development, performance appraisal, and Reward management. HR also concerns itself with organizational change and industrial relations, that is, the balancing of organizational practices with requirements arising from collective bargaining and from governmental laws.

Exam Probability: **Low**

27. *Answer choices:*

(see index for correct answer)

- a. Perceived organizational support
- b. Organizational orientations
- c. Bonus payment
- d. Organization chart

Guidance: level 1

In business strategy, _____ is establishing a competitive advantage by having the lowest cost of operation in the industry. _____ is often driven by company efficiency, size, scale, scope and cumulative experience. A _____ strategy aims to exploit scale of production, well-defined scope and other economies, producing highly standardized products, using advanced technology. In recent years, more and more companies have chosen a strategic mix to achieve market leadership. These patterns consist of simultaneous _____, superior customer service and product leadership. Walmart has succeeded across the world due to its _____ strategy. The company has cut down on exesses at every point of production and thus are able to provide the consumers with quality products at low prices.

Exam Probability: **Low**

28. *Answer choices:*

(see index for correct answer)

- a. imperative
- b. interpersonal communication
- c. Cost leadership
- d. deep-level diversity

Guidance: level 1

:: Business terms ::

Centralisation or _____ is the process by which the activities of an organization, particularly those regarding planning and decision-making, framing strategy and policies become concentrated within a particular geographical location group. This moves the important decision-making and planning powers within the center of the organisation.

Exam Probability: **High**

29. *Answer choices:*

(see index for correct answer)

- a. year-to-date
- b. front office
- c. organic growth
- d. Centralization

Guidance: level 1

:: Time management ::

_____ is the process of planning and exercising conscious control of time spent on specific activities, especially to increase effectiveness, efficiency, and productivity. It involves a juggling act of various demands upon a person relating to work, social life, family, hobbies, personal interests and commitments with the finiteness of time. Using time effectively gives the person "choice" on spending/managing activities at their own time and expediency.

Exam Probability: **High**

30. *Answer choices:*

(see index for correct answer)

- a. Sufficient unto the day is the evil thereof
- b. Time Trek
- c. HabitRPG
- d. Time management

Guidance: level 1

:: Decision theory ::

A _____ is a decision support tool that uses a tree-like model of decisions and their possible consequences, including chance event outcomes, resource costs, and utility. It is one way to display an algorithm that only contains conditional control statements.

Exam Probability: **Low**

31. *Answer choices:*

(see index for correct answer)

- a. Optimal stopping
- b. Cognitive bias
- c. Ophelimity

- d. Ellsberg paradox

Guidance: level 1

:: ::

_____ is a kind of action that occur as two or more objects have an effect upon one another. The idea of a two-way effect is essential in the concept of _____ , as opposed to a one-way causal effect. A closely related term is interconnectivity, which deals with the _____ s of _____ s within systems: combinations of many simple _____ s can lead to surprising emergent phenomena. _____ has different tailored meanings in various sciences. Changes can also involve _____ .

Exam Probability: **Low**

32. *Answer choices:*

(see index for correct answer)

- a. Sarbanes-Oxley act of 2002
- b. personal values
- c. Interaction
- d. empathy

Guidance: level 1

:: Management ::

_____ is the identification, evaluation, and prioritization of risks followed by coordinated and economical application of resources to minimize, monitor, and control the probability or impact of unfortunate events or to maximize the realization of opportunities.

Exam Probability: **High**

33. *Answer choices:*

(see index for correct answer)

- a. Defensive expenditures
- b. Central administration
- c. Context analysis
- d. Business relationship management

Guidance: level 1

:: Project management ::

In political science, an _____ is a means by which a petition signed by a certain minimum number of registered voters can force a government to choose to either enact a law or hold a public vote in parliament in what is called indirect _____, or under direct _____, the proposition is immediately put to a plebiscite or referendum, in what is called a Popular initiated Referendum or citizen-initiated referendum).

Exam Probability: **High**

34. Answer choices:

(see index for correct answer)

- a. Fast-track construction
- b. Association for Project Management
- c. The Transformation Project
- d. Project management 2.0

Guidance: level 1

:: ::

_____ is the process of two or more people or organizations working together to complete a task or achieve a goal. _____ is similar to cooperation. Most _____ requires leadership, although the form of leadership can be social within a decentralized and egalitarian group. Teams that work collaboratively often access greater resources, recognition and rewards when facing competition for finite resources.

Exam Probability: **Medium**

35. Answer choices:

(see index for correct answer)

- a. Collaboration
- b. hierarchical perspective
- c. process perspective
- d. surface-level diversity

Guidance: level 1

:: Business planning ::

_____ is an organization's process of defining its strategy, or direction, and making decisions on allocating its resources to pursue this strategy. It may also extend to control mechanisms for guiding the implementation of the strategy. _____ became prominent in corporations during the 1960s and remains an important aspect of strategic management. It is executed by strategic planners or strategists, who involve many parties and research sources in their analysis of the organization and its relationship to the environment in which it competes.

Exam Probability: **High**

36. *Answer choices:*

(see index for correct answer)

- a. Customer Demand Planning
- b. Business war games
- c. Gap analysis
- d. Exit planning

Guidance: level 1

:: Elementary mathematics ::

_____ is a numerical measurement of how far apart objects are. In physics or everyday usage, _____ may refer to a physical length or an estimation based on other criteria. In most cases, "_____ from A to B" is interchangeable with "_____ from B to A". In mathematics, a _____ function or metric is a generalization of the concept of physical _____. A metric is a function that behaves according to a specific set of rules, and is a way of describing what it means for elements of some space to be "close to" or "far away from" each other.

Exam Probability: **High**

37. *Answer choices:*

(see index for correct answer)

- a. Mathematical beauty
- b. Algebraic operation
- c. Abscissa
- d. Tally marks

Guidance: level 1

:: Life skills ::

_____, emotional leadership, emotional quotient and _____ quotient, is the capability of individuals to recognize their own emotions and those of others, discern between different feelings and label them appropriately, use emotional information to guide thinking and behavior, and manage and/or adjust emotions to adapt to environments or achieve one's goal.

Exam Probability: **High**

38. *Answer choices:*

(see index for correct answer)

- a. Social intelligence
- b. coping mechanism
- c. emotion work
- d. multiple intelligence

Guidance: level 1

:: Product design ::

> _____ as a verb is to create a new product to be sold by a business to its customers. A very broad coefficient and effective generation and development of ideas through a process that leads to new products. Thus, it is a major aspect of new product development.

Exam Probability: **Low**

39. *Answer choices:*

(see index for correct answer)

- a. Marcus Notley
- b. Nottingham Spirk
- c. Production drawing

- d. Rolf Fehlbaum

Guidance: level 1

:: Asset ::

In financial accounting, an _____ is any resource owned by the business. Anything tangible or intangible that can be owned or controlled to produce value and that is held by a company to produce positive economic value is an _____ . Simply stated, _____ s represent value of ownership that can be converted into cash . The balance sheet of a firm records the monetary value of the _____ s owned by that firm. It covers money and other valuables belonging to an individual or to a business.

Exam Probability: **High**

40. *Answer choices:*

(see index for correct answer)

- a. Asset
- b. Current asset

Guidance: level 1

:: Management ::

_____ is a technique used by some employers to rotate their employees' assigned jobs throughout their employment. Employers practice this technique for a number of reasons. It was designed to promote flexibility of employees and to keep employees interested into staying with the company/organization which employs them. There is also research that shows how _____ s help relieve the stress of employees who work in a job that requires manual labor.

Exam Probability: **High**

41. *Answer choices:*

(see index for correct answer)

- a. Place management
- b. Porter five forces analysis
- c. Context analysis
- d. Job rotation

Guidance: level 1

:: ::

_____ is the means to see, hear, or become aware of something or someone through our fundamental senses. The term _____ derives from the Latin word perceptio, and is the organization, identification, and interpretation of sensory information in order to represent and understand the presented information, or the environment.

Exam Probability: **High**

42. Answer choices:

(see index for correct answer)

- a. Sarbanes-Oxley act of 2002
- b. deep-level diversity
- c. process perspective
- d. Perception

Guidance: level 1

:: Market research ::

> _____ is an organized effort to gather information about target markets or customers. It is a very important component of business strategy. The term is commonly interchanged with marketing research; however, expert practitioners may wish to draw a distinction, in that marketing research is concerned specifically about marketing processes, while _____ is concerned specifically with markets.

Exam Probability: **High**

43. Answer choices:

(see index for correct answer)

- a. Product forecasting
- b. Online panel
- c. Market research
- d. INDEX

Guidance: level 1

:: Legal terms ::

> _____ is a type of meaning in which a phrase, statement or resolution is not explicitly defined, making several interpretations plausible. A common aspect of _____ is uncertainty. It is thus an attribute of any idea or statement whose intended meaning cannot be definitively resolved according to a rule or process with a finite number of steps.

Exam Probability: **Low**

44. *Answer choices:*

(see index for correct answer)

- a. Consent decree
- b. Misconduct
- c. European Authorized Representative
- d. Estray

Guidance: level 1

:: Human resource management ::

_____ means increasing the scope of a job through extending the range of its job duties and responsibilities generally within the same level and periphery. _____ involves combining various activities at the same level in the organization and adding them to the existing job. It is also called the horizontal expansion of job activities. This contradicts the principles of specialisation and the division of labour whereby work is divided into small units, each of which is performed repetitively by an individual worker and the responsibilities are always clear. Some motivational theories suggest that the boredom and alienation caused by the division of labour can actually cause efficiency to fall. Thus, _____ seeks to motivate workers through reversing the process of specialisation. A typical approach might be to replace assembly lines with modular work; instead of an employee repeating the same step on each product, they perform several tasks on a single item. In order for employees to be provided with _____ they will need to be retrained in new fields to understand how each field works.

Exam Probability: **Low**

45. *Answer choices:*

(see index for correct answer)

- a. At-will employment
- b. Mergers and acquisitions
- c. Senior management
- d. Job enlargement

Guidance: level 1

:: Goods ::

In most contexts, the concept of _____ denotes the conduct that should be preferred when posed with a choice between possible actions. _____ is generally considered to be the opposite of evil, and is of interest in the study of morality, ethics, religion and philosophy. The specific meaning and etymology of the term and its associated translations among ancient and contemporary languages show substantial variation in its inflection and meaning depending on circumstances of place, history, religious, or philosophical context.

Exam Probability: **Medium**

46. *Answer choices:*

(see index for correct answer)

- a. excludable
- b. Refined goods
- c. Credence good
- d. Durable good

Guidance: level 1

:: Management ::

In the field of management, _____ involves the formulation and implementation of the major goals and initiatives taken by an organization's top management on behalf of owners, based on consideration of resources and an assessment of the internal and external environments in which the organization operates.

Exam Probability: **High**

47. *Answer choices:*

(see index for correct answer)

- a. Voice of the customer
- b. Personal offshoring
- c. SimulTrain
- d. Radical transparency

Guidance: level 1

:: Strategic management ::

_____ is a strategic planning technique used to help a person or organization identify strengths, weaknesses, opportunities, and threats related to business competition or project planning. It is intended to specify the objectives of the business venture or project and identify the internal and external factors that are favorable and unfavorable to achieving those objectives. Users of a _____ often ask and answer questions to generate meaningful information for each category to make the tool useful and identify their competitive advantage. SWOT has been described as the tried-and-true tool of strategic analysis.

Exam Probability: **High**

48. *Answer choices:*

(see index for correct answer)

- a. Delta model
- b. IFE matrix
- c. Rule of three
- d. SWOT analysis

Guidance: level 1

:: Production and manufacturing ::

> _____ is a theory of management that analyzes and synthesizes workflows. Its main objective is improving economic efficiency, especially labor productivity. It was one of the earliest attempts to apply science to the engineering of processes and to management. _____ is sometimes known as Taylorism after its founder, Frederick Winslow Taylor.

Exam Probability: **High**

49. *Answer choices:*

(see index for correct answer)

- a. Hydrosila
- b. Piece work
- c. Plant layout study
- d. Scientific management

Guidance: level 1

:: Management ::

The term _____ refers to measures designed to increase the degree of autonomy and self-determination in people and in communities in order to enable them to represent their interests in a responsible and self-determined way, acting on their own authority. It is the process of becoming stronger and more confident, especially in controlling one's life and claiming one's rights. _____ as action refers both to the process of self-_____ and to professional support of people, which enables them to overcome their sense of powerlessness and lack of influence, and to recognize and use their resources. To do work with power.

Exam Probability: **Low**

50. *Answer choices:*
(see index for correct answer)

- a. Telescopic observations strategic framework
- b. Certified management consultant
- c. Empowerment
- d. Investment control

Guidance: level 1

:: Evaluation methods ::

In social psychology, _____ is the process of looking at oneself in order to assess aspects that are important to one's identity. It is one of the motives that drive self-evaluation, along with self-verification and self-enhancement. Sedikides suggests that the _____ motive will prompt people to seek information to confirm their uncertain self-concept rather than their certain self-concept and at the same time people use _____ to enhance their certainty of their own self-knowledge. However, the _____ motive could be seen as quite different from the other two self-evaluation motives. Unlike the other two motives through _____ people are interested in the accuracy of their current self view, rather than improving their self-view. This makes _____ the only self-evaluative motive that may cause a person's self-esteem to be damaged.

Exam Probability: **High**

51. *Answer choices:*

(see index for correct answer)

- a. Creative participation
- b. Alternative assessment
- c. Self-assessment
- d. Logic model

Guidance: level 1

:: Management accounting ::

_____ s are costs that change as the quantity of the good or service that a business produces changes. _____ s are the sum of marginal costs over all units produced. They can also be considered normal costs. Fixed costs and _____ s make up the two components of total cost. Direct costs are costs that can easily be associated with a particular cost object. However, not all _____ s are direct costs. For example, variable manufacturing overhead costs are _____ s that are indirect costs, not direct costs. _____ s are sometimes called unit-level costs as they vary with the number of units produced.

Exam Probability: **Medium**

52. *Answer choices:*

(see index for correct answer)

- a. Pre-determined overhead rate
- b. Entity-level controls
- c. activity based costing
- d. Variable cost

Guidance: level 1

:: ::

_____ is the moral stance, political philosophy, ideology, or social outlook that emphasizes the moral worth of the individual. Individualists promote the exercise of one's goals and desires and so value independence and self-reliance and advocate that interests of the individual should achieve precedence over the state or a social group, while opposing external interference upon one's own interests by society or institutions such as the government. _____ is often defined in contrast to totalitarianism, collectivism, and more corporate social forms.

Exam Probability: **Low**

53. *Answer choices:*

(see index for correct answer)

- a. cultural
- b. hierarchical
- c. Individualism
- d. imperative

Guidance: level 1

:: ::

_____ consists of using generic or ad hoc methods in an orderly manner to find solutions to problems. Some of the problem-solving techniques developed and used in philosophy, artificial intelligence, computer science, engineering, mathematics, or medicine are related to mental problem-solving techniques studied in psychology.

Exam Probability: **Low**

54. *Answer choices:*

(see index for correct answer)

- a. Sarbanes-Oxley act of 2002
- b. empathy
- c. Problem solving
- d. similarity-attraction theory

Guidance: level 1

:: ::

A _____, or also known as foreman, overseer, facilitator, monitor, area coordinator, or sometimes gaffer, is the job title of a low level management position that is primarily based on authority over a worker or charge of a workplace. A _____ can also be one of the most senior in the staff at the place of work, such as a Professor who oversees a PhD dissertation. Supervision, on the other hand, can be performed by people without this formal title, for example by parents. The term _____ itself can be used to refer to any personnel who have this task as part of their job description.

Exam Probability: **Low**

55. *Answer choices:*

(see index for correct answer)

- a. hierarchical perspective
- b. Sarbanes-Oxley act of 2002
- c. Character
- d. Supervisor

Guidance: level 1

:: Decision theory ::

A _____ is a deliberate system of principles to guide decisions and achieve rational outcomes. A _____ is a statement of intent, and is implemented as a procedure or protocol. Policies are generally adopted by a governance body within an organization. Policies can assist in both subjective and objective decision making. Policies to assist in subjective decision making usually assist senior management with decisions that must be based on the relative merits of a number of factors, and as a result are often hard to test objectively, e.g. work-life balance _____ . In contrast policies to assist in objective decision making are usually operational in nature and can be objectively tested, e.g. password _____ .

Exam Probability: **Low**

56. *Answer choices:*

(see index for correct answer)

- a. Decision aids
- b. There are known knowns
- c. Analysis paralysis
- d. Expected value of perfect information

Guidance: level 1

:: Telecommuting ::

_____, also called telework, teleworking, working from home, mobile work, remote work, and flexible workplace, is a work arrangement in which employees do not commute or travel to a central place of work, such as an office building, warehouse, or store. Teleworkers in the 21st century often use mobile telecommunications technology such as Wi-Fi-equipped laptop or tablet computers and smartphones to work from coffee shops; others may use a desktop computer and a landline phone at their home. According to a Reuters poll, approximately "one in five workers around the globe, particularly employees in the Middle East, Latin America and Asia, telecommute frequently and nearly 10 percent work from home every day." In the 2000s, annual leave or vacation in some organizations was seen as absence from the workplace rather than ceasing work, and some office employees used telework to continue to check work e-mails while on vacation.

Exam Probability: **High**

57. *Answer choices:*

(see index for correct answer)

- a. OmNovia Technologies
- b. IvanAnywhere
- c. Telecommuting
- d. TalkPoint

Guidance: level 1

:: Production and manufacturing ::

_____ is a set of techniques and tools for process improvement. Though as a shortened form it may be found written as 6S, it should not be confused with the methodology known as 6S .

Exam Probability: **Low**

58. *Answer choices:*

(see index for correct answer)

- a. Six Sigma
- b. Advanced product quality planning
- c. Citect
- d. Verband der Automobilindustrie

Guidance: level 1

:: Business process ::

A _____ or business method is a collection of related, structured activities or tasks by people or equipment which in a specific sequence produce a service or product for a particular customer or customers. _____ es occur at all organizational levels and may or may not be visible to the customers. A _____ may often be visualized as a flowchart of a sequence of activities with interleaving decision points or as a process matrix of a sequence of activities with relevance rules based on data in the process. The benefits of using _____ es include improved customer satisfaction and improved agility for reacting to rapid market change. Process-oriented organizations break down the barriers of structural departments and try to avoid functional silos.

Exam Probability: **Low**

59. *Answer choices:*

(see index for correct answer)

- a. Business process
- b. Bonita BPM
- c. International business development
- d. Change order

Guidance: level 1

Business law

Corporate law (also known as business law) is the body of law governing the rights, relations, and conduct of persons, companies, organizations and businesses. It refers to the legal practice relating to, or the theory of corporations. Corporate law often describes the law relating to matters which derive directly from the life-cycle of a corporation. It thus encompasses the formation, funding, governance, and death of a corporation.

:: ::

The _____ is an intergovernmental organization that is concerned with the regulation of international trade between nations. The WTO officially commenced on 1 January 1995 under the Marrakesh Agreement, signed by 124 nations on 15 April 1994, replacing the General Agreement on Tariffs and Trade , which commenced in 1948. It is the largest international economic organization in the world.

Exam Probability: **Medium**

1. *Answer choices:*

(see index for correct answer)

- a. imperative
- b. open system
- c. corporate values
- d. information systems assessment

Guidance: level 1

:: Contract law ::

_____ , also called an anticipatory breach, is a term in the law of contracts that describes a declaration by the promising party to a contract that he or she does not intend to live up to his or her obligations under the contract.

Exam Probability: **Medium**

2. *Answer choices:*

(see index for correct answer)

- a. Collateral contract
- b. Service plan
- c. Anticipatory repudiation
- d. Collateral warranty

Guidance: level 1

:: Patent law ::

A _____ is generally any statement intended to specify or delimit the scope of rights and obligations that may be exercised and enforced by parties in a legally recognized relationship. In contrast to other terms for legally operative language, the term _____ usually implies situations that involve some level of uncertainty, waiver, or risk.

Exam Probability: **Low**

3. *Answer choices:*

(see index for correct answer)

- a. Design around
- b. Prior art
- c. Industrial applicability
- d. Disclaimer

Guidance: level 1

:: Product liability ::

_____ is the area of law in which manufacturers, distributors, suppliers, retailers, and others who make products available to the public are held responsible for the injuries those products cause. Although the word "product" has broad connotations, _____ as an area of law is traditionally limited to products in the form of tangible personal property.

Exam Probability: **Low**

4. *Answer choices:*

(see index for correct answer)

- a. Product liability
- b. Dalkon Shield
- c. Consumer Protection Act 1987
- d. Domestic Fuels Protection Act

Guidance: level 1

:: ::

An _____ is a contingent motivator. Traditional _____ s are extrinsic motivators which reward actions to yield a desired outcome. The effectiveness of traditional _____ s has changed as the needs of Western society have evolved. While the traditional _____ model is effective when there is a defined procedure and goal for a task, Western society started to require a higher volume of critical thinkers, so the traditional model became less effective. Institutions are now following a trend in implementing strategies that rely on intrinsic motivations rather than the extrinsic motivations that the traditional _____ s foster.

Exam Probability: **High**

5. *Answer choices:*

(see index for correct answer)

- a. functional perspective
- b. information systems assessment
- c. hierarchical
- d. Incentive

Guidance: level 1

:: Services management and marketing ::

> A _____ or servicemark is a trademark used in the United States and several other countries to identify a service rather than a product.

Exam Probability: **High**

6. *Answer choices:*

(see index for correct answer)

- a. Service mark
- b. Viable systems approach
- c. Service design
- d. Backend as a service

Guidance: level 1

:: Promotion and marketing communications ::

In everyday language, _____ refers to exaggerated or false praise. In law, _____ is a promotional statement or claim that expresses subjective rather than objective views, which no "reasonable person" would take literally. _____ serves to "puff up" an exaggerated image of what is being described and is especially featured in testimonials.

Exam Probability: **Medium**

7. *Answer choices:*

(see index for correct answer)

- a. News propaganda
- b. Television advertisement
- c. Puffery
- d. Infoganda

Guidance: level 1

:: Marketing ::

_____ comes from the Latin neg and otsia referring to businessmen who, unlike the patricians, had no leisure time in their industriousness; it held the meaning of business until the 17th century when it took on the diplomatic connotation as a dialogue between two or more people or parties intended to reach a beneficial outcome over one or more issues where a conflict exists with respect to at least one of these issues. Thus, _____ is a process of combining divergent positions into a joint agreement under a decision rule of unanimity.

Exam Probability: **Medium**

8. *Answer choices:*

(see index for correct answer)

- a. Demand generation
- b. Negotiation
- c. Mobile marketing research
- d. Contact centre

Guidance: level 1

:: Ethically disputed business practices ::

_____ is the trading of a public company's stock or other securities by individuals with access to nonpublic information about the company. In various countries, some kinds of trading based on insider information is illegal. This is because it is seen as unfair to other investors who do not have access to the information, as the investor with insider information could potentially make larger profits than a typical investor could make. The rules governing _____ are complex and vary significantly from country to country. The extent of enforcement also varies from one country to another. The definition of insider in one jurisdiction can be broad, and may cover not only insiders themselves but also any persons related to them, such as brokers, associates and even family members. A person who becomes aware of non-public information and trades on that basis may be guilty of a crime.

Exam Probability: **Low**

9. *Answer choices:*

(see index for correct answer)

- a. Sugging
- b. anti-competitive
- c. Creative accounting
- d. Nokku kooli

Guidance: level 1

:: Business law ::

A _____ is a business entity created by two or more parties, generally characterized by shared ownership, shared returns and risks, and shared governance. Companies typically pursue _____s for one of four reasons: to access a new market, particularly emerging markets; to gain scale efficiencies by combining assets and operations; to share risk for major investments or projects; or to access skills and capabilities.

Exam Probability: **Low**

10. *Answer choices:*

(see index for correct answer)

- a. Oppression remedy
- b. Power harassment
- c. Lessor
- d. Financial Security Law of France

Guidance: level 1

:: Monopoly (economics) ::

_____ is a category of property that includes intangible creations of the human intellect. _____ encompasses two types of rights: industrial property rights and copyright. It was not until the 19th century that the term "_____" began to be used, and not until the late 20th century that it became commonplace in the majority of the world.

Exam Probability: **Low**

11. *Answer choices:*

(see index for correct answer)

- a. National Competition Policy
- b. Intellectual property
- c. Copyright law of the European Union
- d. Government-granted monopoly

Guidance: level 1

:: Personal property law ::

> Bailment describes a legal relationship in common law where physical possession of personal property, or a chattel, is transferred from one person to another person who subsequently has possession of the property. It arises when a person gives property to someone else for safekeeping, and is a cause of action independent of contract or tort.

Exam Probability: **Medium**

12. *Answer choices:*

(see index for correct answer)

- a. bailment
- b. Bailee

Guidance: level 1

:: Legal doctrines and principles ::

_____ is a doctrine that a party is responsible for acts of their agents. For example, in the United States, there are circumstances when an employer is liable for acts of employees performed within the course of their employment. This rule is also called the master-servant rule, recognized in both common law and civil law jurisdictions.

Exam Probability: **Low**

13. *Answer choices:*

(see index for correct answer)

- a. Respondeat superior
- b. Parol evidence
- c. Proximate cause
- d. Res ipsa

Guidance: level 1

:: Legal doctrines and principles ::

In the United States, the _____ is a legal rule, based on constitutional law, that prevents evidence collected or analyzed in violation of the defendant's constitutional rights from being used in a court of law. This may be considered an example of a prophylactic rule formulated by the judiciary in order to protect a constitutional right. The _____ may also, in some circumstances at least, be considered to follow directly from the constitutional language, such as the Fifth Amendment's command that no person "shall be compelled in any criminal case to be a witness against himself" and that no person "shall be deprived of life, liberty or property without due process of law".

Exam Probability: **Medium**

14. *Answer choices:*

(see index for correct answer)

- a. Unilateral mistake
- b. Act of state doctrine
- c. Exclusionary rule
- d. Proximate cause

Guidance: level 1

:: Debt ::

_____, in finance and economics, is payment from a borrower or deposit-taking financial institution to a lender or depositor of an amount above repayment of the principal sum, at a particular rate. It is distinct from a fee which the borrower may pay the lender or some third party. It is also distinct from dividend which is paid by a company to its shareholders from its profit or reserve, but not at a particular rate decided beforehand, rather on a pro rata basis as a share in the reward gained by risk taking entrepreneurs when the revenue earned exceeds the total costs.

Exam Probability: **Medium**

15. *Answer choices:*

(see index for correct answer)

- a. Money disorders
- b. Internal debt
- c. Interest
- d. Teacher Loan Forgiveness

Guidance: level 1

:: Communication of falsehoods ::

_____, calumny, vilification, or traducement is the communication of a false statement that harms the reputation of, depending on the law of the country, an individual, business, product, group, government, religion, or nation.

Exam Probability: **Medium**

16. *Answer choices:*

(see index for correct answer)

- a. Mental reservation
- b. Misinformation
- c. Erratum
- d. Circular reporting

Guidance: level 1

:: ::

The _____ is the central philosophical concept in the deontological moral philosophy of Immanuel Kant. Introduced in Kant's 1785 Groundwork of the Metaphysics of Morals, it may be defined as a way of evaluating motivations for action.

Exam Probability: **High**

17. *Answer choices:*

(see index for correct answer)

- a. co-culture
- b. hierarchical perspective
- c. Categorical imperative

- d. levels of analysis

Guidance: level 1

:: ::

> _____ is the production of products for use or sale using labour and machines, tools, chemical and biological processing, or formulation. The term may refer to a range of human activity, from handicraft to high tech, but is most commonly applied to industrial design, in which raw materials are transformed into finished goods on a large scale. Such finished goods may be sold to other manufacturers for the production of other, more complex products, such as aircraft, household appliances, furniture, sports equipment or automobiles, or sold to wholesalers, who in turn sell them to retailers, who then sell them to end users and consumers.

Exam Probability: **High**

18. *Answer choices:*

(see index for correct answer)

- a. empathy
- b. hierarchical perspective
- c. cultural
- d. process perspective

Guidance: level 1

:: Finance ::

A _____, in the law of the United States, is a contract that governs the relationship between the parties to a kind of financial transaction known as a secured transaction. In a secured transaction, the Grantor assigns, grants and pledges to the grantee a security interest in personal property which is referred to as the collateral. Examples of typical collateral are shares of stock, livestock, and vehicles. A _____ is not used to transfer any interest in real property, only personal property. The document used by lenders to obtain a lien on real property is a mortgage or deed of trust.

Exam Probability: **Medium**

19. *Answer choices:*

(see index for correct answer)

- a. ITR-2
- b. CBDC NORTIP
- c. Treasury company
- d. Security agreement

Guidance: level 1

:: Business law ::

In the United States, the United Kingdom, Australia, Canada and South Africa, _____ relates to the doctrines of the law of agency. It is relevant particularly in corporate law and constitutional law. _____ refers to a situation where a reasonable third party would understand that an agent had authority to act. This means a principal is bound by the agent's actions, even if the agent had no actual authority, whether express or implied. It raises an estoppel because the third party is given an assurance, which he relies on and would be inequitable for the principal to deny the authority given. _____ can legally be found, even if actual authority has not been given.

Exam Probability: **Low**

20. *Answer choices:*

(see index for correct answer)

- a. Starting a Business Index
- b. Interest of the company
- c. Installment sale
- d. Advertising regulation

Guidance: level 1

:: ::

A _____ is an aggregate of fundamental principles or established precedents that constitute the legal basis of a polity, organisation or other type of entity, and commonly determine how that entity is to be governed.

Exam Probability: **Medium**

21. *Answer choices:*

(see index for correct answer)

- a. empathy
- b. Constitution
- c. functional perspective
- d. hierarchical perspective

Guidance: level 1

:: Real property law ::

A _____ is any legal instrument in writing which passes, affirms or confirms an interest, right, or property and that is signed, attested, delivered, and in some jurisdictions, sealed. It is commonly associated with transferring title to property. The _____ has a greater presumption of validity and is less rebuttable than an instrument signed by the party to the _____ . A _____ can be unilateral or bilateral. _____ s include conveyances, commissions, licenses, patents, diplomas, and conditionally powers of attorney if executed as _____ s. The _____ is the modern descendant of the medieval charter, and delivery is thought to symbolically replace the ancient ceremony of livery of seisin.

Exam Probability: **Low**

22. *Answer choices:*

(see index for correct answer)

- a. Deed
- b. Curtilage
- c. Mesne profits
- d. Tenants in common 1031 exchange

Guidance: level 1

:: Judgment (law) ::

In law, a _____ is a judgment entered by a court for one party and against another party summarily, i.e., without a full trial. Such a judgment may be issued on the merits of an entire case, or on discrete issues in that case.

Exam Probability: **Medium**

23. *Answer choices:*

(see index for correct answer)

- a. judgment as a matter of law
- b. Summary judgment

Guidance: level 1

:: ::

A _____ is monetary compensation paid by an employer to an employee in exchange for work done. Payment may be calculated as a fixed amount for each task completed, or at an hourly or daily rate, or based on an easily measured quantity of work done.

Exam Probability: **Low**

24. *Answer choices:*

(see index for correct answer)

- a. Sarbanes-Oxley act of 2002
- b. Character
- c. Wage
- d. surface-level diversity

Guidance: level 1

:: Contract law ::

In contract law, _____ is an excuse for the nonperformance of duties under a contract, based on a change in circumstances, the nonoccurrence of which was an underlying assumption of the contract, that makes performance of the contract literally impossible.

Exam Probability: **Medium**

25. *Answer choices:*

(see index for correct answer)

- a. Impossibility
- b. Garnishment
- c. Revocation
- d. Co-signing

Guidance: level 1

:: Legal doctrines and principles ::

The _____ rule is a rule in the Anglo-American common law that governs what kinds of evidence parties to a contract dispute can introduce when trying to determine the specific terms of a contract. The rule also prevents parties who have reduced their agreement to a final written document from later introducing other evidence, such as the content of oral discussions from earlier in the negotiation process, as evidence of a different intent as to the terms of the contract. The rule provides that "extrinsic evidence is inadmissible to vary a written contract". The term "parol" derives from the Anglo-Norman French parol or parole, meaning "word of mouth" or "verbal", and in medieval times referred to oral pleadings in a court case.

Exam Probability: **Medium**

26. *Answer choices:*

(see index for correct answer)

- a. Contributory negligence
- b. unconscionable contract

- c. Parol evidence
- d. Proximate cause

Guidance: level 1

:: ::

A concept of English law, a _____ is an untrue or misleading statement of fact made during negotiations by one party to another, the statement then inducing that other party into the contract. The misled party may normally rescind the contract, and sometimes may be awarded damages as well.

Exam Probability: **Low**

27. *Answer choices:*

(see index for correct answer)

- a. functional perspective
- b. Misrepresentation
- c. similarity-attraction theory
- d. cultural

Guidance: level 1

:: Project management ::

_____ is the right to exercise power, which can be formalized by a state and exercised by way of judges, appointed executives of government, or the ecclesiastical or priestly appointed representatives of a God or other deities.

Exam Probability: **High**

28. *Answer choices:*

(see index for correct answer)

- a. Project network
- b. Problem domain analysis
- c. Authority
- d. Kickoff meeting

Guidance: level 1

:: ::

_____ is a process whereby a person assumes the parenting of another, usually a child, from that person's biological or legal parent or parents. Legal _____ s permanently transfers all rights and responsibilities, along with filiation, from the biological parent or parents.

Exam Probability: **High**

29. *Answer choices:*

(see index for correct answer)

- a. Adoption
- b. functional perspective
- c. imperative
- d. cultural

Guidance: level 1

:: Commercial crimes ::

_____ is the process of concealing the origins of money obtained illegally by passing it through a complex sequence of banking transfers or commercial transactions. The overall scheme of this process returns the money to the launderer in an obscure and indirect way.

Exam Probability: **Low**

30. *Answer choices:*

(see index for correct answer)

- a. Offshore leaks
- b. Money laundering
- c. FATF blacklist
- d. Monopolization

Guidance: level 1

:: Types of business entity ::

A _____ , the basic form of partnership under common law, is in most countries an association of persons or an unincorporated company with the following major features.

Exam Probability: **Medium**

31. *Answer choices:*

(see index for correct answer)

- a. Besloten vennootschap
- b. Public limited company
- c. General partnership
- d. Holding company

Guidance: level 1

:: ::

The words "_____" and "testify" both derive from the Latin word testis, referring to the notion of a disinterested third-party witness.

Exam Probability: **Medium**

32. *Answer choices:*

(see index for correct answer)

- a. Testimony
- b. interpersonal communication
- c. Character
- d. levels of analysis

Guidance: level 1

:: ::

A _____ is an organization, usually a group of people or a company, authorized to act as a single entity and recognized as such in law. Early incorporated entities were established by charter. Most jurisdictions now allow the creation of new _____ s through registration.

Exam Probability: **High**

33. *Answer choices:*

(see index for correct answer)

- a. Sarbanes-Oxley act of 2002
- b. open system
- c. hierarchical
- d. process perspective

Guidance: level 1

:: Business models ::

A _____ is "an autonomous association of persons united voluntarily to meet their common economic, social, and cultural needs and aspirations through a jointly-owned and democratically-controlled enterprise". _____ s may include.

Exam Probability: **High**

34. *Answer choices:*

(see index for correct answer)

- a. Entreship
- b. Dependent growth business model
- c. Copy to China
- d. Paid To Click

Guidance: level 1

:: Chemical industry ::

The _____ for the Protection of Literary and Artistic Works, usually known as the _____ , is an international agreement governing copyright, which was first accepted in Berne, Switzerland, in 1886.

Exam Probability: **High**

35. *Answer choices:*

(see index for correct answer)

- a. High production volume chemicals
- b. Berne Convention
- c. Chemical plant
- d. Chemical leasing

Guidance: level 1

:: ::

In contract law, rescission is an equitable remedy which allows a contractual party to cancel the contract. Parties may _____ if they are the victims of a vitiating factor, such as misrepresentation, mistake, duress, or undue influence. Rescission is the unwinding of a transaction. This is done to bring the parties, as far as possible, back to the position in which they were before they entered into a contract.

Exam Probability: **High**

36. *Answer choices:*

(see index for correct answer)

- a. hierarchical perspective
- b. Rescind
- c. information systems assessment
- d. empathy

Guidance: level 1

:: ::

_____ is the body of law that governs the activities of administrative agencies of government. Government agency action can include rule making, adjudication, or the enforcement of a specific regulatory agenda. _____ is considered a branch of public law. As a body of law, _____ deals with the decision-making of the administrative units of government that are part of a national regulatory scheme in such areas as police law, international trade, manufacturing, the environment, taxation, broadcasting, immigration and transport. _____ expanded greatly during the twentieth century, as legislative bodies worldwide created more government agencies to regulate the social, economic and political spheres of human interaction.

Exam Probability: **Low**

37. *Answer choices:*

(see index for correct answer)

- a. levels of analysis

- b. cultural
- c. co-culture
- d. Administrative law

Guidance: level 1

:: Clauses of the United States Constitution ::

The _____ describes an enumerated power listed in the United States Constitution. The clause states that the United States Congress shall have power "To regulate Commerce with foreign Nations, and among the several States, and with the Indian Tribes." Courts and commentators have tended to discuss each of these three areas of commerce as a separate power granted to Congress. It is common to see the individual components of the _____ referred to under specific terms: the Foreign _____, the Interstate _____, and the Indian _____.

Exam Probability: **Low**

38. *Answer choices:*
(see index for correct answer)

- a. Full Faith and Credit Clause
- b. Full faith and credit
- c. Commerce Clause

Guidance: level 1

:: ::

A _____ is a request to do something, most commonly addressed to a government official or public entity. _____ s to a deity are a form of prayer called supplication.

Exam Probability: **Medium**

39. *Answer choices:*

(see index for correct answer)

- a. Petition
- b. Character
- c. hierarchical perspective
- d. Sarbanes-Oxley act of 2002

Guidance: level 1

:: Business law ::

A _____ is a form of security interest granted over an item of property to secure the payment of a debt or performance of some other obligation. The owner of the property, who grants the _____ , is referred to as the _____ ee and the person who has the benefit of the _____ is referred to as the _____ or or _____ holder.

Exam Probability: **High**

40. *Answer choices:*

(see index for correct answer)

- a. Lien
- b. Registered agent
- c. Uniform Partnership Act
- d. OHADA

Guidance: level 1

:: ::

Business is the activity of making one's living or making money by producing or buying and selling products. Simply put, it is "any activity or enterprise entered into for profit. It does not mean it is a company, a corporation, partnership, or have any such formal organization, but it can range from a street peddler to General Motors."

Exam Probability: **Medium**

41. *Answer choices:*

(see index for correct answer)

- a. co-culture
- b. Firm
- c. cultural
- d. levels of analysis

Guidance: level 1

:: ::

_____, or auditory perception, is the ability to perceive sounds by detecting vibrations, changes in the pressure of the surrounding medium through time, through an organ such as the ear. The academic field concerned with _____ is auditory science.

Exam Probability: **Medium**

42. *Answer choices:*

(see index for correct answer)

- a. hierarchical
- b. empathy
- c. similarity-attraction theory
- d. levels of analysis

Guidance: level 1

:: Competition law ::

In competition law, a _____ is a market in which a particular product or service is sold. It is the intersection of a relevant product market and a relevant geographic market. The European Commission defines a _____ and its product and geographic components as follows.

Exam Probability: **Medium**

43. *Answer choices:*

(see index for correct answer)

- a. Small but significant and non-transitory increase in price
- b. Orange-Book-Standard
- c. Relevant market
- d. Competition law

Guidance: level 1

:: Debt ::

_____ is the trust which allows one party to provide money or resources to another party wherein the second party does not reimburse the first party immediately, but promises either to repay or return those resources at a later date. In other words, _____ is a method of making reciprocity formal, legally enforceable, and extensible to a large group of unrelated people.

Exam Probability: **High**

44. Answer choices:

(see index for correct answer)

- a. Arrears
- b. Compulsive buying disorder
- c. External financing
- d. Debt wall

Guidance: level 1

:: Stock market ::

> _____ is freedom from, or resilience against, potential harm caused by others. Beneficiaries of _____ may be of persons and social groups, objects and institutions, ecosystems or any other entity or phenomenon vulnerable to unwanted change by its environment.

Exam Probability: **Low**

45. Answer choices:

(see index for correct answer)

- a. Security
- b. Trading curb
- c. Greenshoe
- d. P chip

Guidance: level 1

:: ::

A _____ is an individual or institution that legally owns one or more shares of stock in a public or private corporation. _____ s may be referred to as members of a corporation. Legally, a person is not a _____ in a corporation until their name and other details are entered in the corporation's register of _____ s or members.

Exam Probability: **Low**

46. *Answer choices:*

(see index for correct answer)

- a. Shareholder
- b. co-culture
- c. imperative
- d. personal values

Guidance: level 1

:: ::

_____, often abbreviated cert. in the United States, is a process for seeking judicial review and a writ issued by a court that agrees to review. A _____ is issued by a superior court, directing an inferior court, tribunal, or other public authority to send the record of a proceeding for review.

Exam Probability: **High**

47. *Answer choices:*

(see index for correct answer)

- a. open system
- b. functional perspective
- c. empathy
- d. imperative

Guidance: level 1

:: ::

In law, an _____ is the process in which cases are reviewed, where parties request a formal change to an official decision. _____ s function both as a process for error correction as well as a process of clarifying and interpreting law. Although appellate courts have existed for thousands of years, common law countries did not incorporate an affirmative right to _____ into their jurisprudence until the 19th century.

Exam Probability: **High**

48. Answer choices:

(see index for correct answer)

- a. surface-level diversity
- b. empathy
- c. Appeal
- d. personal values

Guidance: level 1

:: Contract law ::

> Offer and acceptance analysis is a traditional approach in contract law. The offer and acceptance formula, developed in the 19th century, identifies a moment of formation when the parties are of one mind. This classical approach to contract formation has been modified by developments in the law of estoppel, misleading conduct, misrepresentation and unjust enrichment.

Exam Probability: **High**

49. Answer choices:

(see index for correct answer)

- a. Listing contract
- b. Broad Agency Announcement
- c. ConsensusDOCS
- d. Job order contracting

Guidance: level 1

:: Legal reasoning ::

_____ is a Latin expression meaning on its first encounter or at first sight. The literal translation would be "at first face" or "at first appearance", from the feminine forms of primus and facies, both in the ablative case. In modern, colloquial and conversational English, a common translation would be "on the face of it". The term _____ is used in modern legal English to signify that upon initial examination, sufficient corroborating evidence appears to exist to support a case. In common law jurisdictions, _____ denotes evidence that, unless rebutted, would be sufficient to prove a particular proposition or fact. The term is used similarly in academic philosophy. Most legal proceedings, in most jurisdictions, require a _____ case to exist, following which proceedings may then commence to test it, and create a ruling.

Exam Probability: **Medium**

50. *Answer choices:*
(see index for correct answer)

- a. Prima facie
- b. deliberation
- c. Reasonable man

Guidance: level 1

:: Legal doctrines and principles ::

In some common law jurisdictions, _____ is a defense to a tort claim based on negligence. If it is available, the defense completely bars plaintiffs from any recovery if they contribute to their own injury through their own negligence.

Exam Probability: **High**

51. *Answer choices:*

(see index for correct answer)

- a. Exclusionary rule
- b. Contributory negligence
- c. Mutual mistake
- d. Acquiescence

Guidance: level 1

:: Legal doctrines and principles ::

In the common law of torts, _____ loquitur is a doctrine that infers negligence from the very nature of an accident or injury in the absence of direct evidence on how any defendant behaved. Although modern formulations differ by jurisdiction, common law originally stated that the accident must satisfy the necessary elements of negligence: duty, breach of duty, causation, and injury. In _____ loquitur, the elements of duty of care, breach, and causation are inferred from an injury that does not ordinarily occur without negligence.

Exam Probability: **Low**

52. *Answer choices:*

(see index for correct answer)

- a. Attractive nuisance doctrine
- b. Res ipsa
- c. Act of state
- d. compulsory acquisition

Guidance: level 1

:: ::

In financial markets, a share is a unit used as mutual funds, limited partnerships, and real estate investment trusts. The owner of _____ in the corporation/company is a shareholder of the corporation. A share is an indivisible unit of capital, expressing the ownership relationship between the company and the shareholder. The denominated value of a share is its face value, and the total of the face value of issued _____ represent the capital of a company, which may not reflect the market value of those _____.

Exam Probability: **High**

53. *Answer choices:*

(see index for correct answer)

- a. hierarchical
- b. process perspective
- c. information systems assessment
- d. Shares

Guidance: level 1

:: ::

In law, a _____ is a coming together of parties to a dispute, to present information in a tribunal, a formal setting with the authority to adjudicate claims or disputes. One form of tribunal is a court. The tribunal, which may occur before a judge, jury, or other designated trier of fact, aims to achieve a resolution to their dispute.

Exam Probability: **Low**

54. *Answer choices:*

(see index for correct answer)

- a. surface-level diversity
- b. personal values
- c. Sarbanes-Oxley act of 2002
- d. Trial

Guidance: level 1

:: ::

In general, _____ is a form of dishonesty or criminal activity undertaken by a person or organization entrusted with a position of authority, often to acquire illicit benefit. _____ may include many activities including bribery and embezzlement, though it may also involve practices that are legal in many countries. Political _____ occurs when an office-holder or other governmental employee acts in an official capacity for personal gain. _____ is most commonplace in kleptocracies, oligarchies, narco-states and mafia states.

Exam Probability: **Medium**

55. *Answer choices:*

(see index for correct answer)

- a. Corruption
- b. deep-level diversity
- c. process perspective
- d. surface-level diversity

Guidance: level 1

:: Real property law ::

A _____ is the grant of authority or rights, stating that the granter formally recognizes the prerogative of the recipient to exercise the rights specified. It is implicit that the granter retains superiority , and that the recipient admits a limited status within the relationship, and it is within that sense that _____ s were historically granted, and that sense is retained in modern usage of the term.

Exam Probability: **High**

56. *Answer choices:*

(see index for correct answer)

- a. Charter
- b. Deed in lieu of foreclosure
- c. Calendars of the Grants of Probate and Letters of Administration
- d. Life estate

Guidance: level 1

:: ::

In the law of evidence, a _____ of a particular fact can be made without the aid of proof in some situations. The invocation of a _____ shifts the burden of proof from one party to the opposing party in a court trial.

Exam Probability: **Medium**

57. *Answer choices:*

(see index for correct answer)

- a. process perspective
- b. deep-level diversity
- c. levels of analysis
- d. personal values

Guidance: level 1

:: ::

_____ , also referred to as orthostasis, is a human position in which the body is held in an upright position and supported only by the feet.

Exam Probability: **High**

58. Answer choices:

(see index for correct answer)

- a. Standing
- b. hierarchical perspective
- c. empathy
- d. imperative

Guidance: level 1

:: Contract law ::

A _____ is a legally-binding agreement which recognises and governs the rights and duties of the parties to the agreement. A _____ is legally enforceable because it meets the requirements and approval of the law. An agreement typically involves the exchange of goods, services, money, or promises of any of those. In the event of breach of _____, the law awards the injured party access to legal remedies such as damages and cancellation.

Exam Probability: **Medium**

59. Answer choices:

(see index for correct answer)

- a. Contract B
- b. Risk of loss
- c. Accommodation
- d. Neo-classical contract

Guidance: level 1

Finance

Finance is a field that is concerned with the allocation (investment) of assets and liabilities over space and time, often under conditions of risk or uncertainty. Finance can also be defined as the science of money management. Participants in the market aim to price assets based on their risk level, fundamental value, and their expected rate of return. Finance can be split into three sub-categories: public finance, corporate finance and personal finance.

:: Banking ::

A _____ is a financial institution that accepts deposits from the public and creates credit. Lending activities can be performed either directly or indirectly through capital markets. Due to their importance in the financial stability of a country, _____ s are highly regulated in most countries. Most nations have institutionalized a system known as fractional reserve _____ ing under which _____ s hold liquid assets equal to only a portion of their current liabilities. In addition to other regulations intended to ensure liquidity, _____ s are generally subject to minimum capital requirements based on an international set of capital standards, known as the Basel Accords.

Exam Probability: **Low**

1. *Answer choices:*

(see index for correct answer)

- a. Prime rate
- b. Bank
- c. Direct bank
- d. Short term deposit

Guidance: level 1

:: Separation of investment and commercial banking ::

A _____ is a type of bank that provides services such as accepting deposits, making business loans, and offering basic investment products that is operated as a business for profit.

Exam Probability: **High**

2. *Answer choices:*

(see index for correct answer)

- a. Commercial bank
- b. Depository institution
- c. Speculation
- d. Bank Holding Company Act

Guidance: level 1

:: Debt ::

_____ is the trust which allows one party to provide money or resources to another party wherein the second party does not reimburse the first party immediately, but promises either to repay or return those resources at a later date. In other words, _____ is a method of making reciprocity formal, legally enforceable, and extensible to a large group of unrelated people.

Exam Probability: **High**

3. *Answer choices:*

(see index for correct answer)

- a. Charge-off
- b. Debt club

- c. Credit
- d. Financial assistance

Guidance: level 1

:: Stock market ::

> A _____ or stock divide increases the number of shares in a company. The price is adjusted such that the before and after market capitalization of the company remains the same and dilution does not occur. Options and warrants are included.

Exam Probability: **Low**

4. *Answer choices:*

(see index for correct answer)

- a. PLUS Markets Group
- b. Security
- c. Stock split
- d. Automated trading system

Guidance: level 1

:: ::

In finance, return is a profit on an investment. It comprises any change in value of the investment, and/or cash flows which the investor receives from the investment, such as interest payments or dividends. It may be measured either in absolute terms or as a percentage of the amount invested. The latter is also called the holding period return.

Exam Probability: **High**

5. *Answer choices:*

(see index for correct answer)

- a. personal values
- b. surface-level diversity
- c. similarity-attraction theory
- d. Rate of return

Guidance: level 1

:: Accounting terminology ::

Total _____ is a method of Accounting cost which entails the full cost of manufacturing or providing a service. TAC includes not just the costs of materials and labour, but also of all manufacturing overheads. The cost of each cost center can be direct or indirect. The direct cost can be easily identified with individual cost centers. Whereas indirect cost cannot be easily identified with the cost center. The distribution of overhead among the departments is called apportionment.

Exam Probability: **Low**

6. *Answer choices:*

(see index for correct answer)

- a. Capital surplus
- b. Capital expenditure
- c. Absorption costing
- d. General ledger

Guidance: level 1

:: ::

_____ is a marketing communication that employs an openly sponsored, non-personal message to promote or sell a product, service or idea. Sponsors of _____ are typically businesses wishing to promote their products or services. _____ is differentiated from public relations in that an advertiser pays for and has control over the message. It differs from personal selling in that the message is non-personal, i.e., not directed to a particular individual. _____ is communicated through various mass media, including traditional media such as newspapers, magazines, television, radio, outdoor _____ or direct mail; and new media such as search results, blogs, social media, websites or text messages. The actual presentation of the message in a medium is referred to as an advertisement, or "ad" or advert for short.

Exam Probability: **Medium**

7. *Answer choices:*

(see index for correct answer)

- a. cultural
- b. Sarbanes-Oxley act of 2002
- c. hierarchical
- d. Advertising

Guidance: level 1

:: Government bonds ::

A _____ or sovereign bond is a bond issued by a national government, generally with a promise to pay periodic interest payments called coupon payments and to repay the face value on the maturity date. The aim of a _____ is to support government spending. _____ s are usually denominated in the country's own currency, in which case the government cannot be forced to default, although it may choose to do so. If a government is close to default on its debt the media often refer to this as a sovereign debt crisis.

Exam Probability: **Low**

8. *Answer choices:*

(see index for correct answer)

- a. Municipal bond
- b. GDP-linked bond
- c. Risk-free bond

- d. TreasuryDirect

Guidance: level 1

:: Accounting journals and ledgers ::

A _____, in accounting, is the logging of a transaction in an accounting journal that shows a company's debit and credit balances. The _____ can consist of several recordings, each of which is either a debit or a credit. The total of the debits must equal the total of the credits or the _____ is considered unbalanced. Journal entries can record unique items or recurring items such as depreciation or bond amortization. In accounting software, journal entries are usually entered using a separate module from accounts payable, which typically has its own subledger, that indirectly affects the general ledger. As a result, journal entries directly change the account balances on the general ledger. A properly documented _____ consists of the correct date, amount that will be debited, amount that will be credited, description of transaction, and unique reference number.

Exam Probability: **Low**

9. *Answer choices:*

(see index for correct answer)

- a. Journal entry
- b. General journal
- c. Check register
- d. Cash receipts journal

Guidance: level 1

:: Accounting terminology ::

A _____ contains all the accounts for recording transactions relating to a company's assets, liabilities, owners' equity, revenue, and expenses. In modern accounting software or ERP, the _____ works as a central repository for accounting data transferred from all subledgers or modules like accounts payable, accounts receivable, cash management, fixed assets, purchasing and projects. The _____ is the backbone of any accounting system which holds financial and non-financial data for an organization. The collection of all accounts is known as the _____ . Each account is known as a ledger account. In a manual or non-computerized system this may be a large book. The statement of financial position and the statement of income and comprehensive income are both derived from the _____ . Each account in the _____ consists of one or more pages. The _____ is where posting to the accounts occurs. Posting is the process of recording amounts as credits , and amounts as debits , in the pages of the _____ . Additional columns to the right hold a running activity total .

Exam Probability: **Low**

10. *Answer choices:*

(see index for correct answer)

- a. Accrual
- b. Mark-to-market
- c. Basis of accounting
- d. General ledger

Guidance: level 1

:: Public finance ::

_____ is the process by which the monetary authority of a country, typically the central bank or currency board, controls either the cost of very short-term borrowing or the money supply, often targeting inflation rate or interest rate to ensure price stability and general trust in the currency.

Exam Probability: **High**

11. *Answer choices:*

(see index for correct answer)

- a. Monetary policy
- b. Private participation in railway share
- c. budget deficit
- d. International Fiscal Association

Guidance: level 1

:: Financial markets ::

A _____ is a market in which people trade financial securities and derivatives such as futures and options at low transaction costs. Securities include stocks and bonds, and precious metals.

Exam Probability: **Low**

12. *Answer choices:*

(see index for correct answer)

- a. Future Trading Act
- b. Financial market
- c. Direct market access
- d. Marketcetera

Guidance: level 1

:: Financial risk ::

_____ is any of various types of risk associated with financing, including financial transactions that include company loans in risk of default. Often it is understood to include only downside risk, meaning the potential for financial loss and uncertainty about its extent.

Exam Probability: **Medium**

13. *Answer choices:*

(see index for correct answer)

- a. Risk-free interest rate
- b. Financial risk
- c. Capital Requirements Directive

- d. Dynamic risk measure

Guidance: level 1

:: Basel II ::

> All businesses take risks based on two factors: the probability an adverse circumstance will come about and the cost of such adverse circumstance. Risk management is the study of how to control risks and balance the possibility of gains.

Exam Probability: **Medium**

14. *Answer choices:*

(see index for correct answer)

- a. Basel II
- b. Standardized approach
- c. Basic indicator approach
- d. Advanced IRB

Guidance: level 1

:: ::

_____ is the collection of mechanisms, processes and relations by which corporations are controlled and operated. Governance structures and principles identify the distribution of rights and responsibilities among different participants in the corporation and include the rules and procedures for making decisions in corporate affairs. _____ is necessary because of the possibility of conflicts of interests between stakeholders, primarily between shareholders and upper management or among shareholders.

Exam Probability: **Medium**

15. *Answer choices:*

(see index for correct answer)

- a. process perspective
- b. cultural
- c. interpersonal communication
- d. Corporate governance

Guidance: level 1

:: Generally Accepted Accounting Principles ::

A _____ , in accrual accounting, is any account where the asset or liability is not realized until a future date , e.g. annuities, charges, taxes, income, etc. The deferred item may be carried, dependent on type of _____ , as either an asset or liability. See also accrual.

Exam Probability: **High**

16. *Answer choices:*

(see index for correct answer)

- a. Deprival value
- b. Expense
- c. Construction in progress
- d. Trial balance

Guidance: level 1

:: Investment ::

_____, and investment appraisal, is the planning process used to determine whether an organization's long term investments such as new machinery, replacement of machinery, new plants, new products, and research development projects are worth the funding of cash through the firm's capitalization structure. It is the process of allocating resources for major capital, or investment, expenditures. One of the primary goals of _____ investments is to increase the value of the firm to the shareholders.

Exam Probability: **Low**

17. *Answer choices:*

(see index for correct answer)

- a. Malinvestment
- b. Bullish
- c. Capital budgeting

- d. Asset Liquidation Marketing Integration Within Asset Management Framework

Guidance: level 1

:: Financial markets ::

In economics and finance, _____ is the practice of taking advantage of a price difference between two or more markets: striking a combination of matching deals that capitalize upon the imbalance, the profit being the difference between the market prices. When used by academics, an _____ is a transaction that involves no negative cash flow at any probabilistic or temporal state and a positive cash flow in at least one state; in simple terms, it is the possibility of a risk-free profit after transaction costs. For example, an _____ opportunity is present when there is the opportunity to instantaneously buy something for a low price and sell it for a higher price.

Exam Probability: **High**

18. *Answer choices:*

(see index for correct answer)

- a. Buying in
- b. Faroese Securities Market
- c. Direct market access
- d. Arbitrage

Guidance: level 1

:: Pension funds ::

_____ s typically have large amounts of money to invest and are the major investors in listed and private companies. They are especially important to the stock market where large institutional investors dominate. The largest 300 _____ s collectively hold about $6 trillion in assets. In January 2008, The Economist reported that Morgan Stanley estimates that _____ s worldwide hold over US$20 trillion in assets, the largest for any category of investor ahead of mutual funds, insurance companies, currency reserves, sovereign wealth funds, hedge funds, or private equity.

Exam Probability: **Low**

19. *Answer choices:*

(see index for correct answer)

- a. Pension led funding
- b. Pension fund
- c. Texas Municipal Retirement System

Guidance: level 1

:: Commerce ::

Continuation of an entity as a _____ is presumed as the basis for financial reporting unless and until the entity's liquidation becomes imminent. Preparation of financial statements under this presumption is commonly referred to as the _____ basis of accounting. If and when an entity's liquidation becomes imminent, financial statements are prepared under the liquidation basis of accounting.

Exam Probability: **Low**

20. *Answer choices:*

(see index for correct answer)

- a. Perfect tender rule
- b. Deal transaction
- c. Closed household economy
- d. Hong Kong Mercantile Exchange

Guidance: level 1

:: Scheduling (computing) ::

Ageing or _____ is the process of becoming older. The term refers especially to human beings, many animals, and fungi, whereas for example bacteria, perennial plants and some simple animals are potentially biologically immortal. In the broader sense, ageing can refer to single cells within an organism which have ceased dividing or to the population of a species.

Exam Probability: **High**

21. Answer choices:

(see index for correct answer)

- a. Affinity mask
- b. Idle
- c. Aging
- d. Random boosting

Guidance: level 1

:: ::

_____ is the withdrawal from one's position or occupation or from one's active working life. A person may also semi-retire by reducing work hours.

Exam Probability: **Low**

22. Answer choices:

(see index for correct answer)

- a. interpersonal communication
- b. surface-level diversity
- c. hierarchical perspective
- d. similarity-attraction theory

Guidance: level 1

:: Real estate ::

Amortisation is paying off an amount owed over time by making planned, incremental payments of principal and interest. To amortise a loan means "to kill it off". In accounting, amortisation refers to charging or writing off an intangible asset's cost as an operational expense over its estimated useful life to reduce a company's taxable income.

Exam Probability: **High**

23. *Answer choices:*

(see index for correct answer)

- a. Coving
- b. Lease and release
- c. Warrant of possession
- d. Amortization

Guidance: level 1

:: ::

_____ is the process of making predictions of the future based on past and present data and most commonly by analysis of trends. A commonplace example might be estimation of some variable of interest at some specified future date. Prediction is a similar, but more general term. Both might refer to formal statistical methods employing time series, cross-sectional or longitudinal data, or alternatively to less formal judgmental methods. Usage can differ between areas of application: for example, in hydrology the terms "forecast" and " _____ " are sometimes reserved for estimates of values at certain specific future times, while the term "prediction" is used for more general estimates, such as the number of times floods will occur over a long period.

Exam Probability: **Medium**

24. *Answer choices:*

(see index for correct answer)

- a. hierarchical perspective
- b. process perspective
- c. deep-level diversity
- d. cultural

Guidance: level 1

:: Margin policy ::

In finance, a _____ is a standardized forward contract, a legal agreement to buy or sell something at a predetermined price at a specified time in the future, between parties not known to each other. The asset transacted is usually a commodity or financial instrument. The predetermined price the parties agree to buy and sell the asset for is known as the forward price. The specified time in the future—which is when delivery and payment occur—is known as the delivery date. Because it is a function of an underlying asset, a _____ is a derivative product.

Exam Probability: **Medium**

25. *Answer choices:*

(see index for correct answer)

- a. Regulation T
- b. Futures contract

Guidance: level 1

:: Finance ::

A _____, publicly-traded company, publicly-held company, publicly-listed company, or public limited company is a corporation whose ownership is dispersed among the general public in many shares of stock which are freely traded on a stock exchange or in over-the-counter markets. In some jurisdictions, public companies over a certain size must be listed on an exchange. A _____ can be listed or unlisted.

Exam Probability: **High**

26. Answer choices:

(see index for correct answer)

- a. Property income
- b. Five risks
- c. Pet banks
- d. Public company

Guidance: level 1

:: ::

> A _____, or holiday, is a leave of absence from a regular occupation, or a specific trip or journey, usually for the purpose of recreation or tourism. People often take a _____ during specific holiday observances, or for specific festivals or celebrations. _____ s are often spent with friends or family.

Exam Probability: **Medium**

27. Answer choices:

(see index for correct answer)

- a. co-culture
- b. cultural
- c. surface-level diversity
- d. process perspective

Guidance: level 1

:: Business law ::

A _____ is an arrangement where parties, known as partners, agree to cooperate to advance their mutual interests. The partners in a _____ may be individuals, businesses, interest-based organizations, schools, governments or combinations. Organizations may partner to increase the likelihood of each achieving their mission and to amplify their reach. A _____ may result in issuing and holding equity or may be only governed by a contract.

Exam Probability: **Medium**

28. *Answer choices:*

(see index for correct answer)

- a. Personal Property Security Act
- b. Bulk transfer
- c. Turnkey
- d. Novated lease

Guidance: level 1

:: Accounting terminology ::

_____ is money owed by a business to its suppliers shown as a liability on a company's balance sheet. It is distinct from notes payable liabilities, which are debts created by formal legal instrument documents.

Exam Probability: **High**

29. *Answer choices:*

(see index for correct answer)

- a. Accounts payable
- b. Statement of financial position
- c. Mark-to-market
- d. Accrued liabilities

Guidance: level 1

:: bad_topic ::

_____ refers to systematic approach to the governance and realization of value from the things that a group or entity is responsible for, over their whole life cycles. It may apply both to tangible assets and to intangible assets . _____ is a systematic process of developing, operating, maintaining, upgrading, and disposing of assets in the most cost-effective manner .

Exam Probability: **Medium**

30. *Answer choices:*

(see index for correct answer)

- a. Cognitive appraisal
- b. Asset management
- c. Text message
- d. Inept

Guidance: level 1

:: Financial markets ::

For an individual, a _____ is the minimum amount of money by which the expected return on a risky asset must exceed the known return on a risk-free asset in order to induce an individual to hold the risky asset rather than the risk-free asset. It is positive if the person is risk averse. Thus it is the minimum willingness to accept compensation for the risk.

Exam Probability: **High**

31. *Answer choices:*

(see index for correct answer)

- a. Copy trading
- b. Crossing network
- c. Risk premium
- d. Fution

Guidance: level 1

:: Financial accounting ::

_____ in accounting is the process of treating investments in associate companies. Equity accounting is usually applied where an investor entity holds 20–50% of the voting stock of the associate company. The investor records such investments as an asset on its balance sheet. The investor's proportional share of the associate company's net income increases the investment, and proportional payments of dividends decrease it. In the investor's income statement, the proportional share of the investor's net income or net loss is reported as a single-line item.

Exam Probability: **High**

32. *Answer choices:*

(see index for correct answer)

- a. Asset swap
- b. Financial Condition Report
- c. Working capital
- d. Accounting identity

Guidance: level 1

:: Investment ::

The _____ is a measure of an investment's rate of return. The term internal refers to the fact that the calculation excludes external factors, such as the risk-free rate, inflation, the cost of capital, or various financial risks.

Exam Probability: **Low**

33. *Answer choices:*

(see index for correct answer)

- a. Internal rate of return
- b. Psychology of previous investment
- c. Active management
- d. The Zulu Principle

Guidance: level 1

:: Business economics ::

In finance, _____ is the risk of losses caused by interest rate changes. The prices of most financial instruments, such as stocks and bonds move inversely with interest rates, so investors are subject to capital loss when rates rise.

Exam Probability: **Medium**

34. *Answer choices:*

(see index for correct answer)

- a. Derived demand
- b. Round-tripping
- c. Average daily rate
- d. Rate risk

Guidance: level 1

:: Asset ::

> In accounting, a _____ is any asset which can reasonably be expected to be sold, consumed, or exhausted through the normal operations of a business within the current fiscal year or operating cycle . Typical _____ s include cash, cash equivalents, short-term investments , accounts receivable, stock inventory, supplies, and the portion of prepaid liabilities which will be paid within a year. In simple words, assets which are held for a short period are known as _____ s. Such assets are expected to be realised in cash or consumed during the normal operating cycle of the business.

Exam Probability: **High**

35. *Answer choices:*

(see index for correct answer)

- a. Asset
- b. Fixed asset

Guidance: level 1

:: Cash flow ::

In corporate finance, _____ or _____ to firm is a way of looking at a business's cash flow to see what is available for distribution among all the securities holders of a corporate entity. This may be useful to parties such as equity holders, debt holders, preferred stock holders, and convertible security holders when they want to see how much cash can be extracted from a company without causing issues to its operations.

Exam Probability: **Low**

36. *Answer choices:*

(see index for correct answer)

- a. Valuation using discounted cash flows
- b. Cash flow
- c. Free cash flow
- d. Invoice discounting

Guidance: level 1

:: Accounting terminology ::

In accounting/accountancy, _____ are journal entries usually made at the end of an accounting period to allocate income and expenditure to the period in which they actually occurred. The revenue recognition principle is the basis of making _____ that pertain to unearned and accrued revenues under accrual-basis accounting. They are sometimes called Balance Day adjustments because they are made on balance day.

Exam Probability: **High**

37. *Answer choices:*

(see index for correct answer)

- a. Capital expenditure
- b. Adjusting entries
- c. managerial accounting
- d. Accounts payable

Guidance: level 1

:: Generally Accepted Accounting Principles ::

A _____ is a reduction of the recognized value of something. In accounting, this is a recognition of the reduced or zero value of an asset. In income tax statements, this is a reduction of taxable income, as a recognition of certain expenses required to produce the income.

Exam Probability: **Low**

38. *Answer choices:*

(see index for correct answer)

- a. Gross sales
- b. Operating income
- c. Write-off
- d. Consolidation

Guidance: level 1

:: International trade ::

> _____ involves the transfer of goods or services from one person or entity to another, often in exchange for money. A system or network that allows _____ is called a market.

Exam Probability: **High**

39. *Answer choices:*

(see index for correct answer)

- a. Price band
- b. Business English
- c. Transfer problem
- d. Globalization

Guidance: level 1

:: Fixed income analysis ::

The _____ , book yield or redemption yield of a bond or other fixed-interest security, such as gilts, is the internal rate of return earned by an investor who buys the bond today at the market price, assuming that the bond is held until maturity, and that all coupon and principal payments are made on schedule. _____ is the discount rate at which the sum of all future cash flows from the bond is equal to the current price of the bond. The YTM is often given in terms of Annual Percentage Rate , but more often market convention is followed. In a number of major markets the convention is to quote annualized yields with semi-annual compounding ; thus, for example, an annual effective yield of 10.25% would be quoted as 10.00%, because $1.05 \times 1.05 = 1.1025$ and $2 \times 5 = 10$.

Exam Probability: **High**

40. *Answer choices:*

(see index for correct answer)

- a. Area yield options contract
- b. 30-day yield
- c. Yield to maturity
- d. Bond convexity closed-form formula

Guidance: level 1

:: Valuation (finance) ::

_____ refers to an assessment of the viability, stability, and profitability of a business, sub-business or project.

Exam Probability: **High**

41. *Answer choices:*

(see index for correct answer)

- a. Benjamin Graham formula
- b. Valuation using multiples
- c. Financial analysis
- d. Period of financial distress

Guidance: level 1

:: Generally Accepted Accounting Principles ::

In accounting and finance, earnings before interest and taxes is a measure of a firm's profit that includes all incomes and expenses except interest expenses and income tax expenses.

Exam Probability: **Low**

42. *Answer choices:*

(see index for correct answer)

- a. Insurance asset management
- b. Petty cash
- c. Treasury stock
- d. Operating Income

Guidance: level 1

:: ::

> _____ is the field of accounting concerned with the summary, analysis and reporting of financial transactions related to a business. This involves the preparation of financial statements available for public use. Stockholders, suppliers, banks, employees, government agencies, business owners, and other stakeholders are examples of people interested in receiving such information for decision making purposes.

Exam Probability: **Medium**

43. *Answer choices:*

(see index for correct answer)

- a. surface-level diversity
- b. Financial accounting
- c. imperative
- d. Character

Guidance: level 1

:: Corporate governance ::

The _____ is the officer of a company that has primary responsibility for managing the company's finances, including financial planning, management of financial risks, record-keeping, and financial reporting. In some sectors, the CFO is also responsible for analysis of data. Some CFOs have the title CFOO for chief financial and operating officer. In the United Kingdom, the typical term for a CFO is finance director. The CFO typically reports to the chief executive officer and the board of directors and may additionally have a seat on the board. The CFO supervises the finance unit and is the chief financial spokesperson for the organization. The CFO directly assists the chief operating officer on all strategic and tactical matters relating to budget management, cost-benefit analysis, forecasting needs, and securing of new funding.

Exam Probability: **High**

44. *Answer choices:*

(see index for correct answer)

- a. President
- b. Chief process officer
- c. Chief financial officer
- d. Chartered Secretaries New Zealand

Guidance: level 1

:: Money market instruments ::

_____ , in the global financial market, is an unsecured promissory note with a fixed maturity of not more than 270 days.

Exam Probability: **Low**

45. *Answer choices:*

(see index for correct answer)

- a. Commercial paper in India
- b. Commercial paper

Guidance: level 1

:: Mathematical finance ::

_____ is the value of an asset at a specific date. It measures the nominal future sum of money that a given sum of money is "worth" at a specified time in the future assuming a certain interest rate, or more generally, rate of return; it is the present value multiplied by the accumulation function. The value does not include corrections for inflation or other factors that affect the true value of money in the future. This is used in time value of money calculations.

Exam Probability: **Medium**

46. *Answer choices:*

(see index for correct answer)

- a. Admissible trading strategy
- b. Risk-neutral measure
- c. Future value
- d. Delta neutral

Guidance: level 1

:: ::

In financial markets, a share is a unit used as mutual funds, limited partnerships, and real estate investment trusts. The owner of _____ in the corporation/company is a shareholder of the corporation. A share is an indivisible unit of capital, expressing the ownership relationship between the company and the shareholder. The denominated value of a share is its face value, and the total of the face value of issued _____ represent the capital of a company, which may not reflect the market value of those _____ .

Exam Probability: **Medium**

47. *Answer choices:*
(see index for correct answer)

- a. information systems assessment
- b. personal values
- c. Shares
- d. levels of analysis

Guidance: level 1

:: Money ::

Cash and _____s are the most liquid current assets found on a business's balance sheet. _____s are short-term commitments "with temporarily idle cash and easily convertible into a known cash amount". An investment normally counts to be a _____ when it has a short maturity period of 90 days or less, and can be included in the cash and _____s balance from the date of acquisition when it carries an insignificant risk of changes in the asset value; with more than 90 days maturity, the asset is not considered as cash and _____s. Equity investments mostly are excluded from _____s, unless they are essentially _____s, for instance, if the preferred shares acquired within a short maturity period and with specified recovery date.

Exam Probability: **Medium**

48. *Answer choices:*

(see index for correct answer)

- a. Cash equivalent
- b. Monetization
- c. Chained dollars
- d. Money creation

Guidance: level 1

:: ::

A _____ is the process of presenting a topic to an audience. It is typically a demonstration, introduction, lecture, or speech meant to inform, persuade, inspire, motivate, or to build good will or to present a new idea or product. The term can also be used for a formal or ritualized introduction or offering, as with the _____ of a debutante. _____ s in certain formats are also known as keynote address.

Exam Probability: **High**

49. *Answer choices:*

(see index for correct answer)

- a. imperative
- b. Sarbanes-Oxley act of 2002
- c. Presentation
- d. corporate values

Guidance: level 1

:: Planning ::

_____ is a high level plan to achieve one or more goals under conditions of uncertainty. In the sense of the "art of the general," which included several subsets of skills including tactics, siegecraft, logistics etc., the term came into use in the 6th century C.E. in East Roman terminology, and was translated into Western vernacular languages only in the 18th century. From then until the 20th century, the word "_____" came to denote "a comprehensive way to try to pursue political ends, including the threat or actual use of force, in a dialectic of wills" in a military conflict, in which both adversaries interact.

Exam Probability: **Low**

50. *Answer choices:*

(see index for correct answer)

- a. Strategic communication
- b. Default effect
- c. School timetable
- d. Territorialist School

Guidance: level 1

:: Taxation ::

In a tax system, the _____ is the ratio at which a business or person is taxed. There are several methods used to present a _____ : statutory, average, marginal, and effective. These rates can also be presented using different definitions applied to a tax base: inclusive and exclusive.

Exam Probability: **Medium**

51. *Answer choices:*

(see index for correct answer)

- a. Tax advisor
- b. Tax rate
- c. Severance tax
- d. Energy tax

Guidance: level 1

:: Mereology ::

_____ , in the abstract, is what belongs to or with something, whether as an attribute or as a component of said thing. In the context of this article, it is one or more components , whether physical or incorporeal, of a person's estate; or so belonging to, as in being owned by, a person or jointly a group of people or a legal entity like a corporation or even a society. Depending on the nature of the _____ , an owner of _____ has the right to consume, alter, share, redefine, rent, mortgage, pawn, sell, exchange, transfer, give away or destroy it, or to exclude others from doing these things, as well as to perhaps abandon it; whereas regardless of the nature of the _____ , the owner thereof has the right to properly use it , or at the very least exclusively keep it.

Exam Probability: **Low**

52. *Answer choices:*

(see index for correct answer)

- a. Non-wellfounded mereology
- b. Simple
- c. Mereotopology
- d. Property

Guidance: level 1

:: Consumer theory ::

_____ is the quantity of a good that consumers are willing and able to purchase at various prices during a given period of time.

Exam Probability: **High**

53. *Answer choices:*
(see index for correct answer)

- a. Quality bias
- b. Convex preferences
- c. Demand
- d. Consumer choice

Guidance: level 1

:: Generally Accepted Accounting Principles ::

Financial statements prepared and presented by a company typically follow an external standard that specifically guides their preparation. These standards vary across the globe and are typically overseen by some combination of the private accounting profession in that specific nation and the various government regulators. Variations across countries may be considerable, making cross-country evaluation of financial data challenging.

Exam Probability: **High**

54. *Answer choices:*

(see index for correct answer)

- a. Operating income
- b. Depreciation
- c. Net income
- d. Income statement

Guidance: level 1

:: ::

A shareholder is an individual or institution that legally owns one or more shares of stock in a public or private corporation. Shareholders may be referred to as members of a corporation. Legally, a person is not a shareholder in a corporation until their name and other details are entered in the corporation's register of shareholders or members.

Exam Probability: **High**

55. *Answer choices:*

(see index for correct answer)

- a. interpersonal communication
- b. functional perspective
- c. Stockholder
- d. open system

Guidance: level 1

:: ::

_____ is the administration of an organization, whether it is a business, a not-for-profit organization, or government body. _____ includes the activities of setting the strategy of an organization and coordinating the efforts of its employees to accomplish its objectives through the application of available resources, such as financial, natural, technological, and human resources. The term " _____ " may also refer to those people who manage an organization.

Exam Probability: **High**

56. *Answer choices:*

(see index for correct answer)

- a. cultural

- b. similarity-attraction theory
- c. Management
- d. corporate values

Guidance: level 1

:: ::

_____ s and acquisitions are transactions in which the ownership of companies, other business organizations, or their operating units are transferred or consolidated with other entities. As an aspect of strategic management, M&A can allow enterprises to grow or downsize, and change the nature of their business or competitive position.

Exam Probability: **Low**

57. *Answer choices:*

(see index for correct answer)

- a. Merger
- b. process perspective
- c. hierarchical perspective
- d. interpersonal communication

Guidance: level 1

:: Financial accounting ::

_____ is a financial metric which represents operating liquidity available to a business, organisation or other entity, including governmental entities. Along with fixed assets such as plant and equipment, _____ is considered a part of operating capital. Gross _____ is equal to current assets. _____ is calculated as current assets minus current liabilities. If current assets are less than current liabilities, an entity has a _____ deficiency, also called a _____ deficit.

Exam Probability: **Medium**

58. *Answer choices:*

(see index for correct answer)

- a. Mark-to-market accounting
- b. Working capital
- c. Accounting identity
- d. Financial Condition Report

Guidance: level 1

:: Stock market ::

_____ is freedom from, or resilience against, potential harm caused by others. Beneficiaries of _____ may be of persons and social groups, objects and institutions, ecosystems or any other entity or phenomenon vulnerable to unwanted change by its environment.

Exam Probability: **Medium**

59. *Answer choices:*

(see index for correct answer)

- a. Shadow stock
- b. Exchange
- c. First Prudential Markets
- d. Security

Guidance: level 1

Human resource management

Human resource (HR) management is the strategic approach to the effective management of organization workers so that they help the business gain a competitive advantage. It is designed to maximize employee performance in service of an employer's strategic objectives. HR is primarily concerned with the management of people within organizations, focusing on policies and on systems. HR departments are responsible for overseeing employee-benefits design, employee recruitment, training and development, performance appraisal, and rewarding (e.g., managing pay and benefit systems). HR also concerns itself with organizational change and industrial relations, that is, the balancing of organizational practices with requirements arising from collective bargaining and from governmental laws.

:: Employment compensation ::

The formula commonly used by compensation professionals to assess the competitiveness of an employee's pay level involves calculating a """ _____ """. _____ is the short form for Comparative ratio.

Exam Probability: **High**

1. *Answer choices:*

(see index for correct answer)

- a. Pension administration in the United States
- b. Defense Base Act
- c. Total Reward
- d. Compa-ratio

Guidance: level 1

:: Ethically disputed business practices ::

An _____ in US labor law refers to certain actions taken by employers or unions that violate the National Labor Relations Act of 1935 29 U.S.C. § 151–169 and other legislation. Such acts are investigated by the National Labor Relations Board .

Exam Probability: **High**

2. *Answer choices:*

(see index for correct answer)

- a. Wage slavery
- b. Reassignment centers
- c. Sugging
- d. Unfair labor practice

Guidance: level 1

:: Employment ::

Onboarding, also known as _____, is management jargon first created in 1988 that refers to the mechanism through which new employees acquire the necessary knowledge, skills, and behaviors in order to become effective organizational members and insiders.

Exam Probability: **Medium**

3. *Answer choices:*
(see index for correct answer)

- a. Contingent workforce
- b. Performance improvement
- c. Organizational socialization
- d. The Kingdom of Could Be You

Guidance: level 1

:: Personal finance ::

_____ is an arrangement in which a portion of an employee's income is paid out at a later date after which the income was earned. Examples of _____ include pensions, retirement plans, and employee stock options. The primary benefit of most _____ is the deferral of tax to the date at which the employee receives the income.

Exam Probability: **Medium**

4. *Answer choices:*

(see index for correct answer)

- a. Home equity
- b. Asset location
- c. Repossession
- d. Deferred compensation

Guidance: level 1

:: Labor ::

The workforce or labour force is the labour pool in employment. It is generally used to describe those working for a single company or industry, but can also apply to a geographic region like a city, state, or country. Within a company, its value can be labelled as its "Workforce in Place". The workforce of a country includes both the employed and the unemployed. The labour force participation rate, LFPR , is the ratio between the labour force and the overall size of their cohort . The term generally excludes the employers or management, and can imply those involved in manual labour. It may also mean all those who are available for work.

Exam Probability: **High**

5. *Answer choices:*

(see index for correct answer)

- a. Haken
- b. Occupational safety and health
- c. Deskilling
- d. Labor force

Guidance: level 1

:: Human resource management ::

_____ is a process for identifying and developing new leaders who can replace old leaders when they leave, retire or die. _____ increases the availability of experienced and capable employees that are prepared to assume these roles as they become available. Taken narrowly, "replacement planning" for key roles is the heart of _____ .

Exam Probability: **Low**

6. *Answer choices:*

(see index for correct answer)

- a. Succession planning
- b. Recruitment process outsourcing
- c. Induction training
- d. Autonomous work group

Guidance: level 1

:: ::

_____ is a method for employees to organize into a labor union in which a majority of employees in a bargaining unit sign authorization forms, or "cards", stating they wish to be represented by the union. Since the National Labor Relations Act became law in 1935, _____ has been an alternative to the National Labor Relations Board's election process. _____ and election are both overseen by the National Labor Relations Board. The difference is that with card sign-up, employees sign authorization cards stating they want a union, the cards are submitted to the NLRB and if more than 50% of the employees submitted cards, the NLRB requires the employer to recognize the union. The NLRA election process is an additional step with the NLRB conducting a secret ballot election after authorization cards are submitted. In both cases the employer never sees the authorization cards or any information that would disclose how individual employees voted.

Exam Probability: **High**

7. Answer choices:

(see index for correct answer)

- a. interpersonal communication
- b. Card check
- c. corporate values
- d. functional perspective

Guidance: level 1

:: Human resource management ::

_____ or work sharing is an employment arrangement where typically two people are retained on a part-time or reduced-time basis to perform a job normally fulfilled by one person working full-time. Since all positions are shared thus leads to a net reduction in per-employee income. The people sharing the job work as a team to complete the job task and are equally responsible for the job workload. Compensation is apportioned between the workers. Working hours, pay and holidays are divided equally. The pay as you go system helps make deductions for national insurance and superannuations are made as a straightforward percentage.

Exam Probability: **Medium**

8. Answer choices:

(see index for correct answer)

- a. Job sharing
- b. Succession planning

- c. The war for talent
- d. Inclusive business

Guidance: level 1

:: ::

_____ is the formal act of giving up or quitting one's office or position. A _____ can occur when a person holding a position gained by election or appointment steps down, but leaving a position upon the expiration of a term, or choosing not to seek an additional term, is not considered _____ .

Exam Probability: **Medium**

9. *Answer choices:*
(see index for correct answer)

- a. Resignation
- b. imperative
- c. co-culture
- d. cultural

Guidance: level 1

:: Trade unions in the United States ::

The _____ is a labor union in the United States and Canada. Formed in 1903 by the merger of The Team Drivers International Union and The Teamsters National Union, the union now represents a diverse membership of blue-collar and professional workers in both the public and private sectors. The union had approximately 1.3 million members in 2013. Formerly known as the _____, Chauffeurs, Warehousemen and Helpers of America, the IBT is a member of the Change to Win Federation and Canadian Labour Congress.

Exam Probability: **High**

10. *Answer choices:*

(see index for correct answer)

- a. California State University Employees Union
- b. Culinary Workers Union
- c. National Nurses United
- d. International Brotherhood of Teamsters

Guidance: level 1

:: ::

_____ is the combination of structured planning and the active management choice of one's own professional career. _____ was first defined in a social work doctoral thesis by Mary Valentich as the implementation of a career strategy through application of career tactics in relation to chosen career orientation. Career orientation referred to the overall design or pattern of one's career, shaped by particular goals and interests and identifiable by particular positions that embody these goals and interests. Career strategy pertains to the individual's general approach to the realization of career goals, and to the specificity of the goals themselves. Two general strategy approaches are adaptive and planned. Career tactics are actions to maintain oneself in a satisfactory employment situation. Tactics may be more or less assertive, with assertiveness in the work situation referring to actions taken to advance one's career interests or to exercise one's legitimate rights while respecting the rights of others.

Exam Probability: **Medium**

11. *Answer choices:*

(see index for correct answer)

- a. similarity-attraction theory
- b. open system
- c. Career management
- d. personal values

Guidance: level 1

:: Human resource management ::

The _____ is a free online database that contains hundreds of occupational definitions to help students, job seekers, businesses and workforce development professionals to understand today's world of work in the United States. It was developed under the sponsorship of the US Department of Labor/Employment and Training Administration through a grant to the North Carolina Employment Security Commission during the 1990s. John L. Holland's vocational model, often referred to as the Holland Codes, is used in the "Interests" section of the O*NET.

Exam Probability: **Medium**

12. *Answer choices:*

(see index for correct answer)

- a. Organizational behavior and human resources
- b. Chief human resources officer
- c. Occupational Information Network
- d. Hemsley Fraser

Guidance: level 1

:: Psychometrics ::

Electronic assessment, also known as e-assessment, _____, computer assisted/mediated assessment and computer-based assessment, is the use of information technology in various forms of assessment such as educational assessment, health assessment, psychiatric assessment, and psychological assessment. This may utilize an online computer connected to a network. This definition embraces a wide range of student activity ranging from the use of a word processor to on-screen testing. Specific types of e-assessment include multiple choice, online/electronic submission, computerized adaptive testing and computerized classification testing.

Exam Probability: **Low**

13. *Answer choices:*

(see index for correct answer)

- a. Visual analogue scale
- b. Francis Galton
- c. Online assessment
- d. Intra-rater reliability

Guidance: level 1

:: Nepotism ::

_____ is the granting of favour to relatives in various fields, including business, politics, entertainment, sports, religion and other activities. The term originated with the assignment of nephews to important positions by Catholic popes and bishops. Trading parliamentary employment for favors is a modern-day example of _____. Criticism of _____, however, can be found in ancient Indian texts such as the Kural literature.

Exam Probability: **High**

14. *Answer choices:*

(see index for correct answer)

- a. Cardinal-nephew
- b. Nepotism
- c. Cronyism
- d. Monklandsgate

Guidance: level 1

:: Belief ::

_____ is an umbrella term of influence. _____ can attempt to influence a person's beliefs, attitudes, intentions, motivations, or behaviors. In business, _____ is a process aimed at changing a person's attitude or behavior toward some event, idea, object, or other person, by using written, spoken words or visual tools to convey information, feelings, or reasoning, or a combination thereof. _____ is also an often used tool in the pursuit of personal gain, such as election campaigning, giving a sales pitch, or in trial advocacy. _____ can also be interpreted as using one's personal or positional resources to change people's behaviors or attitudes. Systematic _____ is the process through which attitudes or beliefs are leveraged by appeals to logic and reason. Heuristic _____ on the other hand is the process through which attitudes or beliefs are leveraged by appeals to habit or emotion.

Exam Probability: **High**

15. *Answer choices:*

(see index for correct answer)

- a. Persuasion
- b. Ignorance
- c. Real life
- d. Affective disposition theory

Guidance: level 1

:: Leadership ::

_____ is a theory of leadership where a leader works with teams to identify needed change, creating a vision to guide the change through inspiration, and executing the change in tandem with committed members of a group; it is an integral part of the Full Range Leadership Model. _____ serves to enhance the motivation, morale, and job performance of followers through a variety of mechanisms; these include connecting the follower's sense of identity and self to a project and to the collective identity of the organization; being a role model for followers in order to inspire them and to raise their interest in the project; challenging followers to take greater ownership for their work, and understanding the strengths and weaknesses of followers, allowing the leader to align followers with tasks that enhance their performance.

Exam Probability: **Low**

16. *Answer choices:*

(see index for correct answer)

- a. Authentic leadership
- b. Transactional leadership
- c. Integral leadership
- d. servant leader

Guidance: level 1

:: Occupations ::

_____ means a restricted practice or a restriction on the use of an occupational title, requiring a license. A license created under a "practice act" requires a license before performing a certain activity, such as driving a car on public roads. A license created under a "title act" restricts the use of a given occupational title to licensees, but anyone can perform the activity itself under a less restricted title. For example, in Oregon, anyone can practice counseling, but only licensees can call themselves "Licensed Professional Counselors." Thus depending on the type of law, practicing without a license may carry civil or criminal penalties or may be perfectly legal. For some occupations and professions, licensing is often granted through a professional body or a licensing board composed of practitioners who oversee the applications for licenses. This often involves accredited training and examinations, but varies a great deal for different activities and in different countries.

Exam Probability: **High**

17. *Answer choices:*

(see index for correct answer)

- a. Union organizer
- b. Occupational prestige
- c. Statistician
- d. Licensure

Guidance: level 1

:: Bankruptcy ::

_____ is the concept of a person or group of people taking precedence over another person or group because the former is either older than the latter or has occupied a particular position longer than the latter. _____ is present between parents and children and may be present in other common relationships, such as among siblings of different ages or between workers and their managers.

Exam Probability: **High**

18. *Answer choices:*

(see index for correct answer)

- a. Seniority
- b. Personal bankruptcy
- c. Assisted person
- d. FitzPatrick 1932

Guidance: level 1

:: Employment compensation ::

_____ s is a method for companies to give their management or employees a bonus if the company performs well financially. Such a method is called a `plan`. SARs resemble employee stock options in that the holder/employee benefits from an increase in stock price. They differ from options in that the holder/employee does not have to purchase anything to receive the proceeds. They are not required to pay the exercise price, but just receive the amount of the increase in cash or stock.

Exam Probability: **Low**

19. *Answer choices:*

(see index for correct answer)

- a. Labour law
- b. Stock appreciation right
- c. Profit sharing
- d. Wages for housework

Guidance: level 1

:: Survey methodology ::

An _____ is a conversation where questions are asked and answers are given. In common parlance, the word "_____" refers to a one-on-one conversation between an _____ er and an _____ ee. The _____ er asks questions to which the _____ ee responds, usually so information may be transferred from _____ ee to _____ er. Sometimes, information can be transferred in both directions. It is a communication, unlike a speech, which produces a one-way flow of information.

Exam Probability: **Medium**

20. *Answer choices:*

(see index for correct answer)

- a. Self-report

- b. Survey sampling
- c. Interview
- d. National Health Interview Survey

Guidance: level 1

:: Management ::

_____ or executive pay is composed of the financial compensation and other non-financial awards received by an executive from their firm for their service to the organization. It is typically a mixture of salary, bonuses, shares of or call options on the company stock, benefits, and perquisites, ideally configured to take into account government regulations, tax law, the desires of the organization and the executive, and rewards for performance.

Exam Probability: **Low**

21. *Answer choices:*

(see index for correct answer)

- a. Systems analysis
- b. Executive compensation
- c. U-procedure and Theory U
- d. Management buyout

Guidance: level 1

:: Outsourcing ::

_____ is the practice of sourcing from the global market for goods and services across geopolitical boundaries. _____ often aims to exploit global efficiencies in the delivery of a product or service. These efficiencies include low cost skilled labor, low cost raw material and other economic factors like tax breaks and low trade tariffs. A large number of Information Technology projects and Services, including IS Applications and Mobile Apps and database services are outsourced globally to countries like Pakistan and India for more economical pricing.

Exam Probability: **High**

22. *Answer choices:*

(see index for correct answer)

- a. Global sourcing
- b. Transition methodology
- c. Application Management Services Framework
- d. Vested outsourcing

Guidance: level 1

:: Validity (statistics) ::

_____ is a type of evidence that can be gathered to defend the use of a test for predicting other outcomes. It is a parameter used in sociology, psychology, and other psychometric or behavioral sciences. _____ is demonstrated when a test correlates well with a measure that has previously been validated. The two measures may be for the same construct, but more often used for different, but presumably related, constructs.

Exam Probability: **High**

23. *Answer choices:*

(see index for correct answer)

- a. Predictive validity
- b. Incremental validity
- c. Validation
- d. Concurrent validity

Guidance: level 1

:: Employment compensation ::

In government contracting, a _____ is defined as the hourly wage, usual benefits and overtime, paid to the majority of workers, laborers, and mechanics within a particular area. This is usually the union wage.

Exam Probability: **Medium**

24. Answer choices:

(see index for correct answer)

- a. Dearness allowance
- b. My Family Care
- c. Prevailing wage
- d. Defense Base Act

Guidance: level 1

:: Business law ::

A pre-entry _____ is a form of union security agreement under which the employer agrees to hire union members only, and employees must remain members of the union at all times in order to remain employed. This is different from a post-entry _____ , which is an agreement requiring all employees to join the union if they are not already members. In a union shop, the union must accept as a member any person hired by the employer.

Exam Probability: **Low**

25. Answer choices:

(see index for correct answer)

- a. Power harassment
- b. Trading while insolvent
- c. Refusal to deal
- d. Closed shop

Guidance: level 1

:: Industrial relations ::

> _____ or employee satisfaction is a measure of workers' contentedness with their job, whether or not they like the job or individual aspects or facets of jobs, such as nature of work or supervision. _____ can be measured in cognitive, affective, and behavioral components. Researchers have also noted that _____ measures vary in the extent to which they measure feelings about the job, or cognitions about the job.

Exam Probability: **High**

26. *Answer choices:*

(see index for correct answer)

- a. Workforce Investment Board
- b. European Journal of Industrial Relations
- c. Job satisfaction
- d. Injury prevention

Guidance: level 1

:: Belief ::

_____ is the ability to acquire knowledge without proof, evidence, or conscious reasoning, or without understanding how the knowledge was acquired. Different writers give the word "_____" a great variety of different meanings, ranging from direct access to unconscious knowledge, unconscious cognition, inner sensing, inner insight to unconscious pattern-recognition and the ability to understand something instinctively, without the need for conscious reasoning.

Exam Probability: **High**

27. *Answer choices:*

(see index for correct answer)

- a. Urdoxa
- b. Belief in luck
- c. Doctrine
- d. Sententia fidei proxima

Guidance: level 1

:: Training ::

_____ is the process of ensuring compliance with laws, regulations, rules, standards, or social norms. By enforcing laws and regulations, governments attempt to effectuate successful implementation of policies.

Exam Probability: **Medium**

28. *Answer choices:*

(see index for correct answer)

- a. Training
- b. Simulation game
- c. American Council on Exercise
- d. Enforcement

Guidance: level 1

:: Social psychology ::

> In social psychology, _____ is the phenomenon of a person exerting less effort to achieve a goal when he or she works in a group than when working alone. This is seen as one of the main reasons groups are sometimes less productive than the combined performance of their members working as individuals, but should be distinguished from the accidental coordination problems that groups sometimes experience.

Exam Probability: **High**

29. *Answer choices:*

(see index for correct answer)

- a. self-disclosure
- b. Prosocial
- c. Cross-cultural leadership
- d. fear appeal

Guidance: level 1

:: ::

A _____ is a fund into which a sum of money is added during an employee's employment years, and from which payments are drawn to support the person's retirement from work in the form of periodic payments. A _____ may be a "defined benefit plan" where a fixed sum is paid regularly to a person, or a "defined contribution plan" under which a fixed sum is invested and then becomes available at retirement age. _____ s should not be confused with severance pay; the former is usually paid in regular installments for life after retirement, while the latter is typically paid as a fixed amount after involuntary termination of employment prior to retirement.

Exam Probability: **High**

30. *Answer choices:*
(see index for correct answer)

- a. process perspective
- b. surface-level diversity
- c. cultural
- d. Sarbanes-Oxley act of 2002

Guidance: level 1

:: Job interview ::

A _____ is a job interview in which the applicant is presented with a challenging business scenario that he/she must investigate and propose a solution to. _____s are designed to test the candidate's analytical skills and "soft" skills within a realistic business context. The case is often a business situation or a business case that the interviewer has worked on in real life.

Exam Probability: **Medium**

31. *Answer choices:*

(see index for correct answer)

- a. Exit interview
- b. Mock interview
- c. Case interview
- d. Microsoft interview

Guidance: level 1

:: United States employment discrimination case law ::

_____, 411 U.S. 792, is a US employment law case by the United States Supreme Court regarding the burdens and nature of proof in proving a Title VII case and the order in which plaintiffs and defendants present proof. It was the seminal case in the McDonnell Douglas burden-shifting framework.

Exam Probability: **Low**

32. Answer choices:

(see index for correct answer)

- a. Price Waterhouse v. Hopkins
- b. McDonnell Douglas Corp. v. Green
- c. New York City Transit Authority v. Beazer
- d. Gross v. FBL Financial Services, Inc.

Guidance: level 1

:: ::

_____ is a form of development in which a person called a coach supports a learner or client in achieving a specific personal or professional goal by providing training and guidance. The learner is sometimes called a coachee. Occasionally, _____ may mean an informal relationship between two people, of whom one has more experience and expertise than the other and offers advice and guidance as the latter learns; but _____ differs from mentoring in focusing on specific tasks or objectives, as opposed to more general goals or overall development.

Exam Probability: **High**

33. Answer choices:

(see index for correct answer)

- a. corporate values
- b. functional perspective

- c. Coaching
- d. imperative

Guidance: level 1

:: Industrial agreements ::

> _____ is a process of negotiation between employers and a group of employees aimed at agreements to regulate working salaries, working conditions, benefits, and other aspects of workers' compensation and rights for workers. The interests of the employees are commonly presented by representatives of a trade union to which the employees belong. The collective agreements reached by these negotiations usually set out wage scales, working hours, training, health and safety, overtime, grievance mechanisms, and rights to participate in workplace or company affairs.

Exam Probability: **Low**

34. *Answer choices:*

(see index for correct answer)

- a. McCrone Agreement
- b. Pattern bargaining
- c. Workplace Authority
- d. Collective bargaining

Guidance: level 1

:: Validity (statistics) ::

_____ is "the degree to which a test measures what it claims, or purports, to be measuring." In the classical model of test validity, _____ is one of three main types of validity evidence, alongside content validity and criterion validity. Modern validity theory defines _____ as the overarching concern of validity research, subsuming all other types of validity evidence.

Exam Probability: **Medium**

35. *Answer choices:*

(see index for correct answer)

- a. Statistical conclusion validity
- b. Incremental validity
- c. External validity
- d. Construct validity

Guidance: level 1

:: Human resource management ::

_____ expands the capacity of individuals to perform in leadership roles within organizations. Leadership roles are those that facilitate execution of a company's strategy through building alignment, winning mindshare and growing the capabilities of others. Leadership roles may be formal, with the corresponding authority to make decisions and take responsibility, or they may be informal roles with little official authority .

Exam Probability: **Low**

36. *Answer choices:*

(see index for correct answer)

- a. Leadership development
- b. Bradford Factor
- c. Inclusion
- d. Aspiring Minds

Guidance: level 1

:: Working time ::

The shift plan, rota or roster is the central component of a shift schedule in shift work. The schedule includes considerations of shift overlap, shift change times and alignment with the clock, vacation, training, shift differentials, holidays, etc. The shift plan determines the sequence of work and free days within a shift system.

Exam Probability: **Low**

37. *Answer choices:*

(see index for correct answer)

- a. Bunting v. Oregon
- b. Waiting for the Weekend
- c. Graveyard shift
- d. Double burden

Guidance: level 1

:: Management ::

_____ is the kind of knowledge that is difficult to transfer to another person by means of writing it down or verbalizing it. For example, that London is in the United Kingdom is a piece of explicit knowledge that can be written down, transmitted, and understood by a recipient. However, the ability to speak a language, ride a bicycle, knead dough, play a musical instrument, or design and use complex equipment requires all sorts of knowledge that is not always known explicitly, even by expert practitioners, and which is difficult or impossible to explicitly transfer to other people.

Exam Probability: **Low**

38. *Answer choices:*

(see index for correct answer)

- a. Managerialism
- b. Tacit knowledge

- c. Decentralized decision-making
- d. Maryland StateStat

Guidance: level 1

:: Options (finance) ::

_____ is a contractual agreement between a corporation and recipients of phantom shares that bestow upon the grantee the right to a cash payment at a designated time or in association with a designated event in the future, which payment is to be in an amount tied to the market value of an equivalent number of shares of the corporation's stock. Thus, the amount of the payout will increase as the stock price rises, and decrease if the stock falls, but without the recipient actually receiving any stock. Like other forms of stock-based compensation plans, _____ broadly serves to align the interests of recipients and shareholders, incent contribution to share value, and encourage the retention or continued participation of contributors. Recipients are typically employees, but may also be directors, third-party vendors, or others.

Exam Probability: **Low**

39. *Answer choices:*
(see index for correct answer)

- a. Covered call
- b. Naked call
- c. Cash or share option
- d. Phantom stock

Guidance: level 1

:: ::

The U.S. _____ is a federal agency that administers and enforces civil rights laws against workplace discrimination. The EEOC investigates discrimination complaints based on an individual's race, children, national origin, religion, sex, age, disability, sexual orientation, gender identity, genetic information, and retaliation for reporting, participating in, and/or opposing a discriminatory practice.

Exam Probability: **Medium**

40. *Answer choices:*

(see index for correct answer)

- a. Equal Employment Opportunity Commission
- b. open system
- c. co-culture
- d. imperative

Guidance: level 1

:: Business law ::

_____ or employment relations is the multidisciplinary academic field that studies the employment relationship; that is, the complex interrelations between employers and employees, labor/trade unions, employer organizations and the state.

Exam Probability: **Medium**

41. *Answer choices:*

(see index for correct answer)

- a. Power harassment
- b. Limited liability company
- c. Industrial relations
- d. Negative option billing

Guidance: level 1

:: Human resource management ::

_____ refers to the anticipation of required human capital for an organization and the planning to meet those needs. The field increased in popularity after McKinsey's 1997 research and the 2001 book on The War for Talent. _____ in this context does not refer to the management of entertainers.

Exam Probability: **Low**

42. *Answer choices:*

(see index for correct answer)

- a. Behavioral Competencies
- b. Talent management
- c. Vendor on premises
- d. Individual development plan

Guidance: level 1

:: Organizational behavior ::

> In organizational behavior and industrial and organizational psychology, _____ is an individual's psychological attachment to the organization. The basis behind many of these studies was to find ways to improve how workers feel about their jobs so that these workers would become more committed to their organizations. _____ predicts work variables such as turnover, organizational citizenship behavior, and job performance. Some of the factors such as role stress, empowerment, job insecurity and employability, and distribution of leadership have been shown to be connected to a worker's sense of _____ .

Exam Probability: **Low**

43. *Answer choices:*

(see index for correct answer)

- a. Informal organization
- b. Organizational citizenship behavior

- c. Civic virtue
- d. Administrative Behavior

Guidance: level 1

:: ::

A trade union is an association of workers forming a legal unit or legal personhood, usually called a "bargaining unit", which acts as bargaining agent and legal representative for a unit of employees in all matters of law or right arising from or in the administration of a collective agreement. Labour unions typically fund the formal organisation, head office, and legal team functions of the labour union through regular fees or union dues. The delegate staff of the labour union representation in the workforce are made up of workplace volunteers who are appointed by members in democratic elections.

Exam Probability: **High**

44. *Answer choices:*

(see index for correct answer)

- a. Labor union
- b. surface-level diversity
- c. functional perspective
- d. process perspective

Guidance: level 1

In business strategy, _____ is establishing a competitive advantage by having the lowest cost of operation in the industry. _____ is often driven by company efficiency, size, scale, scope and cumulative experience. A _____ strategy aims to exploit scale of production, well-defined scope and other economies, producing highly standardized products, using advanced technology. In recent years, more and more companies have chosen a strategic mix to achieve market leadership. These patterns consist of simultaneous _____, superior customer service and product leadership. Walmart has succeeded across the world due to its _____ strategy. The company has cut down on exesses at every point of production and thus are able to provide the consumers with quality products at low prices.

Exam Probability: **Low**

45. *Answer choices:*

(see index for correct answer)

- a. Cost leadership
- b. information systems assessment
- c. process perspective
- d. hierarchical

Guidance: level 1

_____ is a common standard in United States labor law arbitration that is used in labor union contracts in the United States as a form of job security.

Exam Probability: **High**

46. *Answer choices:*

(see index for correct answer)

- a. functional perspective
- b. deep-level diversity
- c. Just cause
- d. imperative

Guidance: level 1

:: Sociological theories ::

A _____ is a systematic process for determining and addressing needs, or "gaps" between current conditions and desired conditions or "wants". The discrepancy between the current condition and wanted condition must be measured to appropriately identify the need. The need can be a desire to improve current performance or to correct a deficiency.

Exam Probability: **Medium**

47. *Answer choices:*

(see index for correct answer)

- a. social construction
- b. Needs assessment
- c. social constructionism
- d. comfort zone

Guidance: level 1

:: ::

> The causes of _____ are heavily debated. Classical economics, new classical economics, and the Austrian School of economics argued that market mechanisms are reliable means of resolving _____ . These theories argue against interventions imposed on the labor market from the outside, such as unionization, bureaucratic work rules, minimum wage laws, taxes, and other regulations that they claim discourage the hiring of workers. Keynesian economics emphasizes the cyclical nature of _____ and recommends government interventions in the economy that it claims will reduce _____ during recessions. This theory focuses on recurrent shocks that suddenly reduce aggregate demand for goods and services and thus reduce demand for workers. Keynesian models recommend government interventions designed to increase demand for workers; these can include financial stimuli, publicly funded job creation, and expansionist monetary policies. Its namesake economist, John Maynard Keynes, believed that the root cause of _____ is the desire of investors to receive more money rather than produce more products, which is not possible without public bodies producing new money. A third group of theories emphasize the need for a stable supply of capital and investment to maintain full employment. On this view, government should guarantee full employment through fiscal policy, monetary policy and trade policy as stated, for example, in the US Employment Act of 1946, by counteracting private sector or trade investment volatility, and reducing inequality.

Exam Probability: **Medium**

48. *Answer choices:*

(see index for correct answer)

- a. information systems assessment
- b. interpersonal communication
- c. surface-level diversity
- d. Unemployment

Guidance: level 1

:: Psychometrics ::

A _____ is a set of categories designed to elicit information about a quantitative or a qualitative attribute. In the social sciences, particularly psychology, common examples are the Likert response scale and 1-10 _____ s in which a person selects the number which is considered to reflect the perceived quality of a product.

Exam Probability: **Medium**

49. *Answer choices:*

(see index for correct answer)

- a. Attribute Hierarchy Method
- b. Sequential probability ratio test

- c. Rating scale
- d. Test

Guidance: level 1

:: Employment compensation ::

A _____ is the minimum income necessary for a worker to meet their basic needs. Needs are defined to include food, housing, and other essential needs such as clothing. The goal of a _____ is to allow a worker to afford a basic but decent standard of living. Due to the flexible nature of the term "needs", there is not one universally accepted measure of what a _____ is and as such it varies by location and household type.

Exam Probability: **Low**

50. *Answer choices:*

(see index for correct answer)

- a. Fringe benefits tax
- b. Living wage
- c. Annual leave
- d. Health Reimbursement Account

Guidance: level 1

:: Human resource management ::

_____ means increasing the scope of a job through extending the range of its job duties and responsibilities generally within the same level and periphery. _____ involves combining various activities at the same level in the organization and adding them to the existing job. It is also called the horizontal expansion of job activities. This contradicts the principles of specialisation and the division of labour whereby work is divided into small units, each of which is performed repetitively by an individual worker and the responsibilities are always clear. Some motivational theories suggest that the boredom and alienation caused by the division of labour can actually cause efficiency to fall. Thus, _____ seeks to motivate workers through reversing the process of specialisation. A typical approach might be to replace assembly lines with modular work; instead of an employee repeating the same step on each product, they perform several tasks on a single item. In order for employees to be provided with _____ they will need to be retrained in new fields to understand how each field works.

Exam Probability: **High**

51. *Answer choices:*

(see index for correct answer)

- a. CEO succession
- b. Voluntary redundancy
- c. Management by observation
- d. Expense management

Guidance: level 1

:: Systems thinking ::

In business management, a _____ is a company that facilitates the learning of its members and continuously transforms itself. The concept was coined through the work and research of Peter Senge and his colleagues.

Exam Probability: **High**

52. *Answer choices:*

(see index for correct answer)

- a. Tt30
- b. Scenario analysis
- c. Learning organization
- d. Future history

Guidance: level 1

:: International trade ::

_____ or globalisation is the process of interaction and integration among people, companies, and governments worldwide. As a complex and multifaceted phenomenon, _____ is considered by some as a form of capitalist expansion which entails the integration of local and national economies into a global, unregulated market economy. _____ has grown due to advances in transportation and communication technology. With the increased global interactions comes the growth of international trade, ideas, and culture. _____ is primarily an economic process of interaction and integration that's associated with social and cultural aspects. However, conflicts and diplomacy are also large parts of the history of _____, and modern _____.

Exam Probability: **Medium**

53. *Answer choices:*

(see index for correct answer)

- a. Balanced trade
- b. Globalization
- c. Asian Clearing Union
- d. Hilton Quota

Guidance: level 1

:: Validity (statistics) ::

_____ is the extent to which a test accurately measures what it is supposed to measure. In the fields of psychological testing and educational testing, "validity refers to the degree to which evidence and theory support the interpretations of test scores entailed by proposed uses of tests". Although classical models divided the concept into various "validities", the currently dominant view is that validity is a single unitary construct.

Exam Probability: **Medium**

54. *Answer choices:*

(see index for correct answer)

- a. Convergent validity
- b. Test validity

- c. Statistical conclusion validity
- d. External validity

Guidance: level 1

:: Trade unions ::

An _____ is a form of union security agreement where the employer may hire union or non-union workers, and employees need not join the union in order to remain employed. However, the non-union worker must pay a fee to cover collective bargaining costs. The fee paid by non-union members under the _____ is known as the "agency fee".

Exam Probability: **Low**

55. *Answer choices:*
(see index for correct answer)

- a. Union busting
- b. General union
- c. Union wage premium
- d. Agency shop

Guidance: level 1

:: Unemployment ::

In economics, a _____ is a business cycle contraction when there is a general decline in economic activity. Macroeconomic indicators such as GDP, investment spending, capacity utilization, household income, business profits, and inflation fall, while bankruptcies and the unemployment rate rise. In the United Kingdom, it is defined as a negative economic growth for two consecutive quarters.

Exam Probability: **Medium**

56. *Answer choices:*

(see index for correct answer)

- a. Frictional unemployment
- b. NAIRU
- c. Recession
- d. Mount Street Club

Guidance: level 1

:: Human resource management ::

_____ is the strategic approach to the effective management of people in an organization so that they help the business to gain a competitive advantage. It is designed to maximize employee performance in service of an employer's strategic objectives. HR is primarily concerned with the management of people within organizations, focusing on policies and on systems. HR departments are responsible for overseeing employee-benefits design, employee recruitment, training and development, performance appraisal, and Reward management . HR also concerns itself with organizational change and industrial relations, that is, the balancing of organizational practices with requirements arising from collective bargaining and from governmental laws.

Exam Probability: **High**

57. *Answer choices:*

(see index for correct answer)

- a. Human resource accounting
- b. Personal development planning
- c. Work activity management
- d. Leadership development

Guidance: level 1

:: Employment ::

_____ is a relationship between two parties, usually based on a contract where work is paid for, where one party, which may be a corporation, for profit, not-for-profit organization, co-operative or other entity is the employer and the other is the employee. Employees work in return for payment, which may be in the form of an hourly wage, by piecework or an annual salary, depending on the type of work an employee does or which sector she or he is working in. Employees in some fields or sectors may receive gratuities, bonus payment or stock options. In some types of _____ , employees may receive benefits in addition to payment. Benefits can include health insurance, housing, disability insurance or use of a gym. _____ is typically governed by _____ laws, regulations or legal contracts.

Exam Probability: **Low**

58. *Answer choices:*
(see index for correct answer)

- a. Temporary duty assignment
- b. Extreme Blue
- c. Paradox of toil
- d. Liaison officer

Guidance: level 1

:: Recruitment ::

A _____ is a quantitative research method commonly employed in survey research. The aim of this approach is to ensure that each interview is presented with exactly the same questions in the same order. This ensures that answers can be reliably aggregated and that comparisons can be made with confidence between sample subgroups or between different survey periods.

Exam Probability: **High**

59. *Answer choices:*

(see index for correct answer)

- a. Structured interview
- b. Referral recruitment
- c. Global Career Development Facilitator
- d. Video resume

Guidance: level 1

Information systems

Information systems (IS) are formal, sociotechnical, organizational systems designed to collect, process, store, and distribute information. In a sociotechnical perspective Information Systems are composed by four components: technology, process, people and organizational structure.

:: ::

A _____ is a system designed to capture, store, manipulate, analyze, manage, and present spatial or geographic data. GIS applications are tools that allow users to create interactive queries , analyze spatial information, edit data in maps, and present the results of all these operations. GIS sometimes refers to geographic information science , the science underlying geographic concepts, applications, and systems.

Exam Probability: **Medium**

1. *Answer choices:*

(see index for correct answer)

- a. Character
- b. cultural
- c. Sarbanes-Oxley act of 2002
- d. surface-level diversity

Guidance: level 1

:: Satellite navigation systems ::

> _____ Galilei was an Italian astronomer, physicist and engineer, sometimes described as a polymath. _____ has been called the "father of observational astronomy", the "father of modern physics", the "father of the scientific method", and the "father of modern science".

Exam Probability: **High**

2. *Answer choices:*

(see index for correct answer)

- a. Virtual Reference Station
- b. GIOVE Mission
- c. Galileo

- d. GPS tracking server

Guidance: level 1

:: Virtual reality ::

> A _____ is a computer-based simulated environment which may be populated by many users who can create a personal avatar, and simultaneously and independently explore the _____, participate in its activities and communicate with others. These avatars can be textual, two or three-dimensional graphical representations, or live video avatars with auditory and touch sensations. In general, _____s allow for multiple users but single player computer games, such as Skyrim, can also be considered a type of _____.

Exam Probability: **Low**

3. *Answer choices:*

(see index for correct answer)

- a. Collaborative virtual environment
- b. Advanced disaster management simulator
- c. Curzon Memories App
- d. Virtual world

Guidance: level 1

:: Computer access control ::

_____ is the act of confirming the truth of an attribute of a single piece of data claimed true by an entity. In contrast with identification, which refers to the act of stating or otherwise indicating a claim purportedly attesting to a person or thing's identity, _____ is the process of actually confirming that identity. It might involve confirming the identity of a person by validating their identity documents, verifying the authenticity of a website with a digital certificate, determining the age of an artifact by carbon dating, or ensuring that a product is what its packaging and labeling claim to be. In other words, _____ often involves verifying the validity of at least one form of identification.

Exam Probability: **High**

4. *Answer choices:*

(see index for correct answer)

- a. Numina Application Framework
- b. Initiative For Open Authentication
- c. Time-based One-time Password Algorithm
- d. Registered user

Guidance: level 1

:: Data quality ::

_____ or data cleaning is the process of detecting and correcting corrupt or inaccurate records from a record set, table, or database and refers to identifying incomplete, incorrect, inaccurate or irrelevant parts of the data and then replacing, modifying, or deleting the dirty or coarse data. _____ may be performed interactively with data wrangling tools, or as batch processing through scripting.

Exam Probability: **Low**

5. *Answer choices:*

(see index for correct answer)

- a. Dirty data
- b. Data degradation
- c. Data integrity
- d. Data truncation

Guidance: level 1

:: Automatic identification and data capture ::

_____ is human–computer interaction in which a computer is expected to be transported during normal usage, which allows for transmission of data, voice and video. _____ involves mobile communication, mobile hardware, and mobile software. Communication issues include ad hoc networks and infrastructure networks as well as communication properties, protocols, data formats and concrete technologies. Hardware includes mobile devices or device components. Mobile software deals with the characteristics and requirements of mobile applications.

Exam Probability: **Low**

6. *Answer choices:*

(see index for correct answer)

- a. IBeacon
- b. Magnadata Group
- c. Roper Industries
- d. Barcode printer

Guidance: level 1

:: Survey methodology ::

A _____ is the procedure of systematically acquiring and recording information about the members of a given population. The term is used mostly in connection with national population and housing _____ es; other common _____ es include agriculture, business, and traffic _____ es. The United Nations defines the essential features of population and housing _____ es as "individual enumeration, universality within a defined territory, simultaneity and defined periodicity", and recommends that population _____ es be taken at least every 10 years. United Nations recommendations also cover _____ topics to be collected, official definitions, classifications and other useful information to co-ordinate international practice.

Exam Probability: **Medium**

7. *Answer choices:*

(see index for correct answer)

- a. Interview
- b. Census
- c. World Association for Public Opinion Research
- d. Survey sampling

Guidance: level 1

:: Enterprise modelling ::

_____ are large-scale application software packages that support business processes, information flows, reporting, and data analytics in complex organizations. While ES are generally packaged enterprise application software systems they can also be bespoke, custom developed systems created to support a specific organization's needs.

Exam Probability: **Low**

8. *Answer choices:*

(see index for correct answer)

- a. Enterprise systems
- b. Business engineering
- c. Systems modeling
- d. Business reference model

Guidance: level 1

:: Critical thinking ::

> In psychology, _____ is regarded as the cognitive process resulting in the selection of a belief or a course of action among several alternative possibilities. Every _____ process produces a final choice, which may or may not prompt action.

Exam Probability: **High**

9. *Answer choices:*

(see index for correct answer)

- a. Intellectual responsibility
- b. TregoED
- c. SEE-I
- d. Topical logic

Guidance: level 1

:: ::

Sustainability is the process of people maintaining change in a balanced environment, in which the exploitation of resources, the direction of investments, the orientation of technological development and institutional change are all in harmony and enhance both current and future potential to meet human needs and aspirations. For many in the field, sustainability is defined through the following interconnected domains or pillars: environment, economic and social, which according to Fritjof Capra is based on the principles of Systems Thinking. Sub-domains of _____ development have been considered also: cultural, technological and political. While _____ development may be the organizing principle for sustainability for some, for others, the two terms are paradoxical . _____ development is the development that meets the needs of the present without compromising the ability of future generations to meet their own needs. Brundtland Report for the World Commission on Environment and Development introduced the term of _____ development.

Exam Probability: **Medium**

10. *Answer choices:*

(see index for correct answer)

- a. open system
- b. interpersonal communication
- c. Sustainable
- d. Sarbanes-Oxley act of 2002

Guidance: level 1

:: Google services ::

_____ is a time-management and scheduling calendar service developed by Google. It became available in beta release April 13, 2006, and in general release in July 2009, on the web and as mobile apps for the Android and iOS platforms.

Exam Probability: **Medium**

11. *Answer choices:*

(see index for correct answer)

- a. Gizmo5
- b. App Inventor for Android
- c. Google Classroom
- d. Google Voice Search

Guidance: level 1

:: ::

_____ is software designed to provide a platform for other software. Examples of _____ include operating systems like macOS, Ubuntu and Microsoft Windows, computational science software, game engines, industrial automation, and software as a service applications.

Exam Probability: **Medium**

12. *Answer choices:*

(see index for correct answer)

- a. Character
- b. empathy
- c. functional perspective
- d. process perspective

Guidance: level 1

:: Advertising techniques ::

> The _____ is a story from the Trojan War about the subterfuge that the Greeks used to enter the independent city of Troy and win the war. In the canonical version, after a fruitless 10-year siege, the Greeks constructed a huge wooden horse, and hid a select force of men inside including Odysseus. The Greeks pretended to sail away, and the Trojans pulled the horse into their city as a victory trophy. That night the Greek force crept out of the horse and opened the gates for the rest of the Greek army, which had sailed back under cover of night. The Greeks entered and destroyed the city of Troy, ending the war.

Exam Probability: **Low**

13. *Answer choices:*

(see index for correct answer)

- a. Transfer
- b. Testimonial
- c. Two Cunts in a Kitchen

- d. Trojan horse

Guidance: level 1

:: Information technology ::

_____ is the reorientation of product and service designs to focus on the end user as an individual consumer, in contrast with an earlier era of only organization-oriented offerings . Technologies whose first commercialization was at the inter-organization level thus have potential for later _____ . The emergence of the individual consumer as the primary driver of product and service design is most commonly associated with the IT industry, as large business and government organizations dominated the early decades of computer usage and development. Thus the microcomputer revolution, in which electronic computing moved from exclusively enterprise and government use to include personal computing, is a cardinal example of _____ . But many technology-based products, such as calculators and mobile phones, have also had their origins in business markets, and only over time did they become dominated by high-volume consumer usage, as these products commoditized and prices fell. An example of enterprise software that became consumer software is optical character recognition software, which originated with banks and postal systems but eventually became personal productivity software.

Exam Probability: **High**

14. *Answer choices:*

(see index for correct answer)

- a. Local Government ICT Network
- b. IT as a service
- c. Consumerization

- d. Digital transformation

Guidance: level 1

:: E-commerce ::

_____ is the activity of buying or selling of products on online services or over the Internet. Electronic commerce draws on technologies such as mobile commerce, electronic funds transfer, supply chain management, Internet marketing, online transaction processing, electronic data interchange , inventory management systems, and automated data collection systems.

Exam Probability: **Low**

15. *Answer choices:*
(see index for correct answer)

- a. Allstar
- b. Product finder
- c. E-commerce
- d. Primecoin

Guidance: level 1

:: Management ::

A _____ describes the rationale of how an organization creates, delivers, and captures value, in economic, social, cultural or other contexts. The process of _____ construction and modification is also called _____ innovation and forms a part of business strategy.

Exam Probability: **Low**

16. *Answer choices:*

(see index for correct answer)

- a. Authoritarian leadership style
- b. Document automation
- c. Business model
- d. Business economics

Guidance: level 1

:: ::

_____ is a set of values of subjects with respect to qualitative or quantitative variables.

Exam Probability: **High**

17. *Answer choices:*

(see index for correct answer)

- a. functional perspective
- b. Data
- c. interpersonal communication
- d. surface-level diversity

Guidance: level 1

:: Fraud ::

In law, _____ is intentional deception to secure unfair or unlawful gain, or to deprive a victim of a legal right. _____ can violate civil law, a criminal law, or it may cause no loss of money, property or legal right but still be an element of another civil or criminal wrong. The purpose of _____ may be monetary gain or other benefits, for example by obtaining a passport, travel document, or driver's license, or mortgage _____, where the perpetrator may attempt to qualify for a mortgage by way of false statements.

Exam Probability: **Medium**

18. *Answer choices:*

(see index for correct answer)

- a. Fraud
- b. Control fraud
- c. Wangiri
- d. Welfare queen

Guidance: level 1

:: Network management ::

> _____ is the process of administering and managing computer networks. Services provided by this discipline include fault analysis, performance management, provisioning of networks and maintaining the quality of service. Software that enables network administrators to perform their functions is called _____ software.

Exam Probability: **High**

19. *Answer choices:*

(see index for correct answer)

- a. Network management
- b. Big Brother
- c. Network-to-network interface
- d. Sparrowiq

Guidance: level 1

:: ::

_____ is a brand name associated with the development of the _____ web browser. It is now owned by Verizon Media, a subsidiary of Verizon. The brand belonged to the _____ Communications Corporation, an independent American computer services company, whose headquarters were in Mountain View, California, and later Dulles, Virginia. The browser was once dominant but lost to Internet Explorer and other competitors after the so-called first browser war, its market share falling from more than 90 percent in the mid-1990s to less than 1 percent in 2006.

Exam Probability: **Medium**

20. *Answer choices:*

(see index for correct answer)

- a. surface-level diversity
- b. corporate values
- c. open system
- d. interpersonal communication

Guidance: level 1

:: Internet privacy ::

An _____ is a private network accessible only to an organization's staff. Often, a wide range of information and services are available on an organization's internal _____ that are unavailable to the public, unlike the Internet. A company-wide _____ can constitute an important focal point of internal communication and collaboration, and provide a single starting point to access internal and external resources. In its simplest form, an _____ is established with the technologies for local area networks and wide area networks . Many modern _____ s have search engines, user profiles, blogs, mobile apps with notifications, and events planning within their infrastructure.

Exam Probability: **Medium**

21. *Answer choices:*

(see index for correct answer)

- a. Cypherpunks
- b. Intranet
- c. WikiScanner
- d. Electronic envelope

Guidance: level 1

:: E-commerce ::

Electronic governance or e-governance is the application of information and communication technology for delivering government services, exchange of information, communication transactions, integration of various stand-alone systems and services between government-to-citizen, government-to-business, _____ , government-to-employees as well as back-office processes and interactions within the entire government framework. Through e-governance, government services are made available to citizens in a convenient, efficient, and transparent manner. The three main target groups that can be distinguished in governance concepts are government, citizens, andbusinesses/interest groups. In e-governance, there are no distinct boundaries.

Exam Probability: **Medium**

22. *Answer choices:*

(see index for correct answer)

- a. Mobilpenge
- b. ISO 8583
- c. Consumer-to-consumer
- d. Free Shipping Day

Guidance: level 1

:: Monopoly (economics) ::

A _____ exists when a specific person or enterprise is the only supplier of a particular commodity. This contrasts with a monopsony which relates to a single entity's control of a market to purchase a good or service, and with oligopoly which consists of a few sellers dominating a market. Monopolies are thus characterized by a lack of economic competition to produce the good or service, a lack of viable substitute goods, and the possibility of a high _____ price well above the seller's marginal cost that leads to a high _____ profit. The verb monopolise or monopolize refers to the process by which a company gains the ability to raise prices or exclude competitors. In economics, a _____ is a single seller. In law, a _____ is a business entity that has significant market power, that is, the power to charge overly high prices. Although monopolies may be big businesses, size is not a characteristic of a _____ . A small business may still have the power to raise prices in a small industry.

Exam Probability: **High**

23. *Answer choices:*

(see index for correct answer)

- a. Herfindahl index
- b. Privatization
- c. Monopoly
- d. Concentration ratio

Guidance: level 1

:: Information technology organisations ::

The Internet Corporation for Assigned Names and Numbers is a nonprofit organization responsible for coordinating the maintenance and procedures of several databases related to the namespaces and numerical spaces of the Internet, ensuring the network's stable and secure operation. _____ performs the actual technical maintenance work of the Central Internet Address pools and DNS root zone registries pursuant to the Internet Assigned Numbers Authority function contract. The contract regarding the IANA stewardship functions between _____ and the National Telecommunications and Information Administration of the United States Department of Commerce ended on October 1, 2016, formally transitioning the functions to the global multistakeholder community.

Exam Probability: **High**

24. *Answer choices:*

(see index for correct answer)

- a. GreenNet
- b. Cyber City, Kochi
- c. Logic Programming Associates
- d. International Medical Informatics Association

Guidance: level 1

:: Fraud ::

_____ is the deliberate use of someone else's identity, usually as a method to gain a financial advantage or obtain credit and other benefits in the other person's name, and perhaps to the other person's disadvantage or loss. The person whose identity has been assumed may suffer adverse consequences, especially if they are held responsible for the perpetrator's actions.
_____ occurs when someone uses another's personally identifying information, like their name, identifying number, or credit card number, without their permission, to commit fraud or other crimes. The term _____ was coined in 1964. Since that time, the definition of _____ has been statutorily prescribed throughout both the U.K. and the United States as the theft of personally identifying information, generally including a person's name, date of birth, social security number, driver's license number, bank account or credit card numbers, PIN numbers, electronic signatures, fingerprints, passwords, or any other information that can be used to access a person's financial resources.

Exam Probability: **Low**

25. *Answer choices:*

(see index for correct answer)

- a. Identity theft
- b. Swatting
- c. Missing trader fraud
- d. Pharma fraud

Guidance: level 1

:: Data management ::

_____ is a data management concept concerning the capability that enables an organization to ensure that high data quality exists throughout the complete lifecycle of the data. The key focus areas of _____ include availability, usability, consistency, data integrity and data security and includes establishing processes to ensure effective data management throughout the enterprise such as accountability for the adverse effects of poor data quality and ensuring that the data which an enterprise has can be used by the entire organization.

Exam Probability: **Low**

26. *Answer choices:*

(see index for correct answer)

- a. Navigational database
- b. Query language
- c. Data profiling
- d. Master data management

Guidance: level 1

:: E-commerce ::

Electronic governance or e-governance is the application of information and communication technology for delivering government services, exchange of information, communication transactions, integration of various stand-alone systems and services between _____ , government-to-business , government-to-government , government-to-employees as well as back-office processes and interactions within the entire government framework. Through e-governance, government services are made available to citizens in a convenient, efficient, and transparent manner. The three main target groups that can be distinguished in governance concepts are government, citizens, andbusinesses/interest groups. In e-governance, there are no distinct boundaries.

Exam Probability: **High**

27. *Answer choices:*

(see index for correct answer)

- a. E-procurement
- b. Playism
- c. Transport Layer Security
- d. Government-to-citizen

Guidance: level 1

:: Sensitivity analysis ::

_____ is the study of how the uncertainty in the output of a mathematical model or system can be divided and allocated to different sources of uncertainty in its inputs. A related practice is uncertainty analysis, which has a greater focus on uncertainty quantification and propagation of uncertainty; ideally, uncertainty and _____ should be run in tandem.

Exam Probability: **Medium**

28. *Answer choices:*

(see index for correct answer)

- a. Tornado diagram
- b. Sensitivity analysis
- c. Variance-based sensitivity analysis
- d. Fourier amplitude sensitivity testing

Guidance: level 1

:: Management ::

_____ is the kind of knowledge that is difficult to transfer to another person by means of writing it down or verbalizing it. For example, that London is in the United Kingdom is a piece of explicit knowledge that can be written down, transmitted, and understood by a recipient. However, the ability to speak a language, ride a bicycle, knead dough, play a musical instrument, or design and use complex equipment requires all sorts of knowledge that is not always known explicitly, even by expert practitioners, and which is difficult or impossible to explicitly transfer to other people.

Exam Probability: **Medium**

29. *Answer choices:*

(see index for correct answer)

- a. Preventive action
- b. Reverse innovation
- c. Linear scheduling method
- d. Tacit knowledge

Guidance: level 1

:: Information technology management ::

_____ concerns a cycle of organizational activity: the acquisition of information from one or more sources, the custodianship and the distribution of that information to those who need it, and its ultimate disposition through archiving or deletion.

Exam Probability: **Low**

30. *Answer choices:*

(see index for correct answer)

- a. Information management
- b. EFx Factory
- c. Digital Fuel

- d. Financial management for IT services

Guidance: level 1

:: ::

A _____ is a computer network that interconnects computers within a limited area such as a residence, school, laboratory, university campus or office building. By contrast, a wide area network not only covers a larger geographic distance, but also generally involves leased telecommunication circuits.

Exam Probability: **Medium**

31. *Answer choices:*
(see index for correct answer)

- a. hierarchical perspective
- b. information systems assessment
- c. Local Area Network
- d. deep-level diversity

Guidance: level 1

:: Behavioral and social facets of systemic risk ::

_____ is the difficulty in understanding an issue and effectively making decisions when one has too much information about that issue. Generally, the term is associated with the excessive quantity of daily information. _____ most likely originated from information theory, which are studies in the storage, preservation, communication, compression, and extraction of information. The term, _____, was first used in Bertram Gross' 1964 book, The Managing of Organizations, and it was further popularized by Alvin Toffler in his bestselling 1970 book Future Shock. Speier et al. stated.

Exam Probability: **Medium**

32. *Answer choices:*

(see index for correct answer)

- a. Collective intelligence
- b. recommender
- c. Information overload
- d. Latent human error

Guidance: level 1

:: Management ::

_____ is the identification of an organization's assets, followed by the development, documentation, and implementation of policies and procedures for protecting these assets.

Exam Probability: **Low**

33. *Answer choices:*

(see index for correct answer)

- a. Meeting
- b. Core competency
- c. Empowerment
- d. Integrative thinking

Guidance: level 1

:: Information technology management ::

> _____ is a good-practice framework created by international professional association ISACA for information technology management and IT governance. _____ provides an implementable "set of controls over information technology and organizes them around a logical framework of IT-related processes and enablers."

Exam Probability: **High**

34. *Answer choices:*

(see index for correct answer)

- a. Digital continuity
- b. Infrastructure optimization
- c. Service catalog
- d. COBIT

Guidance: level 1

:: Marketing ::

_____, in marketing, manufacturing, call centres and management, is the use of flexible computer-aided manufacturing systems to produce custom output. Such systems combine the low unit costs of mass production processes with the flexibility of individual customization.

Exam Probability: **High**

35. *Answer choices:*

(see index for correct answer)

- a. Mass customization
- b. Customer acquisition management
- c. Optimal discriminant analysis
- d. Postmodern communication

Guidance: level 1

:: ::

A _____ is server software, or hardware dedicated to running said software, that can satisfy World Wide Web client requests. A _____ can, in general, contain one or more websites. A _____ processes incoming network requests over HTTP and several other related protocols.

Exam Probability: **Medium**

36. *Answer choices:*

(see index for correct answer)

- a. open system
- b. empathy
- c. hierarchical perspective
- d. information systems assessment

Guidance: level 1

:: E-commerce ::

The phrase _____ was originally coined in 1997 by Kevin Duffey at the launch of the Global _____ Forum, to mean "the delivery of electronic commerce capabilities directly into the consumer's hand, anywhere, via wireless technology." Many choose to think of _____ as meaning "a retail outlet in your customer's pocket."

Exam Probability: **High**

37. *Answer choices:*

(see index for correct answer)

- a. Notice and take down
- b. IzzoNet
- c. Consumer-to-consumer
- d. Mobile commerce

Guidance: level 1

:: History of human–computer interaction ::

A _____ , plural mice, is a small rodent characteristically having a pointed snout, small rounded ears, a body-length scaly tail and a high breeding rate. The best known _____ species is the common house _____ . It is also a popular pet. In some places, certain kinds of field mice are locally common. They are known to invade homes for food and shelter.

Exam Probability: **Medium**

38. *Answer choices:*

(see index for correct answer)

- a. IBM 2741
- b. Pilot
- c. Mouse
- d. Mousepad

Guidance: level 1

:: Production economics ::

In microeconomics, _____ are the cost advantages that enterprises obtain due to their scale of operation, with cost per unit of output decreasing with increasing scale.

Exam Probability: **Low**

39. *Answer choices:*

(see index for correct answer)

- a. Economies of scale
- b. Learning-by-doing
- c. Producer's risk
- d. Constant elasticity of transformation

Guidance: level 1

:: Database theory ::

_____ is the organisation of data according to a database model. The designer determines what data must be stored and how the data elements interrelate. With this information, they can begin to fit the data to the database model.

Exam Probability: **Medium**

40. *Answer choices:*

(see index for correct answer)

- a. Principle of orthogonal design
- b. Database design
- c. Temporal database
- d. Attribute domain

Guidance: level 1

:: Multi-agent systems ::

A _____ is a number of Internet-connected devices, each of which is running one or more bots. _____ s can be used to perform distributed denial-of-service attack , steal data, send spam, and allows the attacker to access the device and its connection. The owner can control the _____ using command and control software. The word " _____ " is a combination of the words "robot" and "network". The term is usually used with a negative or malicious connotation.

Exam Probability: **Low**

41. *Answer choices:*

(see index for correct answer)

- a. Botnet
- b. Contract Net Protocol
- c. Argus
- d. Deliberative agent

Guidance: level 1

:: Data interchange standards ::

_____ is the concept of businesses electronically communicating information that was traditionally communicated on paper, such as purchase orders and invoices. Technical standards for EDI exist to facilitate parties transacting such instruments without having to make special arrangements.

Exam Probability: **Low**

42. *Answer choices:*

(see index for correct answer)

- a. ASC X12
- b. Uniform Communication Standard
- c. Electronic data interchange
- d. Common Alerting Protocol

Guidance: level 1

:: Market research ::

_____ s are many different distantly related animals that typically have a long cylindrical tube-like body and no limbs. _____ s vary in size from microscopic to over 1 metre in length for marine polychaete _____ s , 6.7 metres for the African giant earth _____ , Microchaetus rappi, and 58 metres for the marine nemertean _____ , Lineus longissimus. Various types of _____ occupy a small variety of parasitic niches, living inside the bodies of other animals. Free-living _____ species do not live on land, but instead, live in marine or freshwater environments, or underground by burrowing.In biology, " _____ " refers to an obsolete taxon, vermes, used by Carolus Linnaeus and Jean-Baptiste Lamarck for all non-arthropod invertebrate animals, now seen to be paraphyletic. The name stems from the Old English word wyrm. Most animals called " _____ s" are invertebrates, but the term is also used for the amphibian caecilians and the slow _____ Anguis, a legless burrowing lizard. Invertebrate animals commonly called " _____ s" include annelids , nematodes , platyhelminthes , marine nemertean _____ s , marine Chaetognatha , priapulid _____ s, and insect larvae such as grubs and maggots.

Exam Probability: **Medium**

43. *Answer choices:*

(see index for correct answer)

- a. Worm
- b. Online panel
- c. Mall-intercept personal interview
- d. Media-Analyse

Guidance: level 1

:: Payment systems ::

> An _____ is an electronic telecommunications device that enables customers of financial institutions to perform financial transactions, such as cash withdrawals, deposits, transfer funds, or obtaining account information, at any time and without the need for direct interaction with bank staff.

Exam Probability: **High**

44. *Answer choices:*

(see index for correct answer)

- a. Automated teller machine
- b. Pan-European Automated Clearing House
- c. E-toll
- d. Ready Financial

Guidance: level 1

:: Data analysis ::

_____ is a process of inspecting, cleansing, transforming, and modeling data with the goal of discovering useful information, informing conclusions, and supporting decision-making. _____ has multiple facets and approaches, encompassing diverse techniques under a variety of names, and is used in different business, science, and social science domains. In today's business world, _____ plays a role in making decisions more scientific and helping businesses operate more effectively.

Exam Probability: **Low**

45. *Answer choices:*

(see index for correct answer)

- a. Data analysis
- b. Inverse Mills ratio
- c. Empirical distribution function
- d. Variance-stabilizing transformation

Guidance: level 1

:: Human–computer interaction ::

_____ is a database query language for relational databases. It was devised by Moshé M. Zloof at IBM Research during the mid-1970s, in parallel to the development of SQL. It is the first graphical query language, using visual tables where the user would enter commands, example elements and conditions. Many graphical front-ends for databases use the ideas from QBE today. Originally limited only for the purpose of retrieving data, QBE was later extended to allow other operations, such as inserts, deletes and updates, as well as creation of temporary tables.

Exam Probability: **Medium**

46. *Answer choices:*

(see index for correct answer)

- a. 10/GUI
- b. Interactive computing
- c. Implicit data collection
- d. Query by Example

Guidance: level 1

:: ::

Collaborative software or _____ is application software designed to help people involved in a common task to achieve their goals. One of the earliest definitions of collaborative software is "intentional group processes plus software to support them".

Exam Probability: **High**

47. *Answer choices:*

(see index for correct answer)

- a. hierarchical
- b. personal values
- c. imperative
- d. Groupware

Guidance: level 1

:: ::

In linguistics, a _____ is the smallest element that can be uttered in isolation with objective or practical meaning.

Exam Probability: **High**

48. *Answer choices:*

(see index for correct answer)

- a. Word
- b. co-culture
- c. process perspective
- d. similarity-attraction theory

Guidance: level 1

:: Information technology management ::

_____ s or pop-ups are forms of online advertising on the World Wide Web. A pop-up is a graphical user interface display area, usually a small window, that suddenly appears in the foreground of the visual interface. The pop-up window containing an advertisement is usually generated by JavaScript that uses cross-site scripting, sometimes with a secondary payload that uses Adobe Flash. They can also be generated by other vulnerabilities/security holes in browser security.

Exam Probability: **High**

49. *Answer choices:*

(see index for correct answer)

- a. Identity Governance Framework
- b. Storage hypervisor
- c. Pop-up ad
- d. Network configuration and change management

Guidance: level 1

:: Management systems ::

An _____, also known as an <u>Executive support system</u>, is a type of management support system that facilitates and supports senior executive information and decision-making needs. It provides easy access to internal and external information relevant to organizational goals. It is commonly considered a specialized form of decision support system.

Exam Probability: **High**

50. *Answer choices:*

(see index for correct answer)

- a. Executive information system
- b. Business semantics management
- c. Service system
- d. Intelligent enterprise

Guidance: level 1

:: Information technology management ::

_____ is a collective term for all approaches to prepare, support and help individuals, teams, and organizations in making organizational change. The most common change drivers include: technological evolution, process reviews, crisis, and consumer habit changes; pressure from new business entrants, acquisitions, mergers, and organizational restructuring. It includes methods that redirect or redefine the use of resources, business process, budget allocations, or other modes of operation that significantly change a company or organization. Organizational _____ considers the full organization and what needs to change, while _____ may be used solely to refer to how people and teams are affected by such organizational transition. It deals with many different disciplines, from behavioral and social sciences to information technology and business solutions.

Exam Probability: **High**

51. *Answer choices:*

(see index for correct answer)

- a. Telematics
- b. Change management
- c. Change control
- d. One-to-one

Guidance: level 1

:: Data privacy ::

The _____ is an information security standard for organizations that handle branded credit cards from the major card schemes.

Exam Probability: **High**

52. *Answer choices:*

(see index for correct answer)

- a. Unclick
- b. Federal Data Protection and Information Commissioner
- c. Genetic exceptionalism
- d. Payment Card Industry Data Security Standard

Guidance: level 1

:: Fault tolerance ::

_____ is the property that enables a system to continue operating properly in the event of the failure of some of its components. If its operating quality decreases at all, the decrease is proportional to the severity of the failure, as compared to a naively designed system, in which even a small failure can cause total breakdown. _____ is particularly sought after in high-availability or life-critical systems. The ability of maintaining functionality when portions of a system break down is referred to as graceful degradation.

Exam Probability: **High**

53. *Answer choices:*

(see index for correct answer)

- a. Redundancy
- b. Intrusion tolerance
- c. Fault tolerance
- d. Random fault

Guidance: level 1

:: E-commerce ::

_____ is a type of performance-based marketing in which a business rewards one or more affiliates for each visitor or customer brought by the affiliate's own marketing efforts.

Exam Probability: **Medium**

54. *Answer choices:*

(see index for correct answer)

- a. Piano Media
- b. Affiliate marketing
- c. Online food ordering
- d. MOL AccessPortal

Guidance: level 1

:: Big data ::

_____ is the discovery, interpretation, and communication of meaningful patterns in data; and the process of applying those patterns towards effective decision making. In other words, _____ can be understood as the connective tissue between data and effective decision making, within an organization. Especially valuable in areas rich with recorded information, _____ relies on the simultaneous application of statistics, computer programming and operations research to quantify performance.

Exam Probability: **Medium**

55. *Answer choices:*

(see index for correct answer)

- a. Analytics
- b. VoloMetrix
- c. Greenplum
- d. Ninja Metrics

Guidance: level 1

:: Commerce ::

_____, Inc. is an American media-services provider headquartered in Los Gatos, California, founded in 1997 by Reed Hastings and Marc Randolph in Scotts Valley, California. The company's primary business is its subscription-based streaming OTT service which offers online streaming of a library of films and television programs, including those produced in-house. As of April 2019, _____ had over 148 million paid subscriptions worldwide, including 60 million in the United States, and over 154 million subscriptions total including free trials. It is available almost worldwide except in mainland China as well as Syria, North Korea, and Crimea. The company also has offices in the Netherlands, Brazil, India, Japan, and South Korea.
_____ is a member of the Motion Picture Association of America.

Exam Probability: **High**

56. *Answer choices:*

(see index for correct answer)

- a. Netflix
- b. Oxygen bar
- c. Fast track
- d. Bill of sale

Guidance: level 1

:: Virtual reality ::

An _____ , a concept in Hinduism that means "descent", refers to the material appearance or incarnation of a deity on earth. The relative verb to "alight, to make one`s appearance" is sometimes used to refer to any guru or revered human being.

Exam Probability: **Medium**

57. *Answer choices:*

(see index for correct answer)

- a. Endocentric environment
- b. WorldViz
- c. Blue Brain Project
- d. Avizo

Guidance: level 1

:: Internet governance ::

A _____ is one of the domains at the highest level in the hierarchical Domain Name System of the Internet. The _____ names are installed in the root zone of the name space. For all domains in lower levels, it is the last part of the domain name, that is, the last label of a fully qualified domain name. For example, in the domain name www.example.com, the _____ is com. Responsibility for management of most _____ s is delegated to specific organizations by the Internet Corporation for Assigned Names and Numbers , which operates the Internet Assigned Numbers Authority , and is in charge of maintaining the DNS root zone.

Exam Probability: **Low**

58. *Answer choices:*

(see index for correct answer)

- a. Internet governance
- b. Regional Internet registry
- c. GeoTLD
- d. Top-level domain

Guidance: level 1

:: Ubiquitous computing ::

A _____ , chip card, or integrated circuit card is a physical electronic authorization device, used to control access to a resource. It is typically a plastic credit card sized card with an embedded integrated circuit. Many _____ s include a pattern of metal contacts to electrically connect to the internal chip. Others are contactless, and some are both. _____ s can provide personal identification, authentication, data storage, and application processing. Applications include identification, financial, mobile phones , public transit, computer security, schools, and healthcare.
_____ s may provide strong security authentication for single sign-on within organizations. Several nations have deployed _____ s throughout their populations.

Exam Probability: **Medium**

59. *Answer choices:*

(see index for correct answer)

- a. Ubiquitous Communicator
- b. Contactless smart card
- c. Location awareness
- d. Smart card

Guidance: level 1

Marketing

Marketing is the study and management of exchange relationships. Marketing is the business process of creating relationships with and satisfying customers. With its focus on the customer, marketing is one of the premier components of business management.

Marketing is defined by the American Marketing Association as "the activity, set of institutions, and processes for creating, communicating, delivering, and exchanging offerings that have value for customers, clients, partners, and society at large."

:: Consumer theory ::

A _____ is a technical term in psychology, economics and philosophy usually used in relation to choosing between alternatives. For example, someone prefers A over B if they would rather choose A than B.

Exam Probability: **Low**

1. *Answer choices:*

(see index for correct answer)

- a. Business contract hire
- b. Preference
- c. Consumption
- d. Compensated demand

Guidance: level 1

:: ::

A _____ is a professional who provides expert advice in a particular area such as security, management, education, accountancy, law, human resources, marketing, finance, engineering, science or any of many other specialized fields.

Exam Probability: **Medium**

2. *Answer choices:*

(see index for correct answer)

- a. surface-level diversity
- b. Consultant
- c. imperative
- d. cultural

Guidance: level 1

:: Competition regulators ::

The _____ is an independent agency of the United States government, established in 1914 by the _____ Act. Its principal mission is the promotion of consumer protection and the elimination and prevention of anticompetitive business practices, such as coercive monopoly. It is headquartered in the _____ Building in Washington, D.C.

Exam Probability: **High**

3. *Answer choices:*

(see index for correct answer)

- a. Competition Appeal Tribunal
- b. Australian Competition and Consumer Commission
- c. Queensland Competition Authority
- d. Federal Trade Commission

Guidance: level 1

:: ::

_____ , in general use, is a devotion and faithfulness to a nation, cause, philosophy, country, group, or person. Philosophers disagree on what can be an object of _____ , as some argue that _____ is strictly interpersonal and only another human being can be the object of _____ . The definition of _____ in law and political science is the fidelity of an individual to a nation, either one's nation of birth, or one's declared home nation by oath .

Exam Probability: **Low**

4. *Answer choices:*

(see index for correct answer)

- a. open system
- b. deep-level diversity
- c. levels of analysis
- d. Loyalty

Guidance: level 1

:: Direct selling ::

_____ consists of two main business models: single-level marketing, in which a direct seller makes money by buying products from a parent organization and selling them directly to customers, and multi-level marketing, in which the direct seller may earn money from both direct sales to customers and by sponsoring new direct sellers and potentially earning a commission from their efforts.

Exam Probability: **Low**

5. *Answer choices:*

(see index for correct answer)

- a. Direct selling
- b. Direct Selling Association
- c. CVSL
- d. Direct Selling News

Guidance: level 1

:: Business models ::

A _____ is "an autonomous association of persons united voluntarily to meet their common economic, social, and cultural needs and aspirations through a jointly-owned and democratically-controlled enterprise". _____ s may include.

Exam Probability: **Medium**

6. *Answer choices:*

(see index for correct answer)

- a. Co-operative Wholesale Society
- b. Sailing Ship Effect
- c. Microfranchising
- d. Cooperative

Guidance: level 1

:: Marketing ::

_____ comes from the Latin neg and otsia referring to businessmen who, unlike the patricians, had no leisure time in their industriousness; it held the meaning of business until the 17th century when it took on the diplomatic connotation as a dialogue between two or more people or parties intended to reach a beneficial outcome over one or more issues where a conflict exists with respect to at least one of these issues. Thus, _____ is a process of combining divergent positions into a joint agreement under a decision rule of unanimity.

Exam Probability: **Low**

7. *Answer choices:*

(see index for correct answer)

- a. Market orientation
- b. Market share

- c. Processing fluency
- d. Discoverability

Guidance: level 1

:: Communication design ::

An _____ is a series of advertisement messages that share a single idea and theme which make up an integrated marketing communication. An IMC is a platform in which a group of people can group their ideas, beliefs, and concepts into one large media base. _____ s utilize diverse media channels over a particular time frame and target identified audiences.

Exam Probability: **Medium**

8. *Answer choices:*
(see index for correct answer)

- a. Jannuzzi Smith
- b. Advertising campaign
- c. Margaret Calvert
- d. European Design Award

Guidance: level 1

:: Market research ::

_____ is the action of defining, gathering, analyzing, and distributing intelligence about products, customers, competitors, and any aspect of the environment needed to support executives and managers in strategic decision making for an organization.

Exam Probability: **Low**

9. *Answer choices:*

(see index for correct answer)

- a. Preference regression
- b. Respondent error
- c. Focus group
- d. Vehicle Dependability Study

Guidance: level 1

:: Information technology ::

_____ is the use of computers to store, retrieve, transmit, and manipulate data, or information, often in the context of a business or other enterprise. IT is considered to be a subset of information and communications technology. An _____ system is generally an information system, a communications system or, more specifically speaking, a computer system – including all hardware, software and peripheral equipment – operated by a limited group of users.

Exam Probability: **High**

10. Answer choices:

(see index for correct answer)

- a. Legal aspects of computing
- b. Information technology
- c. Geeks Without Bounds
- d. GroupLogic

Guidance: level 1

:: Management ::

In economics and marketing, _____ is the process of distinguishing a product or service from others, to make it more attractive to a particular target market. This involves differentiating it from competitors' products as well as a firm's own products. The concept was proposed by Edward Chamberlin in his 1933 The Theory of Monopolistic Competition.

Exam Probability: **Medium**

11. Answer choices:

(see index for correct answer)

- a. Remedial action
- b. Empowerment
- c. Product differentiation
- d. Maryland StateStat

Guidance: level 1

:: National accounts ::

_____ is a monetary measure of the market value of all the final goods and services produced in a period of time, often annually. GDP per capita does not, however, reflect differences in the cost of living and the inflation rates of the countries; therefore using a basis of GDP per capita at purchasing power parity is arguably more useful when comparing differences in living standards between nations.

Exam Probability: **Low**

12. *Answer choices:*

(see index for correct answer)

- a. capital formation
- b. Gross domestic product
- c. National Income

Guidance: level 1

:: Project management ::

A _____ is a source or supply from which a benefit is produced and it has some utility. _____ s can broadly be classified upon their availability—they are classified into renewable and non-renewable _____ s. Examples of non renewable _____ s are coal ,crude oil natural gas nuclear energy etc. Examples of renewable _____ s are air,water,wind,solar energy etc. They can also be classified as actual and potential on the basis of level of development and use, on the basis of origin they can be classified as biotic and abiotic, and on the basis of their distribution, as ubiquitous and localized . An item becomes a _____ with time and developing technology. Typically, _____ s are materials, energy, services, staff, knowledge, or other assets that are transformed to produce benefit and in the process may be consumed or made unavailable. Benefits of _____ utilization may include increased wealth, proper functioning of a system, or enhanced well-being. From a human perspective a natural _____ is anything obtained from the environment to satisfy human needs and wants. From a broader biological or ecological perspective a _____ satisfies the needs of a living organism .

Exam Probability: **Low**

13. *Answer choices:*

(see index for correct answer)

- a. Value breakdown structure
- b. Deployment Plan
- c. Organizational project management
- d. Project planning

Guidance: level 1

:: ::

In law, an _____ is the process in which cases are reviewed, where parties request a formal change to an official decision. _____ s function both as a process for error correction as well as a process of clarifying and interpreting law. Although appellate courts have existed for thousands of years, common law countries did not incorporate an affirmative right to _____ into their jurisprudence until the 19th century.

Exam Probability: **Medium**

14. *Answer choices:*

(see index for correct answer)

- a. similarity-attraction theory
- b. corporate values
- c. surface-level diversity
- d. personal values

Guidance: level 1

:: ::

A _____ is an organization, usually a group of people or a company, authorized to act as a single entity and recognized as such in law. Early incorporated entities were established by charter. Most jurisdictions now allow the creation of new _____ s through registration.

Exam Probability: **Low**

15. *Answer choices:*

(see index for correct answer)

- a. imperative
- b. corporate values
- c. hierarchical
- d. Corporation

Guidance: level 1

:: Product development ::

In business and engineering, _____ covers the complete process of bringing a new product to market. A central aspect of NPD is product design, along with various business considerations. _____ is described broadly as the transformation of a market opportunity into a product available for sale. The product can be tangible or intangible , though sometimes services and other processes are distinguished from "products." NPD requires an understanding of customer needs and wants, the competitive environment, and the nature of the market.Cost, time and quality are the main variables that drive customer needs. Aiming at these three variables, innovative companies develop continuous practices and strategies to better satisfy customer requirements and to increase their own market share by a regular development of new products. There are many uncertainties and challenges which companies must face throughout the process. The use of best practices and the elimination of barriers to communication are the main concerns for the management of the NPD .

Exam Probability: **Low**

16. *Answer choices:*

(see index for correct answer)

- a. Collaborative product development
- b. DFMA
- c. New product development
- d. Engineering design management

Guidance: level 1

:: Budgets ::

A _____ is a financial plan for a defined period, often one year. It may also include planned sales volumes and revenues, resource quantities, costs and expenses, assets, liabilities and cash flows. Companies, governments, families and other organizations use it to express strategic plans of activities or events in measurable terms.

Exam Probability: **High**

17. *Answer choices:*

(see index for correct answer)

- a. Envelope system
- b. Budget
- c. Operating budget
- d. Budget constraint

Guidance: level 1

:: ::

In production, research, retail, and accounting, a _____ is the value of money that has been used up to produce something or deliver a service, and hence is not available for use anymore. In business, the _____ may be one of acquisition, in which case the amount of money expended to acquire it is counted as _____ . In this case, money is the input that is gone in order to acquire the thing. This acquisition _____ may be the sum of the _____ of production as incurred by the original producer, and further _____ s of transaction as incurred by the acquirer over and above the price paid to the producer. Usually, the price also includes a mark-up for profit over the _____ of production.

Exam Probability: **Medium**

18. *Answer choices:*
(see index for correct answer)

- a. Cost
- b. Sarbanes-Oxley act of 2002
- c. open system
- d. information systems assessment

Guidance: level 1

:: ::

The _____ is a U.S. business-focused, English-language international daily newspaper based in New York City. The Journal, along with its Asian and European editions, is published six days a week by Dow Jones & Company, a division of News Corp. The newspaper is published in the broadsheet format and online. The Journal has been printed continuously since its inception on July 8, 1889, by Charles Dow, Edward Jones, and Charles Bergstresser.

Exam Probability: **High**

19. *Answer choices:*

(see index for correct answer)

- a. information systems assessment
- b. Wall Street Journal
- c. interpersonal communication
- d. Sarbanes-Oxley act of 2002

Guidance: level 1

:: Costs ::

In economics, _____ is the total economic cost of production and is made up of variable cost, which varies according to the quantity of a good produced and includes inputs such as labour and raw materials, plus fixed cost, which is independent of the quantity of a good produced and includes inputs that cannot be varied in the short term: fixed costs such as buildings and machinery, including sunk costs if any. Since cost is measured per unit of time, it is a flow variable.

Exam Probability: **Medium**

20. *Answer choices:*

(see index for correct answer)

- a. Social cost
- b. Travel and subsistence
- c. Total cost
- d. Incremental cost-effectiveness ratio

Guidance: level 1

:: Legal terms ::

A _____ is a person who is called upon to issue a response to a communication made by another. The term is used in legal contexts, in survey methodology, and in psychological conditioning.

Exam Probability: **Low**

21. *Answer choices:*

(see index for correct answer)

- a. Impunity
- b. Respondent
- c. Multiplepoinding
- d. Prerogative

Guidance: level 1

:: Contract law ::

In contract law, a _____ is a promise which is not a condition of the contract or an innominate term: it is a term "not going to the root of the contract", and which only entitles the innocent party to damages if it is breached: i.e. the _____ is not true or the defaulting party does not perform the contract in accordance with the terms of the _____ . A _____ is not guarantee. It is a mere promise. It may be enforced if it is breached by an award for the legal remedy of damages.

Exam Probability: **Low**

22. *Answer choices:*
(see index for correct answer)

- a. Interlineation
- b. Warranty
- c. Broad Agency Announcement
- d. Multimarket contact

Guidance: level 1

:: ::

_____ is a means of protection from financial loss. It is a form of risk management, primarily used to hedge against the risk of a contingent or uncertain loss

Exam Probability: **High**

23. *Answer choices:*

(see index for correct answer)

- a. Insurance
- b. interpersonal communication
- c. similarity-attraction theory
- d. levels of analysis

Guidance: level 1

:: Brand management ::

Marketing communications uses different marketing channels and tools in combination: Marketing communication channels focus on any way a business communicates a message to its desired market, or the market in general. A marketing communication tool can be anything from: advertising, personal selling, direct marketing, sponsorship, communication, and promotion to public relations.

Exam Probability: **High**

24. Answer choices:

(see index for correct answer)

- a. Barloworld Limited
- b. Umbrella brand
- c. E3 Agency Network
- d. Sanrio

Guidance: level 1

:: Brand management ::

_____ refers to the extent to which customers are able to recall or recognise a brand. _____ is a key consideration in consumer behavior, advertising management, brand management and strategy development. The consumer's ability to recognise or recall a brand is central to purchasing decision-making. Purchasing cannot proceed unless a consumer is first aware of a product category and a brand within that category. Awareness does not necessarily mean that the consumer must be able to recall a specific brand name, but he or she must be able to recall sufficient distinguishing features for purchasing to proceed. For instance, if a consumer asks her friend to buy her some gum in a "blue pack", the friend would be expected to know which gum to buy, even though neither friend can recall the precise brand name at the time.

Exam Probability: **Medium**

25. Answer choices:

(see index for correct answer)

- a. Sanrio
- b. Postmodern marketing
- c. Prophet
- d. Brand awareness

Guidance: level 1

:: Organizational structure ::

An _____ defines how activities such as task allocation, coordination, and supervision are directed toward the achievement of organizational aims.

Exam Probability: **Low**

26. *Answer choices:*

(see index for correct answer)

- a. Blessed Unrest
- b. The Starfish and the Spider
- c. Organization of the New York City Police Department
- d. Organizational structure

Guidance: level 1

:: Strategic alliances ::

A _____ is an agreement between two or more parties to pursue a set of agreed upon objectives needed while remaining independent organizations. A _____ will usually fall short of a legal partnership entity, agency, or corporate affiliate relationship. Typically, two companies form a _____ when each possesses one or more business assets or have expertise that will help the other by enhancing their businesses. _____ s can develop in outsourcing relationships where the parties desire to achieve long-term win-win benefits and innovation based on mutually desired outcomes.

Exam Probability: **Medium**

27. *Answer choices:*

(see index for correct answer)

- a. Management contract
- b. Strategic alliance
- c. Defensive termination
- d. Cross-licensing

Guidance: level 1

:: ::

A _____ consists of one people who live in the same dwelling and share meals. It may also consist of a single family or another group of people. A dwelling is considered to contain multiple _____ s if meals or living spaces are not shared. The _____ is the basic unit of analysis in many social, microeconomic and government models, and is important to economics and inheritance.

Exam Probability: **High**

28. *Answer choices:*

(see index for correct answer)

- a. similarity-attraction theory
- b. Household
- c. levels of analysis
- d. surface-level diversity

Guidance: level 1

:: ::

_____ is the administration of an organization, whether it is a business, a not-for-profit organization, or government body. _____ includes the activities of setting the strategy of an organization and coordinating the efforts of its employees to accomplish its objectives through the application of available resources, such as financial, natural, technological, and human resources. The term "_____" may also refer to those people who manage an organization.

Exam Probability: **Low**

29. *Answer choices:*

(see index for correct answer)

- a. deep-level diversity

- b. information systems assessment
- c. Management
- d. cultural

Guidance: level 1

:: ::

_____ is the act of conveying meanings from one entity or group to another through the use of mutually understood signs, symbols, and semiotic rules.

Exam Probability: **Low**

30. *Answer choices:*

(see index for correct answer)

- a. Sarbanes-Oxley act of 2002
- b. hierarchical
- c. process perspective
- d. hierarchical perspective

Guidance: level 1

:: Debt ::

_____ is the trust which allows one party to provide money or resources to another party wherein the second party does not reimburse the first party immediately, but promises either to repay or return those resources at a later date. In other words, _____ is a method of making reciprocity formal, legally enforceable, and extensible to a large group of unrelated people.

Exam Probability: **Low**

31. *Answer choices:*
(see index for correct answer)

- a. Default trap
- b. Tax benefits of debt
- c. Credit cycle
- d. Internal debt

Guidance: level 1

In marketing jargon, product lining is offering several related products for sale individually. Unlike product bundling, where several products are combined into one group, which is then offered for sale as a units, product lining involves offering the products for sale separately. A line can comprise related products of various sizes, types, colors, qualities, or prices. Line depth refers to the number of subcategories a category has. Line consistency refers to how closely related the products that make up the line are. Line vulnerability refers to the percentage of sales or profits that are derived from only a few products in the line.

Exam Probability: **High**

32. *Answer choices:*

(see index for correct answer)

- a. Product line
- b. interpersonal communication
- c. hierarchical perspective
- d. empathy

Guidance: level 1

:: ::

In logic and philosophy, an _____ is a series of statements, called the premises or premisses, intended to determine the degree of truth of another statement, the conclusion. The logical form of an _____ in a natural language can be represented in a symbolic formal language, and independently of natural language formally defined "_____ s" can be made in math and computer science.

Exam Probability: **Low**

33. *Answer choices:*

(see index for correct answer)

- a. Argument
- b. open system
- c. Character
- d. cultural

Guidance: level 1

:: Library science ::

_____ refers to data which is collected by someone who is someone other than the user. Common sources of _____ for social science include censuses, information collected by government departments, organizational records and data that was originally collected for other research purposes. Primary data, by contrast, are collected by the investigator conducting the research.

Exam Probability: **High**

34. *Answer choices:*

(see index for correct answer)

- a. National Agricultural Safety Database
- b. European Association for Grey Literature Exploitation
- c. Bibliomining
- d. Scientific Library of Danylo Halytsky Lviv National Medical University

Guidance: level 1

:: ::

_____ consists of using generic or ad hoc methods in an orderly manner to find solutions to problems. Some of the problem-solving techniques developed and used in philosophy, artificial intelligence, computer science, engineering, mathematics, or medicine are related to mental problem-solving techniques studied in psychology.

Exam Probability: **High**

35. *Answer choices:*

(see index for correct answer)

- a. deep-level diversity

- b. hierarchical
- c. Problem Solving
- d. similarity-attraction theory

Guidance: level 1

:: ::

According to the philosopher Piyush Mathur, "Tangibility is the property that a phenomenon exhibits if it has and/or transports mass and/or energy and/or momentum".

Exam Probability: **Low**

36. *Answer choices:*

(see index for correct answer)

- a. interpersonal communication
- b. process perspective
- c. hierarchical perspective
- d. imperative

Guidance: level 1

:: ::

Distribution is one of the four elements of the marketing mix. Distribution is the process of making a product or service available for the consumer or business user who needs it. This can be done directly by the producer or service provider, or using indirect channels with distributors or intermediaries. The other three elements of the marketing mix are product, pricing, and promotion.

Exam Probability: **Medium**

37. *Answer choices:*

(see index for correct answer)

- a. hierarchical
- b. Distribution channel
- c. hierarchical perspective
- d. cultural

Guidance: level 1

:: Marketing ::

A _____ is an overall experience of a customer that distinguishes an organization or product from its rivals in the eyes of the customer. _____ s are used in business, marketing, and advertising. Name _____ s are sometimes distinguished from generic or store _____ s.

Exam Probability: **High**

38. *Answer choices:*

(see index for correct answer)

- a. Price skimming
- b. Nia effect
- c. Gimmick
- d. Brand

Guidance: level 1

:: ::

> In marketing, a _____ is a ticket or document that can be redeemed for a financial discount or rebate when purchasing a product.

Exam Probability: **Medium**

39. *Answer choices:*

(see index for correct answer)

- a. levels of analysis
- b. Character
- c. cultural
- d. Coupon

Guidance: level 1

:: Evaluation methods ::

In natural and social sciences, and sometimes in other fields, _____ is the systematic empirical investigation of observable phenomena via statistical, mathematical, or computational techniques. The objective of _____ is to develop and employ mathematical models, theories, and hypotheses pertaining to phenomena. The process of measurement is central to _____ because it provides the fundamental connection between empirical observation and mathematical expression of quantitative relationships.

Exam Probability: **Low**

40. *Answer choices:*
(see index for correct answer)

- a. Logic model
- b. Fixtureless in-circuit test
- c. Quantitative research
- d. Video ethnography

Guidance: level 1

:: Marketing techniques ::

_____ is the activity of dividing a broad consumer or business market, normally consisting of existing and potential customers, into sub-groups of consumers based on some type of shared characteristics. In dividing or segmenting markets, researchers typically look for common characteristics such as shared needs, common interests, similar lifestyles or even similar demographic profiles. The overall aim of segmentation is to identify high yield segments – that is, those segments that are likely to be the most profitable or that have growth potential – so that these can be selected for special attention.

Exam Probability: **High**

41. *Answer choices:*

(see index for correct answer)

- a. Product demonstration
- b. Market segmentation
- c. Appeal to fear
- d. Virtual engagement

Guidance: level 1

:: Goods ::

In most contexts, the concept of _____ denotes the conduct that should be preferred when posed with a choice between possible actions. _____ is generally considered to be the opposite of evil, and is of interest in the study of morality, ethics, religion and philosophy. The specific meaning and etymology of the term and its associated translations among ancient and contemporary languages show substantial variation in its inflection and meaning depending on circumstances of place, history, religious, or philosophical context.

Exam Probability: **Medium**

42. *Answer choices:*

(see index for correct answer)

- a. Global public good
- b. Bad
- c. Designer label
- d. Goods and services

Guidance: level 1

:: ::

A _____ is a discussion or informational website published on the World Wide Web consisting of discrete, often informal diary-style text entries. Posts are typically displayed in reverse chronological order, so that the most recent post appears first, at the top of the web page. Until 2009, _____ s were usually the work of a single individual, occasionally of a small group, and often covered a single subject or topic. In the 2010s, "multi-author _____ s" emerged, featuring the writing of multiple authors and sometimes professionally edited. MABs from newspapers, other media outlets, universities, think tanks, advocacy groups, and similar institutions account for an increasing quantity of _____ traffic. The rise of Twitter and other "micro _____ ging" systems helps integrate MABs and single-author _____ s into the news media. _____ can also be used as a verb, meaning to maintain or add content to a _____ .

Exam Probability: **High**

43. *Answer choices:*

(see index for correct answer)

- a. hierarchical perspective
- b. corporate values
- c. Blog
- d. surface-level diversity

Guidance: level 1

:: ::

_____ is the process whereby a business sets the price at which it will sell its products and services, and may be part of the business's marketing plan. In setting prices, the business will take into account the price at which it could acquire the goods, the manufacturing cost, the market place, competition, market condition, brand, and quality of product.

Exam Probability: **Low**

44. *Answer choices:*

(see index for correct answer)

- a. interpersonal communication
- b. hierarchical perspective
- c. Sarbanes-Oxley act of 2002
- d. process perspective

Guidance: level 1

:: Data management ::

_____ is a form of intellectual property that grants the creator of an original creative work an exclusive legal right to determine whether and under what conditions this original work may be copied and used by others, usually for a limited term of years. The exclusive rights are not absolute but limited by limitations and exceptions to _____ law, including fair use. A major limitation on _____ on ideas is that _____ protects only the original expression of ideas, and not the underlying ideas themselves.

Exam Probability: **Medium**

45. *Answer choices:*

(see index for correct answer)

- a. National Information Governance Board for Health and Social Care
- b. Copyright
- c. Operational system
- d. Data monetization

Guidance: level 1

:: Retailing ::

> A _____ is a retail establishment offering a wide range of consumer goods in different product categories known as "departments". In modern major cities, the _____ made a dramatic appearance in the middle of the 19th century, and permanently reshaped shopping habits, and the definition of service and luxury. Similar developments were under way in London, in Paris and in New York.

Exam Probability: **High**

46. *Answer choices:*

(see index for correct answer)

- a. Retail Systems Research
- b. Department store

- c. Automated retailing
- d. Junk shop

Guidance: level 1

:: Advertising ::

A _____ is a document used by creative professionals and agencies to develop creative deliverables: visual design, copy, advertising, web sites, etc. The document is usually developed by the requestor and approved by the creative team of designers, writers, and project managers. In some cases, the project's _____ may need creative director approval before work will commence.

Exam Probability: **Low**

47. *Answer choices:*

(see index for correct answer)

- a. Flighting
- b. Creative brief
- c. 140 Proof
- d. Autosurf

Guidance: level 1

:: Marketing techniques ::

_____, also known as embedded marketing, is a marketing technique where references to specific brands or products are incorporated into another work, such as a film or television program, with specific promotional intent.

Exam Probability: **Low**

48. *Answer choices:*

(see index for correct answer)

- a. Demand-side platform
- b. Product demonstration
- c. Programmatic marketing
- d. Product placement

Guidance: level 1

:: Marketing ::

_____ s are structured marketing strategies designed by merchants to encourage customers to continue to shop at or use the services of businesses associated with each program. These programs exist covering most types of commerce, each one having varying features and rewards-schemes.

Exam Probability: **Medium**

49. *Answer choices:*

(see index for correct answer)

- a. Cultural consumer
- b. Business stature
- c. Cumulative prospect theory
- d. Loyalty program

Guidance: level 1

:: Management ::

A _____ is a promise of value to be delivered, communicated, and acknowledged. It is also a belief from the customer about how value will be delivered, experienced and acquired.

Exam Probability: **High**

50. *Answer choices:*
(see index for correct answer)

- a. Enterprise planning system
- b. Value proposition
- c. Industrial forensics
- d. Supervisory board

Guidance: level 1

:: Contract law ::

A _____ is a legally-binding agreement which recognises and governs the rights and duties of the parties to the agreement. A _____ is legally enforceable because it meets the requirements and approval of the law. An agreement typically involves the exchange of goods, services, money, or promises of any of those. In the event of breach of _____ , the law awards the injured party access to legal remedies such as damages and cancellation.

Exam Probability: **High**

51. *Answer choices:*

(see index for correct answer)

- a. Principles of International Commercial Contracts
- b. Unenforceable
- c. Transmutation agreement
- d. Contract

Guidance: level 1

:: Retailing ::

_____ is the process of selling consumer goods or services to customers through multiple channels of distribution to earn a profit. _____ ers satisfy demand identified through a supply chain. The term "_____ er" is typically applied where a service provider fills the small orders of a large number of individuals, who are end-users, rather than large orders of a small number of wholesale, corporate or government clientele. Shopping generally refers to the act of buying products. Sometimes this is done to obtain final goods, including necessities such as food and clothing; sometimes it takes place as a recreational activity. Recreational shopping often involves window shopping and browsing: it does not always result in a purchase.

Exam Probability: **Medium**

52. *Answer choices:*

(see index for correct answer)

- a. Charity shop
- b. Slatwall
- c. Retail
- d. Home shopping

Guidance: level 1

:: Income ::

In business and accounting, net income is an entity's income minus cost of goods sold, expenses and taxes for an accounting period. It is computed as the residual of all revenues and gains over all expenses and losses for the period, and has also been defined as the net increase in shareholders' equity that results from a company's operations. In the context of the presentation of financial statements, the IFRS Foundation defines net income as synonymous with profit and loss. The difference between revenue and the cost of making a product or providing a service, before deducting overheads, payroll, taxation, and interest payments. This is different from operating income .

Exam Probability: **Medium**

53. *Answer choices:*

(see index for correct answer)

- a. Bottom line
- b. Independent income
- c. Aggregate income
- d. Imputed income

Guidance: level 1

:: Advertising techniques ::

In promotion and of advertising, a _____ or show consists of a person's written or spoken statement extolling the virtue of a product. The term "_____" most commonly applies to the sales-pitches attributed to ordinary citizens, whereas the word "endorsement" usually applies to pitches by celebrities. _____ s can be part of communal marketing. Sometimes, the cartoon character can be a _____ in a commercial.

Exam Probability: **High**

54. *Answer choices:*

(see index for correct answer)

- a. Dolly Dimples
- b. Location-based advertising
- c. Testimonial
- d. Transpromotional

Guidance: level 1

:: ::

Management is the administration of an organization, whether it is a business, a not-for-profit organization, or government body. Management includes the activities of setting the strategy of an organization and coordinating the efforts of its employees to accomplish its objectives through the application of available resources, such as financial, natural, technological, and human resources. The term "management" may also refer to those people who manage an organization.

Exam Probability: **Medium**

55. *Answer choices:*

(see index for correct answer)

- a. empathy
- b. functional perspective
- c. process perspective
- d. personal values

Guidance: level 1

:: Consumer theory ::

_____ is the quantity of a good that consumers are willing and able to purchase at various prices during a given period of time.

Exam Probability: **High**

56. *Answer choices:*

(see index for correct answer)

- a. Rational addiction
- b. Convex preferences
- c. Marshallian demand function
- d. Joint demand

Guidance: level 1

:: Supply chain management terms ::

In business and finance, _____ is a system of organizations, people, activities, information, and resources involved in moving a product or service from supplier to customer. _____ activities involve the transformation of natural resources, raw materials, and components into a finished product that is delivered to the end customer. In sophisticated _____ systems, used products may re-enter the _____ at any point where residual value is recyclable. _____ s link value chains.

Exam Probability: **High**

57. *Answer choices:*

(see index for correct answer)

- a. Widget
- b. Supply chain
- c. Consumable
- d. Last mile

Guidance: level 1

:: Management occupations ::

_____ ship is the process of designing, launching and running a new business, which is often initially a small business. The people who create these businesses are called _____ s.

Exam Probability: **Low**

58. *Answer choices:*

(see index for correct answer)

- a. Directeur sportif
- b. Entrepreneur
- c. Store manager
- d. Director of nursing

Guidance: level 1

:: ::

_____ is the study and management of exchange relationships. _____ is the business process of creating relationships with and satisfying customers. With its focus on the customer, _____ is one of the premier components of business management.

Exam Probability: **High**

59. *Answer choices:*

(see index for correct answer)

- a. Character
- b. empathy
- c. surface-level diversity
- d. Marketing

Guidance: level 1

Manufacturing

Manufacturing is the production of merchandise for use or sale using labor and machines, tools, chemical and biological processing, or formulation. The term may refer to a range of human activity, from handicraft to high tech, but is most commonly applied to industrial design , in which raw materials are transformed into finished goods on a large scale. Such finished goods may be sold to other manufacturers for the production of other, more complex products, such as aircraft, household appliances, furniture, sports equipment or automobiles, or sold to wholesalers, who in turn sell them to retailers, who then sell them to end users and consumers.

:: Consortia ::

A _____ is an association of two or more individuals, companies, organizations or governments with the objective of participating in a common activity or pooling their resources for achieving a common goal.

Exam Probability: **High**

1. *Answer choices:*

(see index for correct answer)

- a. Gang of Nine
- b. SATURN Development Group
- c. Consortium
- d. Grand Alliance

Guidance: level 1

:: Management ::

A _____ is an idea of the future or desired result that a person or a group of people envisions, plans and commits to achieve. People endeavor to reach _____ s within a finite time by setting deadlines.

Exam Probability: **Medium**

2. *Answer choices:*

(see index for correct answer)

- a. Meeting system
- b. Goal
- c. Supervisory board
- d. Planning

Guidance: level 1

:: Costs ::

> The _____ is computed by dividing the total cost of goods available for sale by the total units available for sale. This gives a weighted-average unit cost that is applied to the units in the ending inventory.

Exam Probability: **Low**

3. *Answer choices:*

(see index for correct answer)

- a. Khozraschyot
- b. Prospective costs
- c. Joint cost
- d. Average cost

Guidance: level 1

:: Gas technologies ::

A _____ is a rotary mechanical device that extracts energy from a fluid flow and converts it into useful work. The work produced by a _____ can be used for generating electrical power when combined with a generator. A _____ is a turbomachine with at least one moving part called a rotor assembly, which is a shaft or drum with blades attached. Moving fluid acts on the blades so that they move and impart rotational energy to the rotor. Early _____ examples are windmills and waterwheels.

Exam Probability: **Low**

4. *Answer choices:*

(see index for correct answer)

- a. Turbine
- b. Bartlett Street Lamps
- c. Nitrous oxide engine
- d. Hydrogen purifier

Guidance: level 1

:: Production and manufacturing ::

In industry, _____ is a system of maintaining and improving the integrity of production and quality systems through the machines, equipment, processes, and employees that add business value to an organization.

Exam Probability: **Low**

5. *Answer choices:*

(see index for correct answer)

- a. Countercurrent exchange
- b. Methods-time measurement
- c. Total productive maintenance
- d. Product layout

Guidance: level 1

:: Business process ::

A _____ or business method is a collection of related, structured activities or tasks by people or equipment which in a specific sequence produce a service or product for a particular customer or customers. _____ es occur at all organizational levels and may or may not be visible to the customers. A _____ may often be visualized as a flowchart of a sequence of activities with interleaving decision points or as a process matrix of a sequence of activities with relevance rules based on data in the process. The benefits of using _____ es include improved customer satisfaction and improved agility for reacting to rapid market change. Process-oriented organizations break down the barriers of structural departments and try to avoid functional silos.

Exam Probability: **High**

6. *Answer choices:*

(see index for correct answer)

- a. Sales process engineering
- b. ADONIS
- c. Business Process Definition Metamodel
- d. Business process

Guidance: level 1

:: Quality management ::

_____ ensures that an organization, product or service is consistent. It has four main components: quality planning, quality assurance, quality control and quality improvement. _____ is focused not only on product and service quality, but also on the means to achieve it. _____ , therefore, uses quality assurance and control of processes as well as products to achieve more consistent quality. What a customer wants and is willing to pay for it determines quality. It is written or unwritten commitment to a known or unknown consumer in the market . Thus, quality can be defined as fitness for intended use or, in other words, how well the product performs its intended function

Exam Probability: **Low**

7. *Answer choices:*

(see index for correct answer)

- a. Good Clinical Laboratory Practice
- b. TL 9000
- c. Germanischer Lloyd
- d. Quality management

Guidance: level 1

:: Quality ::

_____ is a concept first outlined by quality expert Joseph M. Juran in publications, most notably Juran on _____ . Designing for quality and innovation is one of the three universal processes of the Juran Trilogy, in which Juran describes what is required to achieve breakthroughs in new products, services, and processes. Juran believed that quality could be planned, and that most quality crises and problems relate to the way in which quality was planned.

Exam Probability: **High**

8. *Answer choices:*

(see index for correct answer)

- a. Market Driven Quality
- b. Cleaning validation
- c. Quality by Design
- d. Process architecture

Guidance: level 1

:: Information systems ::

_____ is the process of creating, sharing, using and managing the knowledge and information of an organisation. It refers to a multidisciplinary approach to achieving organisational objectives by making the best use of knowledge.

Exam Probability: **Low**

9. *Answer choices:*

(see index for correct answer)

- a. Vehicle Information and Communication System
- b. EUCARIS
- c. Information Processes and Technology
- d. Knowledge management

Guidance: level 1

:: Supply chain management terms ::

In business and finance, _____ is a system of organizations, people, activities, information, and resources involved in moving a product or service from supplier to customer. _____ activities involve the transformation of natural resources, raw materials, and components into a finished product that is delivered to the end customer. In sophisticated _____ systems, used products may re-enter the _____ at any point where residual value is recyclable. _____ s link value chains.

Exam Probability: **Low**

10. Answer choices:

(see index for correct answer)

- a. Most valuable customers
- b. Final assembly schedule
- c. Will call
- d. Supply chain

Guidance: level 1

:: Direct marketing ::

> _____ Inc. is an American privately owned multi-level marketing company. According to Direct Selling News, _____ was the sixth largest network marketing company in the world in 2018, with a wholesale volume of US$3.25 billion. _____ is based in Addison, Texas, outside Dallas. The company was founded by _____ Ash in 1963. Richard Rogers, _____ 's son, is the chairman, and David Holl is president and was named CEO in 2006.

Exam Probability: **Medium**

11. Answer choices:

(see index for correct answer)

- a. Direct marketing
- b. Mary Kay
- c. A Common Reader
- d. Forced Free Trial

Guidance: level 1

:: Project management ::

_____ is a marketing activity that does an aggregate plan for the production process, in advance of 6 to 18 months, to give an idea to management as to what quantity of materials and other resources are to be procured and when, so that the total cost of operations of the organization is kept to the minimum over that period.

Exam Probability: **Low**

12. *Answer choices:*
(see index for correct answer)

- a. Operational bill
- b. Organizational project management
- c. Outcomes theory
- d. Milestone

Guidance: level 1

:: ::

An _____ is, most an organized examination or formal evaluation exercise. In engineering activities _____ involves the measurements, tests, and gauges applied to certain characteristics in regard to an object or activity. The results are usually compared to specified requirements and standards for determining whether the item or activity is in line with these targets, often with a Standard _____ Procedure in place to ensure consistent checking. _____ s are usually non-destructive.

Exam Probability: **High**

13. *Answer choices:*
(see index for correct answer)

- a. interpersonal communication
- b. Sarbanes-Oxley act of 2002
- c. functional perspective
- d. Inspection

Guidance: level 1

:: Quality management ::

_____ is a not-for-profit membership foundation in Brussels, established in 1989 to increase the competitiveness of the European economy. The initial impetus for forming _____ was a response to the work of W. Edwards Deming and the development of the concepts of Total Quality Management.

Exam Probability: **Medium**

14. *Answer choices:*

(see index for correct answer)

- a. Regulatory translation
- b. Det Norske Veritas
- c. EFQM
- d. Quality management system

Guidance: level 1

:: Management ::

An _____ is a loosely coupled, self-organizing network of firms that combine their economic output to provide products and services offerings to the market. Firms in the _____ may operate independently, for example, through market mechanisms, or cooperatively through agreements and contracts. They provide value added service or product to the OEM.

Exam Probability: **High**

15. *Answer choices:*

(see index for correct answer)

- a. Extended enterprise
- b. Quality, cost, delivery
- c. Action item
- d. Scenario planning

Guidance: level 1

:: Management ::

In inventory management, _____ is the order quantity that minimizes the total holding costs and ordering costs. It is one of the oldest classical production scheduling models. The model was developed by Ford W. Harris in 1913, but R. H. Wilson, a consultant who applied it extensively, and K. Andler are given credit for their in-depth analysis.

Exam Probability: **High**

16. *Answer choices:*

(see index for correct answer)

- a. Fleet management
- b. Concept of operations
- c. Economic order quantity
- d. Risk management

Guidance: level 1

:: Production and manufacturing ::

An _____ is a manufacturing process in which parts are added as the semi-finished assembly moves from workstation to workstation where the parts are added in sequence until the final assembly is produced. By mechanically moving the parts to the assembly work and moving the semi-finished assembly from work station to work station, a finished product can be assembled faster and with less labor than by having workers carry parts to a stationary piece for assembly.

Exam Probability: **High**

17. *Answer choices:*

(see index for correct answer)

- a. Assembly line
- b. Manufacturing process management
- c. Changeover
- d. Plant layout study

Guidance: level 1

:: Risk analysis ::

Supply-chain risk management is "the implementation of strategies to manage both everyday and exceptional risks along the supply chain based on continuous risk assessment with the objective of reducing vulnerability and ensuring continuity".

Exam Probability: **Low**

18. *Answer choices:*

(see index for correct answer)

- a. Supply chain risk management
- b. Criticality index
- c. Postcautionary principle
- d. Murphy's Law

Guidance: level 1

:: Alchemical processes ::

In chemistry, a _____ is a special type of homogeneous mixture composed of two or more substances. In such a mixture, a solute is a substance dissolved in another substance, known as a solvent. The mixing process of a _____ happens at a scale where the effects of chemical polarity are involved, resulting in interactions that are specific to solvation. The _____ assumes the phase of the solvent when the solvent is the larger fraction of the mixture, as is commonly the case. The concentration of a solute in a _____ is the mass of that solute expressed as a percentage of the mass of the whole _____. The term aqueous _____ is when one of the solvents is water.

Exam Probability: **High**

19. *Answer choices:*

(see index for correct answer)

- a. Putrefying bacteria
- b. Unity of opposites

- c. Digestion
- d. Fixation

Guidance: level 1

:: Business process ::

_____ is the value to an enterprise which is derived from the techniques, procedures, and programs that implement and enhance the delivery of goods and services. _____ is one of the three components of structural capital, itself a component of intellectual capital. _____ can be seen as the value of processes to any entity, whether for profit or not-for profit, but is most commonly used in reference to for-profit entities.

Exam Probability: **Low**

20. *Answer choices:*

(see index for correct answer)

- a. Business communication
- b. Process capital
- c. IBM Blueworks Live
- d. Signavio

Guidance: level 1

:: Natural materials ::

_____ is a finely-grained natural rock or soil material that combines one or more _____ minerals with possible traces of quartz, metal oxides and organic matter. Geologic _____ deposits are mostly composed of phyllosilicate minerals containing variable amounts of water trapped in the mineral structure. _____s are plastic due to particle size and geometry as well as water content, and become hard, brittle and non–plastic upon drying or firing. Depending on the soil's content in which it is found, _____ can appear in various colours from white to dull grey or brown to deep orange-red.

Exam Probability: **Low**

21. *Answer choices:*

(see index for correct answer)

- a. Sprout Watches
- b. Sorbent
- c. Crushed stone
- d. Slate

Guidance: level 1

:: Occupational safety and health ::

_____ is a chemical element with symbol Pb and atomic number 82. It is a heavy metal that is denser than most common materials. _____ is soft and malleable, and also has a relatively low melting point. When freshly cut, _____ is silvery with a hint of blue; it tarnishes to a dull gray color when exposed to air. _____ has the highest atomic number of any stable element and three of its isotopes are endpoints of major nuclear decay chains of heavier elements.

Exam Probability: **Medium**

22. *Answer choices:*

(see index for correct answer)

- a. PIMEX
- b. Bernardino Ramazzini
- c. Occupational Safety and Health Professional Day
- d. Jury stress

Guidance: level 1

:: Unit operations ::

_____ is a discipline of thermal engineering that concerns the generation, use, conversion, and exchange of thermal energy between physical systems. _____ is classified into various mechanisms, such as thermal conduction, thermal convection, thermal radiation, and transfer of energy by phase changes. Engineers also consider the transfer of mass of differing chemical species, either cold or hot, to achieve _____ . While these mechanisms have distinct characteristics, they often occur simultaneously in the same system.

Exam Probability: **Low**

23. *Answer choices:*

(see index for correct answer)

- a. Unit operation
- b. Homogenization
- c. Distillation
- d. Heat transfer

Guidance: level 1

:: Evaluation ::

_____ is a way of preventing mistakes and defects in manufactured products and avoiding problems when delivering products or services to customers; which ISO 9000 defines as "part of quality management focused on providing confidence that quality requirements will be fulfilled". This defect prevention in _____ differs subtly from defect detection and rejection in quality control and has been referred to as a shift left since it focuses on quality earlier in the process.

Exam Probability: **Medium**

24. *Answer choices:*

(see index for correct answer)

- a. Teaching and Learning International Survey
- b. Quality assurance
- c. Ecological indicator
- d. Scale of one to ten

Guidance: level 1

:: Industrial engineering ::

_____, in its contemporary conceptualisation, is a comparison of perceived expectations of a service with perceived performance, giving rise to the equation SQ=P-E. This conceptualistion of _____ has its origins in the expectancy-disconfirmation paradigm.

Exam Probability: **Low**

25. *Answer choices:*

(see index for correct answer)

- a. Health systems engineering
- b. Ergonomic
- c. Service quality
- d. Society of Industrial Engineering

Guidance: level 1

:: Chemical reactions ::

A _____ is a process that leads to the chemical transformation of one set of chemical substances to another. Classically, _____ s encompass changes that only involve the positions of electrons in the forming and breaking of chemical bonds between atoms, with no change to the nuclei, and can often be described by a chemical equation. Nuclear chemistry is a sub-discipline of chemistry that involves the _____ s of unstable and radioactive elements where both electronic and nuclear changes can occur.

Exam Probability: **High**

26. *Answer choices:*

(see index for correct answer)

- a. Ceramide phosphoethanolamine synthase
- b. Lewis acid catalysis
- c. Combination reaction

- d. Chemical reaction

Guidance: level 1

:: Industrial processes ::

A _____ is a device used for high-temperature heating. The name derives from Latin word fornax, which means oven. The heat energy to fuel a _____ may be supplied directly by fuel combustion, by electricity such as the electric arc _____ , or through induction heating in induction _____ s.

Exam Probability: **Medium**

27. *Answer choices:*

(see index for correct answer)

- a. Sinter Plant
- b. Furnace
- c. Tinning
- d. Hoffmann kiln

Guidance: level 1

:: Chemical processes ::

_____ is the understanding and application of the fundamental principles and laws of nature that allow us to transform raw material and energy into products that are useful to society, at an industrial level. By taking advantage of the driving forces of nature such as pressure, temperature and concentration gradients, as well as the law of conservation of mass, process engineers can develop methods to synthesize and purify large quantities of desired chemical products. _____ focuses on the design, operation, control, optimization and intensification of chemical, physical, and biological processes. _____ encompasses a vast range of industries, such as agriculture, automotive, biotechnical, chemical, food, material development, mining, nuclear, petrochemical, pharmaceutical, and software development. The application of systematic computer-based methods to _____ is "process systems engineering".

Exam Probability: **High**

28. *Answer choices:*

(see index for correct answer)

- a. Ether cleavage
- b. Process engineering
- c. Recrystallization
- d. Efflorescence

Guidance: level 1

:: Product development ::

In business and engineering, _____ covers the complete process of bringing a new product to market. A central aspect of NPD is product design, along with various business considerations. _____ is described broadly as the transformation of a market opportunity into a product available for sale. The product can be tangible or intangible , though sometimes services and other processes are distinguished from "products." NPD requires an understanding of customer needs and wants, the competitive environment, and the nature of the market.Cost, time and quality are the main variables that drive customer needs. Aiming at these three variables, innovative companies develop continuous practices and strategies to better satisfy customer requirements and to increase their own market share by a regular development of new products. There are many uncertainties and challenges which companies must face throughout the process. The use of best practices and the elimination of barriers to communication are the main concerns for the management of the NPD .

Exam Probability: **Low**

29. *Answer choices:*

(see index for correct answer)

- a. EXtreme Manufacturing
- b. Product design specification
- c. New product development
- d. Front end innovation

Guidance: level 1

:: ::

A _____ or till is a mechanical or electronic device for registering and calculating transactions at a point of sale. It is usually attached to a drawer for storing cash and other valuables. A modern _____ is usually attached to a printer that can print out receipts for record-keeping purposes.

Exam Probability: **Low**

30. *Answer choices:*

(see index for correct answer)

- a. process perspective
- b. Cash register
- c. hierarchical
- d. similarity-attraction theory

Guidance: level 1

:: E-commerce ::

_____ is the activity of buying or selling of products on online services or over the Internet. Electronic commerce draws on technologies such as mobile commerce, electronic funds transfer, supply chain management, Internet marketing, online transaction processing, electronic data interchange , inventory management systems, and automated data collection systems.

Exam Probability: **High**

31. *Answer choices:*

(see index for correct answer)

- a. Urban Ladder
- b. Eurocheque
- c. GamersGate
- d. E-commerce

Guidance: level 1

:: Semiconductor companies ::

_____ Corporation is a Japanese multinational conglomerate corporation headquartered in Konan, Minato, Tokyo. Its diversified business includes consumer and professional electronics, gaming, entertainment and financial services. The company owns the largest music entertainment business in the world, the largest video game console business and one of the largest video game publishing businesses, and is one of the leading manufacturers of electronic products for the consumer and professional markets, and a leading player in the film and television entertainment industry. _____ was ranked 97th on the 2018 Fortune Global 500 list.

Exam Probability: **Low**

32. *Answer choices:*

(see index for correct answer)

- a. Inotera
- b. Freescale Semiconductor

- c. Arteris
- d. Zilog

Guidance: level 1

:: Asset ::

In financial accounting, an _____ is any resource owned by the business. Anything tangible or intangible that can be owned or controlled to produce value and that is held by a company to produce positive economic value is an _____ . Simply stated, _____ s represent value of ownership that can be converted into cash . The balance sheet of a firm records the monetary value of the _____ s owned by that firm. It covers money and other valuables belonging to an individual or to a business.

Exam Probability: **High**

33. *Answer choices:*

(see index for correct answer)

- a. Fixed asset
- b. Asset

Guidance: level 1

:: Management accounting ::

"_____s are the structural determinants of the cost of an activity, reflecting any linkages or interrelationships that affect it". Therefore we could assume that the _____s determine the cost behavior within the activities, reflecting the links that these have with other activities and relationships that affect them.

Exam Probability: **Medium**

34. *Answer choices:*

(see index for correct answer)

- a. Responsibility center
- b. Managerial risk accounting
- c. Cost driver
- d. Dual overhead rate

Guidance: level 1

:: Help desk ::

Data center management is the collection of tasks performed by those responsible for managing ongoing operation of a data center This includes Business service management and planning for the future.

Exam Probability: **Medium**

35. *Answer choices:*

(see index for correct answer)

- a. OTRS
- b. Computer-aided maintenance
- c. EHelp Corporation
- d. SysAid Technologies

Guidance: level 1

:: Lean manufacturing ::

> _____ is a Japanese term that means "mistake-proofing" or "inadvertent error prevention". A _____ is any mechanism in any process that helps an equipment operator avoid mistakes. Its purpose is to eliminate product defects by preventing, correcting, or drawing attention to human errors as they occur. The concept was formalised, and the term adopted, by Shigeo Shingo as part of the Toyota Production System. It was originally described as baka-yoke, but as this means "fool-proofing" the name was changed to the milder _____ .

Exam Probability: **High**

36. *Answer choices:*
(see index for correct answer)

- a. Heijunka box
- b. Lean accounting
- c. Poka-yoke

- d. Fixed Repeating Schedule

Guidance: level 1

:: Project management ::

> Some scenarios associate "this kind of planning" with learning "life skills". _____ s are necessary, or at least useful, in situations where individuals need to know what time they must be at a specific location to receive a specific service, and where people need to accomplish a set of goals within a set time period.

Exam Probability: **High**

37. *Answer choices:*

(see index for correct answer)

- a. Schedule
- b. Transfer of Burden
- c. The International Association of Project and Program Management
- d. Flexible product development

Guidance: level 1

:: Marketing ::

_____ or stock control can be broadly defined as "the activity of checking a shop's stock." However, a more focused definition takes into account the more science-based, methodical practice of not only verifying a business' inventory but also focusing on the many related facets of inventory management "within an organisation to meet the demand placed upon that business economically." Other facets of _____ include supply chain management, production control, financial flexibility, and customer satisfaction. At the root of _____ , however, is the _____ problem, which involves determining when to order, how much to order, and the logistics of those decisions.

Exam Probability: **High**

38. *Answer choices:*

(see index for correct answer)

- a. Joint product pricing
- b. Inventory control
- c. Product marketing
- d. Inbound marketing automation

Guidance: level 1

:: Industrial equipment ::

_____s are heat exchangers typically used to provide heat to the bottom of industrial distillation columns. They boil the liquid from the bottom of a distillation column to generate vapors which are returned to the column to drive the distillation separation. The heat supplied to the column by the _____ at the bottom of the column is removed by the condenser at the top of the column.

Exam Probability: **Low**

39. *Answer choices:*

(see index for correct answer)

- a. Cellulose insulating material plant
- b. Gravimetric blender
- c. Reboiler
- d. Single-ended recuperative burner

Guidance: level 1

:: Production and manufacturing ::

_____ is the process of determining the production capacity needed by an organization to meet changing demands for its products. In the context of _____, design capacity is the maximum amount of work that an organization is capable of completing in a given period. Effective capacity is the maximum amount of work that an organization is capable of completing in a given period due to constraints such as quality problems, delays, material handling, etc.

Exam Probability: **Medium**

40. *Answer choices:*

(see index for correct answer)

- a. Capacity planning
- b. Division of labour
- c. product lifecycle
- d. Verband der Automobilindustrie

Guidance: level 1

:: Business process ::

> A committee is a body of one or more persons that is subordinate to a deliberative assembly. Usually, the assembly sends matters into a committee as a way to explore them more fully than would be possible if the assembly itself were considering them. Committees may have different functions and their type of work differ depending on the type of the organization and its needs.

Exam Probability: **Low**

41. *Answer choices:*

(see index for correct answer)

- a. Value process management
- b. IBM Blueworks Live

- c. Business process
- d. Business process management

Guidance: level 1

:: Quality control tools ::

A _____ is a type of diagram that represents an algorithm, workflow or process. _____ can also be defined as a diagramatic representation of an algorithm.

Exam Probability: **Medium**

42. *Answer choices:*

(see index for correct answer)

- a. Regression control chart
- b. Robust parameter design
- c. Robustness validation
- d. CUSUM

Guidance: level 1

:: Management ::

In economics and marketing, _____ is the process of distinguishing a product or service from others, to make it more attractive to a particular target market. This involves differentiating it from competitors' products as well as a firm's own products. The concept was proposed by Edward Chamberlin in his 1933 The Theory of Monopolistic Competition.

Exam Probability: **Low**

43. *Answer choices:*

(see index for correct answer)

- a. Responsible autonomy
- b. Product differentiation
- c. Project management simulation
- d. Intopia

Guidance: level 1

:: ::

A _____ consists of an orchestrated and repeatable pattern of business activity enabled by the systematic organization of resources into processes that transform materials, provide services, or process information. It can be depicted as a sequence of operations, the work of a person or group, the work of an organization of staff, or one or more simple or complex mechanisms.

Exam Probability: **High**

44. Answer choices:

(see index for correct answer)

- a. empathy
- b. deep-level diversity
- c. open system
- d. levels of analysis

Guidance: level 1

:: Procurement ::

Purchasing is the formal process of buying goods and services. The _____ can vary from one organization to another, but there are some common key elements.

Exam Probability: **High**

45. Answer choices:

(see index for correct answer)

- a. Inverted Sourcing
- b. Government contract proposal
- c. Purchasing process
- d. Purchasing Managers Index

Guidance: level 1

:: Project management ::

_____ is the right to exercise power, which can be formalized by a state and exercised by way of judges, appointed executives of government, or the ecclesiastical or priestly appointed representatives of a God or other deities.

Exam Probability: **Medium**

46. *Answer choices:*

(see index for correct answer)

- a. Operational bill
- b. Project management office
- c. Resource allocation
- d. Authority

Guidance: level 1

:: Project management ::

A _____ is the approximation of the cost of a program, project, or operation. The _____ is the product of the cost estimating process. The _____ has a single total value and may have identifiable component values. A problem with a cost overrun can be avoided with a credible, reliable, and accurate _____. A cost estimator is the professional who prepares _____s. There are different types of cost estimators, whose title may be preceded by a modifier, such as building estimator, or electrical estimator, or chief estimator. Other professionals such as quantity surveyors and cost engineers may also prepare _____s or contribute to _____s. In the US, according to the Bureau of Labor Statistics, there were 185,400 cost estimators in 2010. There are around 75,000 professional quantity surveyors working in the UK.

Exam Probability: **Low**

47. *Answer choices:*

(see index for correct answer)

- a. Cost estimate
- b. Time limit
- c. Project
- d. American Society of Professional Estimators

Guidance: level 1

:: Debt ::

_____ is the trust which allows one party to provide money or resources to another party wherein the second party does not reimburse the first party immediately, but promises either to repay or return those resources at a later date. In other words, _____ is a method of making reciprocity formal, legally enforceable, and extensible to a large group of unrelated people.

Exam Probability: **Low**

48. *Answer choices:*

(see index for correct answer)

- a. Legal liability
- b. Extendible bond
- c. Teacher Loan Forgiveness
- d. Vulture fund

Guidance: level 1

:: Promotion and marketing communications ::

The _____ of American Manufacturers, now ThomasNet, is an online platform for supplier discovery and product sourcing in the US and Canada. It was once known as the "big green books" and "Thomas Registry", and was a multi-volume directory of industrial product information covering 650,000 distributors, manufacturers and service companies within 67,000-plus industrial categories that is now published on ThomasNet.

Exam Probability: **Medium**

49. *Answer choices:*

(see index for correct answer)

- a. Cross-promotion
- b. Dumb Ways to Die
- c. Thomas Register
- d. Trade promotion management

Guidance: level 1

:: Process management ::

_____ is a statistics package developed at the Pennsylvania State University by researchers Barbara F. Ryan, Thomas A. Ryan, Jr., and Brian L. Joiner in 1972. It began as a light version of OMNITAB 80, a statistical analysis program by NIST. Statistical analysis software such as _____ automates calculations and the creation of graphs, allowing the user to focus more on the analysis of data and the interpretation of results. It is compatible with other _____ , Inc. software.

Exam Probability: **Low**

50. *Answer choices:*

(see index for correct answer)

- a. Throughput

- b. President%27s Quality Award
- c. Six Sigma for ROI
- d. Minitab

Guidance: level 1

:: Lean manufacturing ::

> _____ is the Sino-Japanese word for "improvement". In business, _____ refers to activities that continuously improve all functions and involve all employees from the CEO to the assembly line workers. It also applies to processes, such as purchasing and logistics, that cross organizational boundaries into the supply chain. It has been applied in healthcare, psychotherapy, life-coaching, government, and banking.

Exam Probability: **Medium**

51. *Answer choices:*

(see index for correct answer)

- a. Manufacturing supermarket
- b. Kaizen
- c. Value stream mapping
- d. Agent-assisted automation

Guidance: level 1

:: Natural resources ::

_____s are resources that exist without actions of humankind. This includes all valued characteristics such as magnetic, gravitational, electrical properties and forces etc. On Earth it includes sunlight, atmosphere, water, land along with all vegetation, crops and animal life that naturally subsists upon or within the heretofore identified characteristics and substances.

Exam Probability: **Medium**

52. *Answer choices:*

(see index for correct answer)

- a. Land cover
- b. Consolidated Natural Resources Act of 2008
- c. Natural Resources Acts
- d. Natural resource

Guidance: level 1

:: Distribution, retailing, and wholesaling ::

The _____ is a distribution channel phenomenon in which forecasts yield supply chain inefficiencies. It refers to increasing swings in inventory in response to shifts in customer demand as one moves further up the supply chain. The concept first appeared in Jay Forrester's Industrial Dynamics and thus it is also known as the Forrester effect. The _____ was named for the way the amplitude of a whip increases down its length. The further from the originating signal, the greater the distortion of the wave pattern. In a similar manner, forecast accuracy decreases as one moves upstream along the supply chain. For example, many consumer goods have fairly consistent consumption at retail but this signal becomes more chaotic and unpredictable as the focus moves away from consumer purchasing behavior.

Exam Probability: **High**

53. *Answer choices:*

(see index for correct answer)

- a. Pacific Comics
- b. 350 West Mart Center
- c. Teleflorist
- d. Cash and carry

Guidance: level 1

:: Production and manufacturing ::

_____ is a systematic method to improve the "value" of goods or products and services by using an examination of function. Value, as defined, is the ratio of function to cost. Value can therefore be manipulated by either improving the function or reducing the cost. It is a primary tenet of _____ that basic functions be preserved and not be reduced as a consequence of pursuing value improvements.

Exam Probability: **Medium**

54. *Answer choices:*

(see index for correct answer)

- a. IBM RFID Information Center
- b. Assembly line
- c. Highly accelerated life test
- d. Value engineering

Guidance: level 1

:: ::

In sales, commerce and economics, a _____ is the recipient of a good, service, product or an idea - obtained from a seller, vendor, or supplier via a financial transaction or exchange for money or some other valuable consideration.

Exam Probability: **Low**

55. Answer choices:

(see index for correct answer)

- a. functional perspective
- b. Customer
- c. empathy
- d. information systems assessment

Guidance: level 1

:: Procurement ::

> A _____ is a standard business process whose purpose is to invite suppliers into a bidding process to bid on specific products or services. RfQ generally means the same thing as Call for bids and Invitation for bid.

Exam Probability: **High**

56. Answer choices:

(see index for correct answer)

- a. Request for quotation
- b. Basware
- c. Commodity management
- d. Request price quotation

Guidance: level 1

:: Management ::

Business _____ is a discipline in operations management in which people use various methods to discover, model, analyze, measure, improve, optimize, and automate business processes. BPM focuses on improving corporate performance by managing business processes. Any combination of methods used to manage a company's business processes is BPM. Processes can be structured and repeatable or unstructured and variable. Though not required, enabling technologies are often used with BPM.

Exam Probability: **Low**

57. *Answer choices:*
(see index for correct answer)

- a. SimulTrain
- b. Process management
- c. Financial planning
- d. Vorstand

Guidance: level 1

:: Costs ::

In economics, _____ is the total economic cost of production and is made up of variable cost, which varies according to the quantity of a good produced and includes inputs such as labour and raw materials, plus fixed cost, which is independent of the quantity of a good produced and includes inputs that cannot be varied in the short term: fixed costs such as buildings and machinery, including sunk costs if any. Since cost is measured per unit of time, it is a flow variable.

Exam Probability: **Medium**

58. *Answer choices:*

(see index for correct answer)

- a. Search cost
- b. Total cost
- c. Manufacturing cost
- d. Customer Cost

Guidance: level 1

:: Commercial item transport and distribution ::

_____ in logistics and supply chain management is an organization's use of third-party businesses to outsource elements of its distribution, warehousing, and fulfillment services.

Exam Probability: **Low**

59. *Answer choices:*
(see index for correct answer)

- a. Third-party logistics
- b. Point-to-point transit
- c. Inland navigation
- d. SAP EWM

Guidance: level 1

Commerce

Commerce relates to "the exchange of goods and services, especially on a large scale." It includes legal, economic, political, social, cultural and technological systems that operate in any country or internationally.

:: Information retrieval ::

_____ is a technique used by recommender systems. _____ has two senses, a narrow one and a more general one.

Exam Probability: **High**

1. *Answer choices:*

(see index for correct answer)

- a. Enterprise search
- b. Automatic Content Extraction
- c. Collaborative filtering
- d. Noisy text analytics

Guidance: level 1

:: ::

> In Western musical notation, the staff or stave is a set of five horizontal lines and four spaces that each represent a different musical pitch or in the case of a percussion staff, different percussion instruments. Appropriate music symbols, depending on the intended effect, are placed on the staff according to their corresponding pitch or function. Musical notes are placed by pitch, percussion notes are placed by instrument, and rests and other symbols are placed by convention.

Exam Probability: **Medium**

2. *Answer choices:*

(see index for correct answer)

- a. interpersonal communication
- b. Staff position
- c. Sarbanes-Oxley act of 2002

- d. personal values

Guidance: level 1

:: Manufacturing ::

A _____ is an object used to extend the ability of an individual to modify features of the surrounding environment. Although many animals use simple _____ s, only human beings, whose use of stone _____ s dates back hundreds of millennia, use _____ s to make other _____ s. The set of _____ s needed to perform different tasks that are part of the same activity is called gear or equipment.

Exam Probability: **Medium**

3. *Answer choices:*
(see index for correct answer)

- a. Guitar manufacturing
- b. By-product
- c. International Manufacturing Technology Show
- d. Tool

Guidance: level 1

:: Information technology management ::

_____ s or pop-ups are forms of online advertising on the World Wide Web. A pop-up is a graphical user interface display area, usually a small window, that suddenly appears in the foreground of the visual interface. The pop-up window containing an advertisement is usually generated by JavaScript that uses cross-site scripting, sometimes with a secondary payload that uses Adobe Flash. They can also be generated by other vulnerabilities/security holes in browser security.

Exam Probability: **Low**

4. *Answer choices:*

(see index for correct answer)

- a. Wiki software
- b. Pop-up ad
- c. SFIAPlus
- d. Lean IT

Guidance: level 1

:: Game theory ::

To _____ is to make a deal between different parties where each party gives up part of their demand. In arguments, _____ is a concept of finding agreement through communication, through a mutual acceptance of terms—often involving variations from an original goal or desires.

Exam Probability: **Medium**

5. *Answer choices:*

(see index for correct answer)

- a. Strategic complements
- b. Null move
- c. Compromise
- d. Two-level game theory

Guidance: level 1

:: ::

_____ s and acquisitions are transactions in which the ownership of companies, other business organizations, or their operating units are transferred or consolidated with other entities. As an aspect of strategic management, M&A can allow enterprises to grow or downsize, and change the nature of their business or competitive position.

Exam Probability: **High**

6. *Answer choices:*

(see index for correct answer)

- a. co-culture
- b. personal values
- c. cultural
- d. imperative

Guidance: level 1

:: Decision theory ::

A _____ is a deliberate system of principles to guide decisions and achieve rational outcomes. A _____ is a statement of intent, and is implemented as a procedure or protocol. Policies are generally adopted by a governance body within an organization. Policies can assist in both subjective and objective decision making. Policies to assist in subjective decision making usually assist senior management with decisions that must be based on the relative merits of a number of factors, and as a result are often hard to test objectively, e.g. work-life balance _____ . In contrast policies to assist in objective decision making are usually operational in nature and can be objectively tested, e.g. password _____ .

Exam Probability: **Low**

7. *Answer choices:*

(see index for correct answer)

- a. Wild card
- b. Policy
- c. Option grid
- d. Decision engineering

Guidance: level 1

:: ::

Business Model Canvas is a strategic management and lean startup template for developing new or documenting existing business models. It is a visual chart with elements describing a firm's or product's value proposition, infrastructure, customers, and finances. It assists firms in aligning their activities by illustrating potential trade-offs.

Exam Probability: **Medium**

8. *Answer choices:*

(see index for correct answer)

- a. imperative
- b. personal values
- c. process perspective
- d. Cost structure

Guidance: level 1

:: Auctioneering ::

A _____ is one of several similar kinds of auctions. Most commonly, it means an auction in which the auctioneer begins with a high asking price, and lowers it until some participant accepts the price, or it reaches a predetermined reserve price. This has also been called a clock auction or open-outcry descending-price auction. This type of auction is good for auctioning goods quickly, since a sale never requires more than one bid. Strategically, it's similar to a first-price sealed-bid auction.

Exam Probability: **Medium**

9. *Answer choices:*

(see index for correct answer)

- a. Online trading community
- b. Dutch auction
- c. Online auction
- d. How Much Wood Would a Woodchuck Chuck

Guidance: level 1

:: Insolvency ::

_____ is the process in accounting by which a company is brought to an end in the United Kingdom, Republic of Ireland and United States. The assets and property of the company are redistributed. _____ is also sometimes referred to as winding-up or dissolution, although dissolution technically refers to the last stage of _____ . The process of _____ also arises when customs, an authority or agency in a country responsible for collecting and safeguarding customs duties, determines the final computation or ascertainment of the duties or drawback accruing on an entry.

Exam Probability: **Low**

10. *Answer choices:*

(see index for correct answer)

- a. Liquidation
- b. Liquidator
- c. Insolvency law of Russia
- d. Bankruptcy

Guidance: level 1

:: Goods ::

In most contexts, the concept of _____ denotes the conduct that should be preferred when posed with a choice between possible actions. _____ is generally considered to be the opposite of evil, and is of interest in the study of morality, ethics, religion and philosophy. The specific meaning and etymology of the term and its associated translations among ancient and contemporary languages show substantial variation in its inflection and meaning depending on circumstances of place, history, religious, or philosophical context.

Exam Probability: **Low**

11. *Answer choices:*

(see index for correct answer)

- a. Ordinary good
- b. Club good
- c. Good
- d. Yellow goods

Guidance: level 1

:: ::

_____ Corporation is an American multinational technology company with headquarters in Redmond, Washington. It develops, manufactures, licenses, supports and sells computer software, consumer electronics, personal computers, and related services. Its best known software products are the _____ Windows line of operating systems, the _____ Office suite, and the Internet Explorer and Edge Web browsers. Its flagship hardware products are the Xbox video game consoles and the _____ Surface lineup of touchscreen personal computers. As of 2016, it is the world's largest software maker by revenue, and one of the world's most valuable companies. The word " _____ " is a portmanteau of "microcomputer" and "software". _____ is ranked No. 30 in the 2018 Fortune 500 rankings of the largest United States corporations by total revenue.

Exam Probability: **Medium**

12. *Answer choices:*

(see index for correct answer)

- a. Microsoft
- b. surface-level diversity
- c. cultural
- d. process perspective

Guidance: level 1

:: Commercial item transport and distribution ::

A _____, forwarder, or forwarding agent, also known as a non-vessel operating common carrier, is a person or company that organizes shipments for individuals or corporations to get goods from the manufacturer or producer to a market, customer or final point of distribution. Forwarders contract with a carrier or often multiple carriers to move the goods. A forwarder does not move the goods but acts as an expert in the logistics network. These carriers can use a variety of shipping modes, including ships, airplanes, trucks, and railroads, and often do utilize multiple modes for a single shipment. For example, the _____ may arrange to have cargo moved from a plant to an airport by truck, flown to the destination city, then moved from the airport to a customer's building by another truck.

Exam Probability: **Low**

13. *Answer choices:*

(see index for correct answer)

- a. Cabotage
- b. Freight forwarder
- c. Interchange
- d. Cutaway van chassis

Guidance: level 1

:: Income ::

_____ is a ratio between the net profit and cost of investment resulting from an investment of some resources. A high ROI means the investment's gains favorably to its cost. As a performance measure, ROI is used to evaluate the efficiency of an investment or to compare the efficiencies of several different investments. In purely economic terms, it is one way of relating profits to capital invested. _____ is a performance measure used by businesses to identify the efficiency of an investment or number of different investments.

Exam Probability: **Medium**

14. *Answer choices:*

(see index for correct answer)

- a. Private income
- b. Gratuity
- c. Return of investment
- d. Implied level of government service

Guidance: level 1

:: Public relations ::

_____ is the public visibility or awareness for any product, service or company. It may also refer to the movement of information from its source to the general public, often but not always via the media. The subjects of _____ include people, goods and services, organizations, and works of art or entertainment.

Exam Probability: **Medium**

15. *Answer choices:*

(see index for correct answer)

- a. Aneta Avramova
- b. Media relations
- c. Ice block expedition of 1959
- d. Publicity

Guidance: level 1

:: Payment systems ::

_____ s are part of a payment system issued by financial institutions, such as a bank, to a customer that enables its owner to access the funds in the customer's designated bank accounts, or through a credit account and make payments by electronic funds transfer and access automated teller machines. Such cards are known by a variety of names including bank cards, ATM cards, MAC, client cards, key cards or cash cards.

Exam Probability: **High**

16. *Answer choices:*

(see index for correct answer)

- a. 1LINK
- b. Moneo

- c. Bill of credit
- d. Payment card

Guidance: level 1

:: Commerce ::

_____ relates to "the exchange of goods and services, especially on a large scale". It includes legal, economic, political, social, cultural and technological systems that operate in a country or in international trade.

Exam Probability: **Low**

17. *Answer choices:*
(see index for correct answer)

- a. Commerce
- b. Grain trade
- c. Dumping
- d. Economic entity

Guidance: level 1

:: Payment systems ::

A _____ is any system used to settle financial transactions through the transfer of monetary value. This includes the institutions, instruments, people, rules, procedures, standards, and technologies that make it exchange possible. A common type of _____ is called an operational network that links bank accounts and provides for monetary exchange using bank deposits. Some _____ s also include credit mechanisms, which are essentially a different aspect of payment.

Exam Probability: **High**

18. *Answer choices:*

(see index for correct answer)

- a. OneVu
- b. Moneo
- c. Letters of credit
- d. Electronic Benefit Transfer

Guidance: level 1

:: Industry ::

_____ describes various measures of the efficiency of production. Often , a _____ measure is expressed as the ratio of an aggregate output to a single input or an aggregate input used in a production process, i.e. output per unit of input. Most common example is the labour _____ measure, e.g., such as GDP per worker. There are many different definitions of _____ and the choice among them depends on the purpose of the _____ measurement and/or data availability. The key source of difference between various _____ measures is also usually related to how the outputs and the inputs are aggregated into scalars to obtain such a ratio-type measure of _____ .

Exam Probability: **Low**

19. *Answer choices:*

(see index for correct answer)

- a. Metal hose
- b. Energy policy
- c. Prefabrication
- d. Productivity

Guidance: level 1

:: Production economics ::

In economics and related disciplines, a _____ is a cost in making any economic trade when participating in a market.

Exam Probability: **Low**

20. *Answer choices:*

(see index for correct answer)

- a. Socially optimal firm size
- b. Capacity utilization
- c. Economies of scale
- d. Transaction cost

Guidance: level 1

:: Production economics ::

In economics, _____ is the change in the total cost that arises when the quantity produced is incremented by one unit; that is, it is the cost of producing one more unit of a good. Intuitively, _____ at each level of production includes the cost of any additional inputs required to produce the next unit. At each level of production and time period being considered, _____s include all costs that vary with the level of production, whereas other costs that do not vary with production are fixed and thus have no _____. For example, the _____ of producing an automobile will generally include the costs of labor and parts needed for the additional automobile but not the fixed costs of the factory that have already been incurred. In practice, marginal analysis is segregated into short and long-run cases, so that, over the long run, all costs become marginal. Where there are economies of scale, prices set at _____ will fail to cover total costs, thus requiring a subsidy. _____ pricing is not a matter of merely lowering the general level of prices with the aid of a subsidy; with or without subsidy it calls for a drastic restructuring of pricing practices, with opportunities for very substantial improvements in efficiency at critical points.

Exam Probability: **Low**

21. *Answer choices:*

(see index for correct answer)

- a. Marginal cost
- b. Split-off point
- c. Sharing
- d. Fragmentation

Guidance: level 1

:: ::

_____ is a qualitative measure used to relate the quality of motor vehicle traffic service. LOS is used to analyze roadways and intersections by categorizing traffic flow and assigning quality levels of traffic based on performance measure like vehicle speed, density, congestion, etc.

Exam Probability: **High**

22. *Answer choices:*

(see index for correct answer)

- a. open system
- b. cultural
- c. Character
- d. Level of service

Guidance: level 1

:: Management ::

The term _____ refers to measures designed to increase the degree of autonomy and self-determination in people and in communities in order to enable them to represent their interests in a responsible and self-determined way, acting on their own authority. It is the process of becoming stronger and more confident, especially in controlling one's life and claiming one's rights. _____ as action refers both to the process of self- _____ and to professional support of people, which enables them to overcome their sense of powerlessness and lack of influence, and to recognize and use their resources. To do work with power.

Exam Probability: **High**

23. *Answer choices:*

(see index for correct answer)

- a. One in, one out policy
- b. Empowerment
- c. Event management
- d. Project stakeholder

Guidance: level 1

:: ::

Competition arises whenever at least two parties strive for a goal which cannot be shared: where one's gain is the other's loss.

Exam Probability: **Low**

24. *Answer choices:*

(see index for correct answer)

- a. cultural
- b. Competitor
- c. functional perspective
- d. levels of analysis

Guidance: level 1

:: Monopoly (economics) ::

A _____ exists when a specific person or enterprise is the only supplier of a particular commodity. This contrasts with a monopsony which relates to a single entity's control of a market to purchase a good or service, and with oligopoly which consists of a few sellers dominating a market. Monopolies are thus characterized by a lack of economic competition to produce the good or service, a lack of viable substitute goods, and the possibility of a high _____ price well above the seller's marginal cost that leads to a high _____ profit. The verb monopolise or monopolize refers to the process by which a company gains the ability to raise prices or exclude competitors. In economics, a _____ is a single seller. In law, a _____ is a business entity that has significant market power, that is, the power to charge overly high prices. Although monopolies may be big businesses, size is not a characteristic of a _____ . A small business may still have the power to raise prices in a small industry .

Exam Probability: **Low**

25. *Answer choices:*

(see index for correct answer)

- a. Trust
- b. Monopoly
- c. Demonopolization
- d. Competition Commission

Guidance: level 1

:: ::

_____ refers to the overall process of attracting, shortlisting, selecting and appointing suitable candidates for jobs within an organization. _____ can also refer to processes involved in choosing individuals for unpaid roles. Managers, human resource generalists and _____ specialists may be tasked with carrying out _____ , but in some cases public-sector employment agencies, commercial _____ agencies, or specialist search consultancies are used to undertake parts of the process. Internet-based technologies which support all aspects of _____ have become widespread.

Exam Probability: **Medium**

26. *Answer choices:*

(see index for correct answer)

- a. process perspective
- b. Recruitment
- c. surface-level diversity

- d. open system

Guidance: level 1

:: Supply chain management ::

> _____ is the process of finding and agreeing to terms, and acquiring goods, services, or works from an external source, often via a tendering or competitive bidding process. _____ is used to ensure the buyer receives goods, services, or works at the best possible price when aspects such as quality, quantity, time, and location are compared. Corporations and public bodies often define processes intended to promote fair and open competition for their business while minimizing risks such as exposure to fraud and collusion.

Exam Probability: **High**

27. *Answer choices:*

(see index for correct answer)

- a. Supply chain engineering
- b. Netchain analysis
- c. Procurement
- d. ClearOrbit

Guidance: level 1

:: ::

_____ s is the linguistic and philosophical study of meaning, in language, programming languages, formal logics, and semiotics. It is concerned with the relationship between signifiers—like words, phrases, signs, and symbols—and what they stand for in reality, their denotation.

Exam Probability: **High**

28. *Answer choices:*

(see index for correct answer)

- a. surface-level diversity
- b. Semantic
- c. Sarbanes-Oxley act of 2002
- d. process perspective

Guidance: level 1

:: ::

_____ s are formal, sociotechnical, organizational systems designed to collect, process, store, and distribute information. In a sociotechnical perspective, _____ s are composed by four components: task, people, structure, and technology.

Exam Probability: **High**

29. *Answer choices:*

(see index for correct answer)

- a. hierarchical perspective
- b. information systems assessment
- c. interpersonal communication
- d. Information system

Guidance: level 1

:: ::

A _____ is a fund into which a sum of money is added during an employee's employment years, and from which payments are drawn to support the person's retirement from work in the form of periodic payments. A _____ may be a "defined benefit plan" where a fixed sum is paid regularly to a person, or a "defined contribution plan" under which a fixed sum is invested and then becomes available at retirement age. _____ s should not be confused with severance pay; the former is usually paid in regular installments for life after retirement, while the latter is typically paid as a fixed amount after involuntary termination of employment prior to retirement.

Exam Probability: **Medium**

30. *Answer choices:*

(see index for correct answer)

- a. Pension
- b. Character
- c. corporate values

- d. co-culture

Guidance: level 1

:: E-commerce ::

A _____ is a hosted service offering that acts as an intermediary between business partners sharing standards based or proprietary data via shared business processes. The offered service is referred to as " _____ services".

Exam Probability: **Medium**

31. *Answer choices:*
(see index for correct answer)

- a. IzzoNet
- b. Certificate-based encryption
- c. Virtual enterprise
- d. Tradex Technologies

Guidance: level 1

:: ::

_____ or accountancy is the measurement, processing, and communication of financial information about economic entities such as businesses and corporations. The modern field was established by the Italian mathematician Luca Pacioli in 1494. _____, which has been called the "language of business", measures the results of an organization's economic activities and conveys this information to a variety of users, including investors, creditors, management, and regulators. Practitioners of _____ are known as accountants. The terms "_____" and "financial reporting" are often used as synonyms.

Exam Probability: **Medium**

32. *Answer choices:*

(see index for correct answer)

- a. levels of analysis
- b. hierarchical perspective
- c. Sarbanes-Oxley act of 2002
- d. Accounting

Guidance: level 1

:: Management ::

_____ is a process by which entities review the quality of all factors involved in production. ISO 9000 defines _____ as "A part of quality management focused on fulfilling quality requirements".

Exam Probability: **Low**

33. *Answer choices:*

(see index for correct answer)

- a. Management buyout
- b. Community-based management
- c. Remedial action
- d. Quality control

Guidance: level 1

:: ::

In marketing jargon, product lining is offering several related products for sale individually. Unlike product bundling, where several products are combined into one group, which is then offered for sale as a units, product lining involves offering the products for sale separately. A line can comprise related products of various sizes, types, colors, qualities, or prices. Line depth refers to the number of subcategories a category has. Line consistency refers to how closely related the products that make up the line are. Line vulnerability refers to the percentage of sales or profits that are derived from only a few products in the line.

Exam Probability: **Low**

34. *Answer choices:*

(see index for correct answer)

- a. levels of analysis
- b. Character
- c. Product mix
- d. cultural

Guidance: level 1

:: ::

_____ is an abstract concept of management of complex systems according to a set of rules and trends. In systems theory, these types of rules exist in various fields of biology and society, but the term has slightly different meanings according to context. For example.

Exam Probability: **Low**

35. *Answer choices:*

(see index for correct answer)

- a. Regulation
- b. similarity-attraction theory
- c. functional perspective
- d. Sarbanes-Oxley act of 2002

Guidance: level 1

:: Information technology ::

_____ is the use of computers to store, retrieve, transmit, and manipulate data, or information, often in the context of a business or other enterprise. IT is considered to be a subset of information and communications technology. An _____ system is generally an information system, a communications system or, more specifically speaking, a computer system – including all hardware, software and peripheral equipment – operated by a limited group of users.

Exam Probability: **Low**

36. *Answer choices:*

(see index for correct answer)

- a. Mobile file management
- b. Open collaboration
- c. Information technology
- d. PC Supporters

Guidance: level 1

:: ::

_____ is the principled guide to action taken by the administrative executive branches of the state with regard to a class of issues, in a manner consistent with law and institutional customs.

Exam Probability: **Low**

37. *Answer choices:*

(see index for correct answer)

- a. imperative
- b. Public policy
- c. corporate values
- d. surface-level diversity

Guidance: level 1

:: Free market ::

In economics, a _____ is a system in which the prices for goods and services are determined by the open market and by consumers. In a _____, the laws and forces of supply and demand are free from any intervention by a government or other authority and from all forms of economic privilege, monopolies and artificial scarcities. Proponents of the concept of _____ contrast it with a regulated market in which a government intervenes in supply and demand through various methods, such as tariffs, used to restrict trade and to protect the local economy. In an idealized free-market economy, prices for goods and services are set freely by the forces of supply and demand and are allowed to reach their point of equilibrium without intervention by government policy.

Exam Probability: **Low**

38. *Answer choices:*

(see index for correct answer)

- a. Regulated market
- b. Piece rate

Guidance: level 1

:: E-commerce ::

Customer to customer markets provide an innovative way to allow customers to interact with each other. Traditional markets require business to customer relationships, in which a customer goes to the business in order to purchase a product or service. In customer to customer markets, the business facilitates an environment where customers can sell goods or services to each other. Other types of markets include business to business and business to customer.

Exam Probability: **High**

39. *Answer choices:*

(see index for correct answer)

- a. Affiliate marketing
- b. Standard Interchange Language
- c. APazari Desktop
- d. Consumer-to-consumer

Guidance: level 1

:: Production economics ::

In economics long run is a theoretical concept where all markets are in equilibrium, and all prices and quantities have fully adjusted and are in equilibrium. The long run contrasts with the _____ where there are some constraints and markets are not fully in equilibrium.

Exam Probability: **Medium**

40. *Answer choices:*

(see index for correct answer)

- a. Cost-of-production theory of value
- b. Partial productivity
- c. Short run
- d. Capacity utilization

Guidance: level 1

:: Credit cards ::

A _____ is a payment card issued to users to enable the cardholder to pay a merchant for goods and services based on the cardholder's promise to the card issuer to pay them for the amounts plus the other agreed charges. The card issuer creates a revolving account and grants a line of credit to the cardholder, from which the cardholder can borrow money for payment to a merchant or as a cash advance.

Exam Probability: **Medium**

41. *Answer choices:*

(see index for correct answer)

- a. MPP Global Solutions
- b. Credit card
- c. Payments as a service
- d. Wirecard

Guidance: level 1

:: Debt ::

_____, in finance and economics, is payment from a borrower or deposit-taking financial institution to a lender or depositor of an amount above repayment of the principal sum , at a particular rate. It is distinct from a fee which the borrower may pay the lender or some third party. It is also distinct from dividend which is paid by a company to its shareholders from its profit or reserve, but not at a particular rate decided beforehand, rather on a pro rata basis as a share in the reward gained by risk taking entrepreneurs when the revenue earned exceeds the total costs.

Exam Probability: **Low**

42. *Answer choices:*

(see index for correct answer)

- a. Interest
- b. Debt relief
- c. Extendible bond
- d. Christians Against Poverty

Guidance: level 1

:: ::

_____ is the practical authority granted to a legal body to administer justice within a defined field of responsibility, e.g., Michigan tax law. In federations like the United States, areas of _____ apply to local, state, and federal levels; e.g. the court has _____ to apply federal law.

Exam Probability: **Medium**

43. *Answer choices:*

(see index for correct answer)

- a. Jurisdiction
- b. surface-level diversity
- c. cultural
- d. similarity-attraction theory

Guidance: level 1

:: Marketing techniques ::

_____ is the activity of dividing a broad consumer or business market, normally consisting of existing and potential customers, into sub-groups of consumers based on some type of shared characteristics. In dividing or segmenting markets, researchers typically look for common characteristics such as shared needs, common interests, similar lifestyles or even similar demographic profiles. The overall aim of segmentation is to identify high yield segments – that is, those segments that are likely to be the most profitable or that have growth potential – so that these can be selected for special attention .

Exam Probability: **High**

44. *Answer choices:*

(see index for correct answer)

- a. Beauty whitewash
- b. Blackout dates
- c. Product life cycle
- d. Market segmentation

Guidance: level 1

:: Management ::

_____ is the process of thinking about the activities required to achieve a desired goal. It is the first and foremost activity to achieve desired results. It involves the creation and maintenance of a plan, such as psychological aspects that require conceptual skills. There are even a couple of tests to measure someone's capability of _____ well. As such, _____ is a fundamental property of intelligent behavior. An important further meaning, often just called " _____ " is the legal context of permitted building developments.

Exam Probability: **Low**

45. *Answer choices:*
(see index for correct answer)

- a. Crisis management
- b. Toxic leader
- c. Intopia
- d. Semiconductor consolidation

Guidance: level 1

:: ::

_____ is a means of protection from financial loss. It is a form of risk management, primarily used to hedge against the risk of a contingent or uncertain loss

Exam Probability: **Medium**

46. *Answer choices:*

(see index for correct answer)

- a. levels of analysis
- b. co-culture
- c. functional perspective
- d. open system

Guidance: level 1

:: ::

The _____ is a political and economic union of 28 member states that are located primarily in Europe. It has an area of 4,475,757 km2 and an estimated population of about 513 million. The EU has developed an internal single market through a standardised system of laws that apply in all member states in those matters, and only those matters, where members have agreed to act as one. EU policies aim to ensure the free movement of people, goods, services and capital within the internal market, enact legislation in justice and home affairs and maintain common policies on trade, agriculture, fisheries and regional development. For travel within the Schengen Area, passport controls have been abolished. A monetary union was established in 1999 and came into full force in 2002 and is composed of 19 EU member states which use the euro currency.

Exam Probability: **High**

47. *Answer choices:*

(see index for correct answer)

- a. surface-level diversity
- b. co-culture
- c. European Union
- d. personal values

Guidance: level 1

:: Market research ::

_____ is an organized effort to gather information about target markets or customers. It is a very important component of business strategy. The term is commonly interchanged with marketing research; however, expert practitioners may wish to draw a distinction, in that marketing research is concerned specifically about marketing processes, while _____ is concerned specifically with markets.

Exam Probability: **Medium**

48. *Answer choices:*

(see index for correct answer)

- a. CRISIL
- b. Multistage sampling
- c. Zyfin
- d. Market research

Guidance: level 1

:: ::

A _____ is an organization, usually a group of people or a company, authorized to act as a single entity and recognized as such in law. Early incorporated entities were established by charter. Most jurisdictions now allow the creation of new _____ s through registration.

Exam Probability: **High**

49. *Answer choices:*

(see index for correct answer)

- a. deep-level diversity
- b. Corporation
- c. levels of analysis
- d. corporate values

Guidance: level 1

:: ::

In international relations, _____ is – from the perspective of governments – a voluntary transfer of resources from one country to another.

Exam Probability: **Low**

50. *Answer choices:*

(see index for correct answer)

- a. Character
- b. imperative
- c. surface-level diversity
- d. functional perspective

Guidance: level 1

:: Business law ::

> A _____ is a group of people who jointly supervise the activities of an organization, which can be either a for-profit business, nonprofit organization, or a government agency. Such a board's powers, duties, and responsibilities are determined by government regulations and the organization's own constitution and bylaws. These authorities may specify the number of members of the board, how they are to be chosen, and how often they are to meet.

Exam Probability: **Low**

51. *Answer choices:*

(see index for correct answer)

- a. Doing business as
- b. Stick licensing
- c. Board of directors

- d. Wrongful trading

Guidance: level 1

:: International trade ::

An _____ is a good brought into a jurisdiction, especially across a national border, from an external source. The party bringing in the good is called an _____ er. An _____ in the receiving country is an export from the sending country. _____ ation and exportation are the defining financial transactions of international trade.

Exam Probability: **High**

52. *Answer choices:*
(see index for correct answer)

- a. New Zealand Meat Producers Board
- b. Import
- c. Flying geese paradigm
- d. Sea lane

Guidance: level 1

:: Securities (finance) ::

A _____ is a container that is traditionally constructed from stiff fibers, and can be made from a range of materials, including wood splints, runners, and cane. While most _____s are made from plant materials, other materials such as horsehair, baleen, or metal wire can be used. _____s are generally woven by hand. Some _____s are fitted with a lid, while others are left open on top.

Exam Probability: **Medium**

53. *Answer choices:*

(see index for correct answer)

- a. Insurance-Linked Securities
- b. UNIDROIT
- c. Non-DVP
- d. Basket

Guidance: level 1

:: Export and import control ::

" _____ " means the Government Service which is responsible for the administration of _____ law and the collection of duties and taxes and which also has the responsibility for the application of other laws and regulations relating to the importation, exportation, movement or storage of goods.

Exam Probability: **Medium**

54. Answer choices:

(see index for correct answer)

- a. CoCom
- b. Customs Modernization Act
- c. Export Management and Compliance Program
- d. Export of cryptography

Guidance: level 1

:: Stock market ::

The _____ of a corporation is all of the shares into which ownership of the corporation is divided. In American English, the shares are commonly known as " _____ s". A single share of the _____ represents fractional ownership of the corporation in proportion to the total number of shares. This typically entitles the _____ holder to that fraction of the company's earnings, proceeds from liquidation of assets , or voting power, often dividing these up in proportion to the amount of money each _____ holder has invested. Not all _____ is necessarily equal, as certain classes of _____ may be issued for example without voting rights, with enhanced voting rights, or with a certain priority to receive profits or liquidation proceeds before or after other classes of shareholders.

Exam Probability: **High**

55. Answer choices:

(see index for correct answer)

- a. Initial public offering
- b. Thinkorswim
- c. Avanza
- d. Volume-weighted average price

Guidance: level 1

:: Industry ::

> A _____ is a set of sequential operations established in a factory where materials are put through a refining process to produce an end-product that is suitable for onward consumption; or components are assembled to make a finished article.

Exam Probability: **High**

56. *Answer choices:*
(see index for correct answer)

- a. Unexpected events
- b. Production line
- c. Eco-industrial development
- d. Consciousness Industry

Guidance: level 1

:: Marketing ::

_____ is a concept introduced in a book of the same name in 1999 by marketing expert Seth Godin. _____ is a non-traditional marketing technique that advertises goods and services when advance consent is given.

Exam Probability: **Medium**

57. *Answer choices:*
(see index for correct answer)

- a. Permission marketing
- b. Business-to-employee
- c. Markup
- d. Mobile marketing research

Guidance: level 1

:: E-commerce ::

_____ is a method of e-commerce where shoppers' friends become involved in the shopping experience. _____ attempts to use technology to mimic the social interactions found in physical malls and stores. With the rise of mobile devices, _____ is now extending beyond the online world and into the offline world of shopping.

Exam Probability: **Medium**

58. *Answer choices:*

(see index for correct answer)

- a. ICOCA
- b. Social shopping
- c. Helpling
- d. UN/CEFACT

Guidance: level 1

:: Summary statistics ::

> _____ is the number of occurrences of a repeating event per unit of time. It is also referred to as temporal _____ , which emphasizes the contrast to spatial _____ and angular _____ . The period is the duration of time of one cycle in a repeating event, so the period is the reciprocal of the _____ . For example: if a newborn baby's heart beats at a _____ of 120 times a minute, its period—the time interval between beats—is half a second . _____ is an important parameter used in science and engineering to specify the rate of oscillatory and vibratory phenomena, such as mechanical vibrations, audio signals , radio waves, and light.

Exam Probability: **High**

59. *Answer choices:*

(see index for correct answer)

- a. Mean percentage error
- b. Frequency distribution

- c. L-moment
- d. weighted mean

Guidance: level 1

Business ethics

Business ethics (also known as corporate ethics) is a form of applied ethics or professional ethics, that examines ethical principles and moral or ethical problems that can arise in a business environment. It applies to all aspects of business conduct and is relevant to the conduct of individuals and entire organizations. These ethics originate from individuals, organizational statements or from the legal system. These norms, values, ethical, and unethical practices are what is used to guide business. They help those businesses maintain a better connection with their stakeholders.

The _____ , founded in 1912, is a private, nonprofit organization whose self-described mission is to focus on advancing marketplace trust, consisting of 106 independently incorporated local BBB organizations in the United States and Canada, coordinated under the Council of _____ s in Arlington, Virginia.

Exam Probability: **Low**

1. *Answer choices:*

(see index for correct answer)

- a. imperative
- b. Sarbanes-Oxley act of 2002
- c. Better Business Bureau
- d. similarity-attraction theory

Guidance: level 1

:: Anti-capitalism ::

_____ is a range of economic and social systems characterised by social ownership of the means of production and workers' self-management, as well as the political theories and movements associated with them. Social ownership can be public, collective or cooperative ownership, or citizen ownership of equity. There are many varieties of _____ and there is no single definition encapsulating all of them, with social ownership being the common element shared by its various forms.

Exam Probability: **Low**

2. *Answer choices:*

(see index for correct answer)

- a. Feminist Theory: From Margin to Center
- b. Stalinism
- c. Anti-Capitalist Convergence
- d. Anti-capitalist

Guidance: level 1

:: Organizational structure ::

> An _____ defines how activities such as task allocation, coordination, and supervision are directed toward the achievement of organizational aims.

Exam Probability: **Low**

3. *Answer choices:*

(see index for correct answer)

- a. Blessed Unrest
- b. Unorganisation
- c. Automated Bureaucracy
- d. Organizational structure

Guidance: level 1

:: ::

> In ecology, a _____ is the type of natural environment in which a particular species of organism lives. It is characterized by both physical and biological features. A species' _____ is those places where it can find food, shelter, protection and mates for reproduction.

Exam Probability: **High**

4. *Answer choices:*

(see index for correct answer)

- a. Character
- b. corporate values
- c. Habitat
- d. functional perspective

Guidance: level 1

:: Television terminology ::

A _____ organization, also known as a non-business entity, not-for-profit organization, or _____ institution, is dedicated to furthering a particular social cause or advocating for a shared point of view. In economic terms, it is an organization that uses its surplus of the revenues to further achieve its ultimate objective, rather than distributing its income to the organization's shareholders, leaders, or members. _____ s are tax exempt or charitable, meaning they do not pay income tax on the money that they receive for their organization. They can operate in religious, scientific, research, or educational settings.

Exam Probability: **Low**

5. *Answer choices:*

(see index for correct answer)

- a. Nonprofit
- b. distance learning
- c. multiplexing
- d. Satellite television

Guidance: level 1

:: Electronic waste ::

_____ or e-waste describes discarded electrical or electronic devices. Used electronics which are destined for refurbishment, reuse, resale, salvage, recycling through material recovery, or disposal are also considered e-waste. Informal processing of e-waste in developing countries can lead to adverse human health effects and environmental pollution.

Exam Probability: **Low**

6. *Answer choices:*

(see index for correct answer)

- a. Techreturns
- b. World Reuse, Repair and Recycling Association
- c. Electronic waste
- d. Global waste trade

Guidance: level 1

:: Ethical banking ::

A _____ or community development finance institution - abbreviated in both cases to CDFI - is a financial institution that provides credit and financial services to underserved markets and populations, primarily in the USA but also in the UK. A CDFI may be a community development bank, a community development credit union , a community development loan fund , a community development venture capital fund , a microenterprise development loan fund, or a community development corporation.

Exam Probability: **Low**

7. *Answer choices:*

(see index for correct answer)

- a. The Co-operative Bank

- b. Community development financial institution
- c. ShoreBank
- d. GLS Bank

Guidance: level 1

:: Statutory law ::

_____ or statute law is written law set down by a body of legislature or by a singular legislator. This is as opposed to oral or customary law; or regulatory law promulgated by the executive or common law of the judiciary. Statutes may originate with national, state legislatures or local municipalities.

Exam Probability: **Low**

8. *Answer choices:*

(see index for correct answer)

- a. ratification
- b. Statutory law
- c. statute law
- d. incorporation by reference

Guidance: level 1

:: Minimum wage ::

A _____ is the lowest remuneration that employers can legally pay their workers—the price floor below which workers may not sell their labor. Most countries had introduced _____ legislation by the end of the 20th century.

Exam Probability: **High**

9. *Answer choices:*

(see index for correct answer)

- a. Minimum wage in the United States
- b. Minimum wage
- c. Working poor
- d. Minimum wage in Taiwan

Guidance: level 1

:: Ethically disputed business practices ::

_____ is the trading of a public company's stock or other securities by individuals with access to nonpublic information about the company. In various countries, some kinds of trading based on insider information is illegal. This is because it is seen as unfair to other investors who do not have access to the information, as the investor with insider information could potentially make larger profits than a typical investor could make. The rules governing _____ are complex and vary significantly from country to country. The extent of enforcement also varies from one country to another. The definition of insider in one jurisdiction can be broad, and may cover not only insiders themselves but also any persons related to them, such as brokers, associates and even family members. A person who becomes aware of non-public information and trades on that basis may be guilty of a crime.

Exam Probability: **High**

10. *Answer choices:*

(see index for correct answer)

- a. Copyright troll
- b. Insider trading
- c. Market saturation
- d. Spamming

Guidance: level 1

:: ::

In regulatory jurisdictions that provide for it, _____ is a group of laws and organizations designed to ensure the rights of consumers as well as fair trade, competition and accurate information in the marketplace. The laws are designed to prevent the businesses that engage in fraud or specified unfair practices from gaining an advantage over competitors. They may also provides additional protection for those most vulnerable in society. _____ laws are a form of government regulation that aim to protect the rights of consumers. For example, a government may require businesses to disclose detailed information about products—particularly in areas where safety or public health is an issue, such as food.

Exam Probability: **Medium**

11. *Answer choices:*

(see index for correct answer)

- a. Sarbanes-Oxley act of 2002
- b. hierarchical
- c. empathy
- d. Consumer Protection

Guidance: level 1

:: Social enterprise ::

Corporate social responsibility is a type of international private business self-regulation. While once it was possible to describe CSR as an internal organisational policy or a corporate ethic strategy, that time has passed as various international laws have been developed and various organisations have used their authority to push it beyond individual or even industry-wide initiatives. While it has been considered a form of corporate self-regulation for some time, over the last decade or so it has moved considerably from voluntary decisions at the level of individual organisations, to mandatory schemes at regional, national and even transnational levels.

Exam Probability: **Medium**

12. *Answer choices:*

(see index for correct answer)

- a. Social venture
- b. Social enterprise

Guidance: level 1

:: Social responsibility ::

The United Nations Global Compact is a non-binding United Nations pact to encourage businesses worldwide to adopt sustainable and socially responsible policies, and to report on their implementation. The _____ is a principle-based framework for businesses, stating ten principles in the areas of human rights, labor, the environment and anti-corruption. Under the Global Compact, companies are brought together with UN agencies, labor groups and civil society. Cities can join the Global Compact through the Cities Programme.

Exam Probability: **High**

13. *Answer choices:*

(see index for correct answer)

- a. UN Global Compact
- b. Footprints network
- c. Socially responsible marketing
- d. Strategic corporate social responsibility

Guidance: level 1

:: United States federal labor legislation ::

The _____ of 1988 is a United States federal law that generally prevents employers from using polygraph tests, either for pre-employment screening or during the course of employment, with certain exemptions.

Exam Probability: **High**

14. *Answer choices:*

(see index for correct answer)

- a. Workforce Investment Act of 1998
- b. Employee Polygraph Protection Act
- c. Federal Emergency Relief Administration
- d. Hiring Incentives to Restore Employment Act

Guidance: level 1

:: ::

> _____ is an eight-block-long street running roughly northwest to southeast from Broadway to South Street, at the East River, in the Financial District of Lower Manhattan in New York City. Over time, the term has become a metonym for the financial markets of the United States as a whole, the American financial services industry , or New York–based financial interests.

Exam Probability: **High**

15. *Answer choices:*

(see index for correct answer)

- a. functional perspective
- b. Wall Street
- c. interpersonal communication
- d. personal values

Guidance: level 1

:: ::

A _____ is a form of business network, for example, a local organization of businesses whose goal is to further the interests of businesses. Business owners in towns and cities form these local societies to advocate on behalf of the business community. Local businesses are members, and they elect a board of directors or executive council to set policy for the chamber. The board or council then hires a President, CEO or Executive Director, plus staffing appropriate to size, to run the organization.

Exam Probability: **Medium**

16. *Answer choices:*

(see index for correct answer)

- a. Chamber of Commerce
- b. open system
- c. process perspective
- d. deep-level diversity

Guidance: level 1

:: Public relations terminology ::

_____ , also called "green sheen", is a form of spin in which green PR or green marketing is deceptively used to promote the perception that an organization's products, aims or policies are environmentally friendly. Evidence that an organization is _____ often comes from pointing out the spending differences: when significantly more money or time has been spent advertising being "green", than is actually spent on environmentally sound practices. _____ efforts can range from changing the name or label of a product to evoke the natural environment on a product that contains harmful chemicals to multimillion-dollar marketing campaigns portraying highly polluting energy companies as eco-friendly. Publicized accusations of _____ have contributed to the term's increasing use.

Exam Probability: **Medium**

17. *Answer choices:*
(see index for correct answer)

- a. Junk science
- b. Green PR
- c. Corporate pathos
- d. Greenwashing

Guidance: level 1

:: ::

The _____ is an 1848 political pamphlet by the German philosophers Karl Marx and Friedrich Engels. Commissioned by the Communist League and originally published in London just as the Revolutions of 1848 began to erupt, the Manifesto was later recognised as one of the world's most influential political documents. It presents an analytical approach to the class struggle and the conflicts of capitalism and the capitalist mode of production, rather than a prediction of communism's potential future forms.

Exam Probability: **Low**

18. *Answer choices:*

(see index for correct answer)

- a. imperative
- b. deep-level diversity
- c. process perspective
- d. Communist Manifesto

Guidance: level 1

:: Water law ::

The _____ is the primary federal law in the United States governing water pollution. Its objective is to restore and maintain the chemical, physical, and biological integrity of the nation's waters; recognizing the responsibilities of the states in addressing pollution and providing assistance to states to do so, including funding for publicly owned treatment works for the improvement of wastewater treatment; and maintaining the integrity of wetlands. It is one of the United States' first and most influential modern environmental laws. As with many other major U.S. federal environmental statutes, it is administered by the U.S. Environmental Protection Agency , in coordination with state governments. Its implementing regulations are codified at 40 C.F.R. Subchapters D, N, and O .

Exam Probability: **Low**

19. *Answer choices:*

(see index for correct answer)

- a. Clean Water Act
- b. Water law
- c. The Helsinki Rules on the Uses of the Waters of International Rivers
- d. Water quality law

Guidance: level 1

:: Management ::

_____ is the identification, evaluation, and prioritization of risks followed by coordinated and economical application of resources to minimize, monitor, and control the probability or impact of unfortunate events or to maximize the realization of opportunities.

Exam Probability: **Low**

20. *Answer choices:*

(see index for correct answer)

- a. Risk management
- b. Porter five forces analysis
- c. manager's right to manage
- d. Staff management

Guidance: level 1

:: Utilitarianism ::

_____ is a school of thought that argues that the pursuit of pleasure and intrinsic goods are the primary or most important goals of human life. A hedonist strives to maximize net pleasure. However upon finally gaining said pleasure, happiness may remain stationary.

Exam Probability: **Low**

21. *Answer choices:*

(see index for correct answer)

- a. Paradox of hedonism
- b. Consequentialism
- c. Hedonism
- d. Global Happiness Organization

Guidance: level 1

:: Natural gas ::

> _____ is a naturally occurring hydrocarbon gas mixture consisting primarily of methane, but commonly including varying amounts of other higher alkanes, and sometimes a small percentage of carbon dioxide, nitrogen, hydrogen sulfide, or helium. It is formed when layers of decomposing plant and animal matter are exposed to intense heat and pressure under the surface of the Earth over millions of years. The energy that the plants originally obtained from the sun is stored in the form of chemical bonds in the gas.

Exam Probability: **Medium**

22. *Answer choices:*

(see index for correct answer)

- a. Eurogas
- b. Liquefied natural gas
- c. Associated petroleum gas
- d. Natural gas

Guidance: level 1

:: ::

Revenge is a form of justice enacted in the absence or defiance of the norms of formal law and jurisprudence. Often, revenge is defined as being a harmful action against a person or group in response to a grievance, be it real or perceived. It is used to punish a wrong by going outside the law. Francis Bacon described revenge as a kind of "wild justice" that "does... offend the law [and] putteth the law out of office." Primitive justice or retributive justice is often differentiated from more formal and refined forms of justice such as distributive justice and divine judgment.

Exam Probability: **Low**

23. *Answer choices:*

(see index for correct answer)

- a. deep-level diversity
- b. hierarchical perspective
- c. Retaliation
- d. surface-level diversity

Guidance: level 1

:: Majority–minority relations ::

It was established as axiomatic in anthropological research by Franz Boas in the first few decades of the 20th century and later popularized by his students. Boas first articulated the idea in 1887: "civilization is not something absolute, but ... is relative, and ... our ideas and conceptions are true only so far as our civilization goes". However, Boas did not coin the term.

Exam Probability: **High**

24. *Answer choices:*

(see index for correct answer)

- a. Cultural relativism
- b. cultural dissonance
- c. positive discrimination

Guidance: level 1

:: Utilitarianism ::

_____ is a family of consequentialist ethical theories that promotes actions that maximize happiness and well-being for the majority of a population. Although different varieties of _____ admit different characterizations, the basic idea behind all of them is to in some sense maximize utility, which is often defined in terms of well-being or related concepts. For instance, Jeremy Bentham, the founder of _____, described utility as

Exam Probability: **Medium**

25. *Answer choices:*

(see index for correct answer)

- a. Utilitarianism
- b. Average and total utilitarianism
- c. The Theory of Good and Evil
- d. Act utilitarianism

Guidance: level 1

:: Parental leave ::

_____, or family leave, is an employee benefit available in almost all countries. The term " _____ " may include maternity, paternity, and adoption leave; or may be used distinctively from "maternity leave" and "paternity leave" to describe separate family leave available to either parent to care for small children. In some countries and jurisdictions, "family leave" also includes leave provided to care for ill family members. Often, the minimum benefits and eligibility requirements are stipulated by law.

Exam Probability: **Low**

26. *Answer choices:*

(see index for correct answer)

- a. Geduldig v. Aiello

- b. Maternity and Parental Leave, etc Regulations 1999
- c. Sara Hlupekile Longwe
- d. Equal Opportunities Commission v Secretary of State for Trade and Industry

Guidance: level 1

:: ::

_____ is the introduction of contaminants into the natural environment that cause adverse change. _____ can take the form of chemical substances or energy, such as noise, heat or light. Pollutants, the components of _____ , can be either foreign substances/energies or naturally occurring contaminants. _____ is often classed as point source or nonpoint source _____ .In 2015, _____ killed 9 million people in the world.

Exam Probability: **Medium**

27. *Answer choices:*

(see index for correct answer)

- a. functional perspective
- b. Pollution
- c. deep-level diversity
- d. hierarchical

Guidance: level 1

:: Law ::

_____ is a body of law which defines the role, powers, and structure of different entities within a state, namely, the executive, the parliament or legislature, and the judiciary; as well as the basic rights of citizens and, in federal countries such as the United States and Canada, the relationship between the central government and state, provincial, or territorial governments.

Exam Probability: **Low**

28. *Answer choices:*

(see index for correct answer)

- a. Legal case
- b. Constitutional law

Guidance: level 1

:: Price fixing convictions ::

_____ AG is a German multinational conglomerate company headquartered in Berlin and Munich and the largest industrial manufacturing company in Europe with branch offices abroad.

Exam Probability: **High**

29. *Answer choices:*

(see index for correct answer)

- a. SK Foods
- b. Grolsch Brewery
- c. Archer Daniels Midland
- d. Siemens

Guidance: level 1

:: Business ethics ::

A _____ is a person who exposes any kind of information or activity that is deemed illegal, unethical, or not correct within an organization that is either private or public. The information of alleged wrongdoing can be classified in many ways: violation of company policy/rules, law, regulation, or threat to public interest/national security, as well as fraud, and corruption. Those who become _____ s can choose to bring information or allegations to surface either internally or externally. Internally, a _____ can bring his/her accusations to the attention of other people within the accused organization such as an immediate supervisor. Externally, a _____ can bring allegations to light by contacting a third party outside of an accused organization such as the media, government, law enforcement, or those who are concerned. _____ s, however, take the risk of facing stiff reprisal and retaliation from those who are accused or alleged of wrongdoing.

Exam Probability: **Low**

30. *Answer choices:*

(see index for correct answer)

- a. Fair value
- b. Whistleblower
- c. Creative destruction
- d. Precarity

Guidance: level 1

:: Corporate governance ::

> _____ refers to the practice of members of a corporate board of directors serving on the boards of multiple corporations. A person that sits on multiple boards is known as a multiple director. Two firms have a direct interlock if a director or executive of one firm is also a director of the other, and an indirect interlock if a director of each sits on the board of a third firm. This practice, although widespread and lawful, raises questions about the quality and independence of board decisions.

Exam Probability: **High**

31. *Answer choices:*

(see index for correct answer)

- a. Chief privacy officer
- b. Interlocking directorate
- c. Financial mismanagement
- d. Chief operating officer

Guidance: level 1

:: Fraud ::

In law, _____ is intentional deception to secure unfair or unlawful gain, or to deprive a victim of a legal right. _____ can violate civil law, a criminal law, or it may cause no loss of money, property or legal right but still be an element of another civil or criminal wrong. The purpose of _____ may be monetary gain or other benefits, for example by obtaining a passport, travel document, or driver's license, or mortgage _____, where the perpetrator may attempt to qualify for a mortgage by way of false statements.

Exam Probability: **High**

32. *Answer choices:*

(see index for correct answer)

- a. Fraud
- b. Statute of frauds
- c. Telemarketing fraud
- d. Shell corporation

Guidance: level 1

:: Environmental economics ::

_____ is the process of people maintaining change in a balanced environment, in which the exploitation of resources, the direction of investments, the orientation of technological development and institutional change are all in harmony and enhance both current and future potential to meet human needs and aspirations. For many in the field, _____ is defined through the following interconnected domains or pillars: environment, economic and social, which according to Fritjof Capra is based on the principles of Systems Thinking. Sub-domains of sustainable development have been considered also: cultural, technological and political. While sustainable development may be the organizing principle for _____ for some, for others, the two terms are paradoxical. Sustainable development is the development that meets the needs of the present without compromising the ability of future generations to meet their own needs. Brundtland Report for the World Commission on Environment and Development introduced the term of sustainable development.

Exam Probability: **Low**

33. *Answer choices:*

(see index for correct answer)

- a. Harrington paradox
- b. European Association of Environmental and Resource Economists
- c. Sustainability
- d. Emission intensity

Guidance: level 1

:: Advertising techniques ::

The _____ is a story from the Trojan War about the subterfuge that the Greeks used to enter the independent city of Troy and win the war. In the canonical version, after a fruitless 10-year siege, the Greeks constructed a huge wooden horse, and hid a select force of men inside including Odysseus. The Greeks pretended to sail away, and the Trojans pulled the horse into their city as a victory trophy. That night the Greek force crept out of the horse and opened the gates for the rest of the Greek army, which had sailed back under cover of night. The Greeks entered and destroyed the city of Troy, ending the war.

Exam Probability: **Medium**

34. *Answer choices:*

(see index for correct answer)

- a. Transfer
- b. Below the line
- c. Trojan horse
- d. Testimonial

Guidance: level 1

:: Business ethics ::

_____ is a type of harassment technique that relates to a sexual nature and the unwelcome or inappropriate promise of rewards in exchange for sexual favors. _____ includes a range of actions from mild transgressions to sexual abuse or assault. Harassment can occur in many different social settings such as the workplace, the home, school, churches, etc. Harassers or victims may be of any gender.

Exam Probability: **High**

35. *Answer choices:*

(see index for correct answer)

- a. Conscious business
- b. Terror-free investing
- c. Sexual harassment
- d. Foreign official

Guidance: level 1

:: Minimum wage ::

The _____ are working people whose incomes fall below a given poverty line due to lack of work hours and/or low wages. Largely because they are earning such low wages, the _____ face numerous obstacles that make it difficult for many of them to find and keep a job, save up money, and maintain a sense of self-worth.

Exam Probability: **High**

36. *Answer choices:*

(see index for correct answer)

- a. Guaranteed minimum income
- b. Minimum wage in the United States
- c. Minimum Wage Fairness Act
- d. Minimum wage in Taiwan

Guidance: level 1

:: Anti-competitive behaviour ::

_____ is a secret cooperation or deceitful agreement in order to deceive others, although not necessarily illegal, as a conspiracy. A secret agreement between two or more parties to limit open competition by deceiving, misleading, or defrauding others of their legal rights, or to obtain an objective forbidden by law typically by defrauding or gaining an unfair market advantage is an example of _____ . It is an agreement among firms or individuals to divide a market, set prices, limit production or limit opportunities.It can involve "unions, wage fixing, kickbacks, or misrepresenting the independence of the relationship between the colluding parties". In legal terms, all acts effected by _____ are considered void.

Exam Probability: **Medium**

37. *Answer choices:*

(see index for correct answer)

- a. Third line forcing
- b. Collusion
- c. Byrd Amendment
- d. Bid rigging

Guidance: level 1

:: Timber industry ::

The _____ is an international non-profit, multi-stakeholder organization established in 1993 to promote responsible management of the world's forests. The FSC does this by setting standards on forest products, along with certifying and labeling them as eco-friendly.

Exam Probability: **Low**

38. *Answer choices:*

(see index for correct answer)

- a. Forest Stewardship Council
- b. Moisture meter
- c. West Coast lumber trade
- d. Timber pirate

Guidance: level 1

The Ethics & Compliance Initiative was formed in 2015 and consists of three nonprofit organizations: the Ethics Research Center, the Ethics & Compliance Association, and the Ethics & Compliance Certification Institute. Based in Arlington, Virginia, United States, ECI is devoted to the advancement of high ethical standards and practices in public and private institutions, and provides research about ethical standards, workplace integrity, and compliance practices and processes.

Exam Probability: **Medium**

39. *Answer choices:*

(see index for correct answer)

- a. Sarbanes-Oxley act of 2002
- b. surface-level diversity
- c. cultural
- d. Ethics Resource Center

Guidance: level 1

An _____ is the release of a liquid petroleum hydrocarbon into the environment, especially the marine ecosystem, due to human activity, and is a form of pollution. The term is usually given to marine _____ s, where oil is released into the ocean or coastal waters, but spills may also occur on land. _____ s may be due to releases of crude oil from tankers, offshore platforms, drilling rigs and wells, as well as spills of refined petroleum products and their by-products, heavier fuels used by large ships such as bunker fuel, or the spill of any oily refuse or waste oil.

Exam Probability: **Low**

40. *Answer choices:*

(see index for correct answer)

- a. deep-level diversity
- b. imperative
- c. open system
- d. Oil spill

Guidance: level 1

:: Globalization-related theories ::

_____ is an economic system based on the private ownership of the means of production and their operation for profit. Characteristics central to _____ include private property, capital accumulation, wage labor, voluntary exchange, a price system, and competitive markets. In a capitalist market economy, decision-making and investment are determined by every owner of wealth, property or production ability in financial and capital markets, whereas prices and the distribution of goods and services are mainly determined by competition in goods and services markets.

Exam Probability: **Low**

41. *Answer choices:*

(see index for correct answer)

- a. Capitalism
- b. post-industrial
- c. Economic Development

Guidance: level 1

:: Types of marketing ::

_____ is an advertisement strategy in which a company uses surprise and/or unconventional interactions in order to promote a product or service. It is a type of publicity. The term was popularized by Jay Conrad Levinson's 1984 book _____.

Exam Probability: **High**

42. Answer choices:

(see index for correct answer)

- a. Customer advocacy
- b. Guerrilla Marketing
- c. Limited edition candy
- d. Social pull marketing

Guidance: level 1

:: ::

The Catholic Church, also known as the Roman Catholic Church, is the largest Christian church, with approximately 1.3 billion baptised Catholics worldwide as of 2017. As the world's oldest continuously functioning international institution, it has played a prominent role in the history and development of Western civilisation. The church is headed by the Bishop of Rome, known as the pope. Its central administration, the Holy See, is in the Vatican City, an enclave within the city of Rome in Italy.

Exam Probability: **Low**

43. Answer choices:

(see index for correct answer)

- a. levels of analysis
- b. hierarchical perspective
- c. Catholicism

- d. imperative

Guidance: level 1

:: ::

The Federal National Mortgage Association, commonly known as _____, is a United States government-sponsored enterprise and, since 1968, a publicly traded company. Founded in 1938 during the Great Depression as part of the New Deal, the corporation's purpose is to expand the secondary mortgage market by securitizing mortgage loans in the form of mortgage-backed securities, allowing lenders to reinvest their assets into more lending and in effect increasing the number of lenders in the mortgage market by reducing the reliance on locally based savings and loan associations. Its brother organization is the Federal Home Loan Mortgage Corporation, better known as Freddie Mac. As of 2018, _____ is ranked #21 on the Fortune 500 rankings of the largest United States corporations by total revenue.

Exam Probability: **Low**

44. *Answer choices:*

(see index for correct answer)

- a. information systems assessment
- b. hierarchical
- c. surface-level diversity
- d. Fannie Mae

Guidance: level 1

:: Financial regulatory authorities of the United States ::

The _____ is an agency of the United States government responsible for consumer protection in the financial sector. CFPB's jurisdiction includes banks, credit unions, securities firms, payday lenders, mortgage-servicing operations, foreclosure relief services, debt collectors and other financial companies operating in the United States.

Exam Probability: **Medium**

45. *Answer choices:*
(see index for correct answer)

- a. Securities Investor Protection Corporation
- b. Federal Reserve Board
- c. National Futures Association
- d. Internal Revenue Service

Guidance: level 1

:: Auditing ::

_____, as defined by accounting and auditing, is a process for assuring of an organization's objectives in operational effectiveness and efficiency, reliable financial reporting, and compliance with laws, regulations and policies. A broad concept, _____ involves everything that controls risks to an organization.

Exam Probability: **Low**

46. *Answer choices:*

(see index for correct answer)

- a. Internal control
- b. Communication audit
- c. RSM International
- d. security audit

Guidance: level 1

:: Production and manufacturing ::

_____ is a set of techniques and tools for process improvement. Though as a shortened form it may be found written as 6S, it should not be confused with the methodology known as 6S.

Exam Probability: **Low**

47. *Answer choices:*

(see index for correct answer)

- a. Manufacturing process management
- b. Production engineering
- c. Six Sigma
- d. Digital prototyping

Guidance: level 1

:: Auditing ::

_____ refers to the independence of the internal auditor or of the external auditor from parties that may have a financial interest in the business being audited. Independence requires integrity and an objective approach to the audit process. The concept requires the auditor to carry out his or her work freely and in an objective manner.

Exam Probability: **Low**

48. *Answer choices:*

(see index for correct answer)

- a. International Association of Airline Internal Auditors
- b. Joint audit
- c. Auditor independence
- d. Auditing Standards Board

Guidance: level 1

:: Renewable energy ::

> A _____ is a fuel that is produced through contemporary biological processes, such as agriculture and anaerobic digestion, rather than a fuel produced by geological processes such as those involved in the formation of fossil fuels, such as coal and petroleum, from prehistoric biological matter. If the source biomatter can regrow quickly, the resulting fuel is said to be a form of renewable energy.

Exam Probability: **Low**

49. *Answer choices:*

(see index for correct answer)

- a. Solar thermal collector
- b. Tidal power
- c. Biofuel
- d. Waste heat recovery unit

Guidance: level 1

:: ::

Sustainability is the process of people maintaining change in a balanced environment, in which the exploitation of resources, the direction of investments, the orientation of technological development and institutional change are all in harmony and enhance both current and future potential to meet human needs and aspirations. For many in the field, sustainability is defined through the following interconnected domains or pillars: environment, economic and social, which according to Fritjof Capra is based on the principles of Systems Thinking. Sub-domains of _____ development have been considered also: cultural, technological and political. While _____ development may be the organizing principle for sustainability for some, for others, the two terms are paradoxical . _____ development is the development that meets the needs of the present without compromising the ability of future generations to meet their own needs. Brundtland Report for the World Commission on Environment and Development introduced the term of _____ development.

Exam Probability: **Low**

50. *Answer choices:*

(see index for correct answer)

- a. levels of analysis
- b. interpersonal communication
- c. surface-level diversity
- d. Sustainable

Guidance: level 1

:: United States law ::

The ABA _____, created by the American Bar Association, are a set of rules that prescribe baseline standards of legal ethics and professional responsibility for lawyers in the United States. They were promulgated by the ABA House of Delegates upon the recommendation of the Kutak Commission in 1983. The rules are merely recommendations, or models, and are not themselves binding. However, having a common set of Model Rules facilitates a common discourse on legal ethics, and simplifies professional responsibility training as well as the day-to-day application of such rules. As of 2015, 49 states and four territories have adopted the rules in whole or in part, of which the most recent to do so was the Commonwealth of the Northern Mariana Islands in March 2015. California is the only state that has not adopted the ABA Model Rules, while Puerto Rico is the only U.S. jurisdiction outside of confederation has not adopted them but instead has its own Código de Ética Profesional.

Exam Probability: **Medium**

51. *Answer choices:*

(see index for correct answer)

- a. Pro se
- b. Model Rules of Professional Conduct

Guidance: level 1

:: Fraud ::

In the United States, _____ is the claiming of Medicare health care reimbursement to which the claimant is not entitled. There are many different types of _____, all of which have the same goal: to collect money from the Medicare program illegitimately.

Exam Probability: **Medium**

52. *Answer choices:*

(see index for correct answer)

- a. Overbilling
- b. Accreditation mill
- c. Insurance fraud
- d. Employment fraud

Guidance: level 1

:: Coal ::

_____ is a combustible black or brownish-black sedimentary rock, formed as rock strata called _____ seams. _____ is mostly carbon with variable amounts of other elements; chiefly hydrogen, sulfur, oxygen, and nitrogen. _____ is formed if dead plant matter decays into peat and over millions of years the heat and pressure of deep burial converts the peat into _____. Vast deposits of _____ originates in former wetlands—called _____ forests—that covered much of the Earth's tropical land areas during the late Carboniferous and Permian times.

Exam Probability: **Low**

53. *Answer choices:*

(see index for correct answer)

- a. Gyttja
- b. Coal measures
- c. Sporinite
- d. Coal

Guidance: level 1

:: Carbon finance ::

The _____ is an international treaty which extends the 1992 United Nations Framework Convention on Climate Change that commits state parties to reduce greenhouse gas emissions, based on the scientific consensus that global warming is occurring and it is extremely likely that human-made CO2 emissions have predominantly caused it. The _____ was adopted in Kyoto, Japan on 11 December 1997 and entered into force on 16 February 2005. There are currently 192 parties to the Protocol.

Exam Probability: **Medium**

54. *Answer choices:*
(see index for correct answer)

- a. Renewable Energy Payments
- b. Inter-American Development Bank
- c. Carbon retirement
- d. Kyoto Protocol

Guidance: level 1

:: United States federal trade legislation ::

The _____ of 1914 established the Federal Trade Commission. The Act, signed into law by Woodrow Wilson in 1914, outlaws unfair methods of competition and outlaws unfair acts or practices that affect commerce.

Exam Probability: **Medium**

55. *Answer choices:*
(see index for correct answer)

- a. Federal Trade Commission Act
- b. Export Administration Act of 1979
- c. Tariff of 1883
- d. Tariff of Abominations

Guidance: level 1

:: Industrial ecology ::

_____ is a strategy for reducing the amount of waste created and released into the environment, particularly by industrial facilities, agriculture, or consumers. Many large corporations view P2 as a method of improving the efficiency and profitability of production processes by technology advancements. Legislative bodies have enacted P2 measures, such as the _____ Act of 1990 and the Clean Air Act Amendments of 1990 by the United States Congress.

Exam Probability: **Low**

56. *Answer choices:*

(see index for correct answer)

- a. Energetics
- b. Earth systems engineering and management
- c. Anthropogenic metabolism
- d. Avoided burden

Guidance: level 1

:: Anti-Revisionism ::

_____, officially the German Democratic Republic, was a country that existed from 1949 to 1990, when the eastern portion of Germany was part of the Eastern Bloc during the Cold War. It described itself as a socialist "workers` and peasants` state", and the territory was administered and occupied by Soviet forces at the end of World War II — the Soviet Occupation Zone of the Potsdam Agreement, bounded on the east by the Oder–Neisse line. The Soviet zone surrounded West Berlin but did not include it; as a result, West Berlin remained outside the jurisdiction of the GDR.

Exam Probability: **Medium**

57. *Answer choices:*
(see index for correct answer)

- a. East Germany
- b. Ho Chi Minh Thought
- c. Hoxhaism
- d. New Communist Movement

Guidance: level 1

:: ::

_____ is a private Dominican liberal arts college in Madison, Wisconsin. The college occupies a 55 acres campus overlooking the shores of Lake Wingra.

Exam Probability: **Low**

58. Answer choices:

(see index for correct answer)

- a. levels of analysis
- b. surface-level diversity
- c. Edgewood College
- d. Sarbanes-Oxley act of 2002

Guidance: level 1

:: ::

_____ Ltd. is the world's 2nd largest offshore drilling contractor and is based in Vernier, Switzerland. The company has offices in 20 countries, including Switzerland, Canada, United States, Norway, Scotland, India, Brazil, Singapore, Indonesia and Malaysia.

Exam Probability: **High**

59. Answer choices:

(see index for correct answer)

- a. functional perspective
- b. empathy
- c. levels of analysis
- d. surface-level diversity

Guidance: level 1

Accounting

Accounting or accountancy is the measurement, processing, and communication of financial information about economic entities such as businesses and corporations. The modern field was established by the Italian mathematician Luca Pacioli in 1494. Accounting, which has been called the "language of business", measures the results of an organization's economic activities and conveys this information to a variety of users, including investors, creditors, management, and regulators.

:: Tax avoidance ::

_____ s are any method of reducing taxable income resulting in a reduction of the payments to tax collecting entities, including state and federal governments. The methodology can vary depending on local and international tax laws.

Exam Probability: **High**

1. *Answer choices:*

(see index for correct answer)

- a. Tax exile
- b. Tax shelter
- c. Corporate inversion
- d. Lagarde list

Guidance: level 1

:: ::

A work order is usually a task or a job for a customer, that can be scheduled or assigned to someone. Such an order may be from a customer request or created internally within the organization. Work orders may also be created as follow ups to Inspections or Audits. A work order may be for products or services.

Exam Probability: **Medium**

2. *Answer choices:*

(see index for correct answer)

- a. Job order
- b. Sarbanes-Oxley act of 2002
- c. open system
- d. empathy

Guidance: level 1

:: Accounting terminology ::

> _____ is money owed by a business to its suppliers shown as a liability on a company's balance sheet. It is distinct from notes payable liabilities, which are debts created by formal legal instrument documents.

Exam Probability: **High**

3. *Answer choices:*

(see index for correct answer)

- a. Accrued liabilities
- b. Accounts payable
- c. Capital appreciation
- d. Absorption costing

Guidance: level 1

:: Basic financial concepts ::

_____ is a sustained increase in the general price level of goods and services in an economy over a period of time. When the general price level rises, each unit of currency buys fewer goods and services; consequently, _____ reflects a reduction in the purchasing power per unit of money a loss of real value in the medium of exchange and unit of account within the economy. The measure of _____ is the _____ rate, the annualized percentage change in a general price index, usually the consumer price index, over time. The opposite of _____ is deflation.

Exam Probability: **Medium**

4. *Answer choices:*

(see index for correct answer)

- a. Inflation
- b. Deflation
- c. Present value of costs
- d. Present value of benefits

Guidance: level 1

:: Business models ::

A _____ is a company that owns enough voting stock in another firm to control management and operation by influencing or electing its board of directors. The company is deemed a subsidiary of the _____ .

Exam Probability: **Medium**

5. *Answer choices:*

(see index for correct answer)

- a. Home business
- b. Low-cost carrier
- c. Parent company
- d. Subsidiary

Guidance: level 1

:: Management accounting ::

The _____ is a professional membership organization headquartered in Montvale, New Jersey, United States, operating in four global regions: The Americas, Asia/Pacific, Europe, and Middle East/India.

Exam Probability: **High**

6. *Answer choices:*

(see index for correct answer)

- a. Responsibility center
- b. Revenue center
- c. Dual overhead rate
- d. Cost accounting

Guidance: level 1

:: Financial ratios ::

_____ or interest coverage ratio is a measure of a company's ability to honor its debt payments. It may be calculated as either EBIT or EBITDA divided by the total interest payable.

Exam Probability: **Medium**

7. *Answer choices:*

(see index for correct answer)

- a. Sortino ratio
- b. Times interest earned
- c. Retention rate
- d. Sales density

Guidance: level 1

:: ::

An _____ is an asset that lacks physical substance. It is defined in opposition to physical assets such as machinery and buildings. An _____ is usually very hard to evaluate. Patents, copyrights, franchises, goodwill, trademarks, and trade names. The general interpretation also includes software and other intangible computer based assets are all examples of _____s. _____s generally—though not necessarily—suffer from typical market failures of non-rivalry and non-excludability.

Exam Probability: **Low**

8. *Answer choices:*

(see index for correct answer)

- a. surface-level diversity
- b. hierarchical perspective
- c. levels of analysis
- d. imperative

Guidance: level 1

:: Valuation (finance) ::

_____ refers to an assessment of the viability, stability, and profitability of a business, sub-business or project.

Exam Probability: **High**

9. *Answer choices:*

(see index for correct answer)

- a. The Appraisal Foundation
- b. Chepakovich valuation model
- c. International Valuation Standards Council
- d. Sum of perpetuities method

Guidance: level 1

:: ::

In the field of analysis of algorithms in computer science, the _____ is a method of amortized analysis based on accounting. The _____ often gives a more intuitive account of the amortized cost of an operation than either aggregate analysis or the potential method. Note, however, that this does not guarantee such analysis will be immediately obvious; often, choosing the correct parameters for the _____ requires as much knowledge of the problem and the complexity bounds one is attempting to prove as the other two methods.

Exam Probability: **High**

10. *Answer choices:*

(see index for correct answer)

- a. Accounting method
- b. similarity-attraction theory

- c. hierarchical perspective
- d. Character

Guidance: level 1

:: Banking ::

> A _____ is a financial institution that accepts deposits from the public and creates credit. Lending activities can be performed either directly or indirectly through capital markets. Due to their importance in the financial stability of a country, _____ s are highly regulated in most countries. Most nations have institutionalized a system known as fractional reserve _____ ing under which _____ s hold liquid assets equal to only a portion of their current liabilities. In addition to other regulations intended to ensure liquidity, _____ s are generally subject to minimum capital requirements based on an international set of capital standards, known as the Basel Accords.

Exam Probability: **High**

11. *Answer choices:*

(see index for correct answer)

- a. Variance risk premium
- b. Bank
- c. Prime rate
- d. Real-time posting

Guidance: level 1

:: Generally Accepted Accounting Principles ::

_____ is a measure of a fixed or current asset's worth when held in inventory, in the field of accounting. NRV is part of the Generally Accepted Accounting Principles and International Financial Reporting Standards that apply to valuing inventory, so as to not overstate or understate the value of inventory goods. _____ is generally equal to the selling price of the inventory goods less the selling costs. Therefore, it is expected sales price less selling costs. NRV prevents overstating or understating of an assets value. NRV is the price cap when using the Lower of Cost or Market Rule.

Exam Probability: **Low**

12. *Answer choices:*

(see index for correct answer)

- a. Vendor-specific objective evidence
- b. Net realizable value
- c. Provision
- d. Gross profit

Guidance: level 1

:: Marketing ::

_____ or stock is the goods and materials that a business holds for the ultimate goal of resale.

Exam Probability: **Low**

13. *Answer choices:*

(see index for correct answer)

- a. One Town One Product
- b. Brandjacking
- c. Inventory
- d. Osborne effect

Guidance: level 1

:: Budgets ::

An _____ is the annual budget of an activity stated in terms of Budget Classification Code, functional/subfunctional categories and cost accounts. It contains estimates of the total value of resources required for the performance of the operation including reimbursable work or services for others. It also includes estimates of workload in terms of total work units identified by cost accounts.

Exam Probability: **High**

14. *Answer choices:*

(see index for correct answer)

- a. Budgeted cost of work scheduled
- b. Participatory budgeting
- c. Operating budget
- d. Public budgeting

Guidance: level 1

:: Real estate ::

An _____ is to, interest in, or legal liability on real property that does not prohibit passing title to the property but that may diminish its value. _____ s can be classified in several ways. They may be financial or non-financial. Alternatively, they may be divided into those that affect title or those that affect the use or physical condition of the encumbered property. _____ s include security interests, liens, servitudes, leases, restrictions, encroachments, and air and subsurface rights. Also, those considered as potentially making the title defeasible are _____ s, for example, charging orders, building orders and structure alteration. _____ : charge upon or claim against land arising out of private grant or a contract.

Exam Probability: **Low**

15. *Answer choices:*

(see index for correct answer)

- a. Habendum clause
- b. Deeds registration

- c. Encumbrance
- d. Double closing

Guidance: level 1

:: Management accounting ::

" _____ s are the structural determinants of the cost of an activity, reflecting any linkages or interrelationships that affect it". Therefore we could assume that the _____ s determine the cost behavior within the activities, reflecting the links that these have with other activities and relationships that affect them.

Exam Probability: **High**

16. *Answer choices:*
(see index for correct answer)

- a. Chartered Institute of Management Accountants
- b. Cost driver
- c. Variable Costing
- d. Semi-variable cost

Guidance: level 1

:: ::

A _____ is an organization, usually a group of people or a company, authorized to act as a single entity and recognized as such in law. Early incorporated entities were established by charter. Most jurisdictions now allow the creation of new _____ s through registration.

Exam Probability: **High**

17. *Answer choices:*

(see index for correct answer)

- a. personal values
- b. Corporation
- c. empathy
- d. information systems assessment

Guidance: level 1

:: ::

An _____ is a contingent motivator. Traditional _____ s are extrinsic motivators which reward actions to yield a desired outcome. The effectiveness of traditional _____ s has changed as the needs of Western society have evolved. While the traditional _____ model is effective when there is a defined procedure and goal for a task, Western society started to require a higher volume of critical thinkers, so the traditional model became less effective. Institutions are now following a trend in implementing strategies that rely on intrinsic motivations rather than the extrinsic motivations that the traditional _____ s foster.

Exam Probability: **High**

18. *Answer choices:*

(see index for correct answer)

- a. open system
- b. co-culture
- c. Character
- d. Incentive

Guidance: level 1

:: Management accounting ::

_____ , or dollar contribution per unit, is the selling price per unit minus the variable cost per unit. "Contribution" represents the portion of sales revenue that is not consumed by variable costs and so contributes to the coverage of fixed costs. This concept is one of the key building blocks of break-even analysis.

Exam Probability: **Medium**

19. *Answer choices:*

(see index for correct answer)

- a. Management accounting
- b. Certified Management Accountants of Canada

- c. Contribution margin
- d. RCA open-source application

Guidance: level 1

:: Manufacturing ::

_____ costs are all manufacturing costs that are related to the cost object but cannot be traced to that cost object in an economically feasible way.

Exam Probability: **Low**

20. *Answer choices:*
(see index for correct answer)

- a. Engineering bill of materials
- b. Manufacturing overhead
- c. By-product
- d. Fixture

Guidance: level 1

:: Inventory ::

_____ is the amount of inventory a company has in stock at the end of its fiscal year. It is closely related with _____ cost, which is the amount of money spent to get these goods in stock. It should be calculated at the lower of cost or market.

Exam Probability: **Low**

21. *Answer choices:*

(see index for correct answer)

- a. Reorder point
- b. just-in-time manufacturing
- c. Ending inventory
- d. Item-level tagging

Guidance: level 1

:: Loans ::

In corporate finance, a _____ is a medium- to long-term debt instrument used by large companies to borrow money, at a fixed rate of interest. The legal term " _____ " originally referred to a document that either creates a debt or acknowledges it, but in some countries the term is now used interchangeably with bond, loan stock or note. A _____ is thus like a certificate of loan or a loan bond evidencing the fact that the company is liable to pay a specified amount with interest and although the money raised by the _____ s becomes a part of the company's capital structure, it does not become share capital. Senior _____ s get paid before subordinate _____ s, and there are varying rates of risk and payoff for these categories.

Exam Probability: **High**

22. *Answer choices:*

(see index for correct answer)

- a. Structural adjustment loan
- b. Loan
- c. Collateralized loan obligation
- d. Fixed interest

Guidance: level 1

:: Debt ::

A _____ is a monetary amount owed to a creditor that is unlikely to be paid and, or which the creditor is not willing to take action to collect for various reasons, often due to the debtor not having the money to pay, for example due to a company going into liquidation or insolvency. There are various technical definitions of what constitutes a _____ , depending on accounting conventions, regulatory treatment and the institution provisioning. In the USA, bank loans with more than ninety days' arrears become "problem loans". Accounting sources advise that the full amount of a _____ be written off to the profit and loss account or a provision for _____ s as soon as it is foreseen.

Exam Probability: **Low**

23. *Answer choices:*

(see index for correct answer)

- a. Teacher Loan Forgiveness
- b. Tax benefits of debt
- c. Charge-off
- d. Arrears

Guidance: level 1

:: Expense ::

An _____ is the right to reimbursement of money spent by employees for work-related purposes. Some common _____ s are: administrative expense, amortization expense, bad debt expense, cost of goods sold, depreciation expense, freight-out, income tax expense, insurance expense, interest expense, loss on disposal of plant assets, maintenance and repairs expense, rent expense, salaries and wages expense, selling expense, supplies expense and utilities expense.

Exam Probability: **Medium**

24. *Answer choices:*

(see index for correct answer)

- a. Accretion expense
- b. Corporate travel
- c. Tax expense
- d. Interest expense

Guidance: level 1

:: Management accounting ::

In _____ or managerial accounting, managers use the provisions of accounting information in order to better inform themselves before they decide matters within their organizations, which aids their management and performance of control functions.

Exam Probability: **Medium**

25. *Answer choices:*

(see index for correct answer)

- a. Operating profit margin
- b. Management accounting
- c. Responsibility center
- d. Institute of Certified Management Accountants

Guidance: level 1

:: Stock market ::

_____ is a form of stock which may have any combination of features not possessed by common stock including properties of both an equity and a debt instrument, and is generally considered a hybrid instrument. _____s are senior to common stock, but subordinate to bonds in terms of claim and may have priority over common stock in the payment of dividends and upon liquidation. Terms of the _____ are described in the issuing company's articles of association or articles of incorporation.

Exam Probability: **High**

26. *Answer choices:*
(see index for correct answer)

- a. China Concepts Stock
- b. Indian Depository Receipt
- c. Selling climax
- d. Bagholder

Guidance: level 1

:: Debt ::

A _____ is a party that has a claim on the services of a second party. It is a person or institution to whom money is owed. The first party, in general, has provided some property or service to the second party under the assumption that the second party will return an equivalent property and service. The second party is frequently called a debtor or borrower. The first party is called the _____, which is the lender of property, service, or money.

Exam Probability: **High**

27. *Answer choices:*

(see index for correct answer)

- a. Creditor
- b. Peak debt
- c. Consumer debt
- d. Sum certain

Guidance: level 1

:: ::

> _____ is a process whereby a person assumes the parenting of another, usually a child, from that person's biological or legal parent or parents. Legal _____ s permanently transfers all rights and responsibilities, along with filiation, from the biological parent or parents.

Exam Probability: **High**

28. *Answer choices:*

(see index for correct answer)

- a. open system
- b. cultural
- c. co-culture

- d. Adoption

Guidance: level 1

:: SEC filings ::

_____ is a prescribed regulation under the US Securities Act of 1933 that lays out reporting requirements for various SEC filings used by public companies. Companies are also often called issuers , filers or registrants .

Exam Probability: **High**

29. *Answer choices:*

(see index for correct answer)

- a. Schedule 13D
- b. Form 4
- c. Form 6K
- d. Form 3

Guidance: level 1

:: Management ::

The _____ is a strategy performance management tool – a semi-standard structured report, that can be used by managers to keep track of the execution of activities by the staff within their control and to monitor the consequences arising from these actions.

Exam Probability: **Medium**

30. *Answer choices:*

(see index for correct answer)

- a. Statistical process control
- b. Certified Energy Manager
- c. Completed Staff Work
- d. Balanced scorecard

Guidance: level 1

A _____ is a form of public administration which, in a majority of contexts, exists as the lowest tier of administration within a given state. The term is used to contrast with offices at state level, which are referred to as the central government, national government, or federal government and also to supranational government which deals with governing institutions between states. _____s generally act within powers delegated to them by legislation or directives of the higher level of government. In federal states, _____ generally comprises the third tier of government, whereas in unitary states, _____ usually occupies the second or third tier of government, often with greater powers than higher-level administrative divisions.

Exam Probability: **High**

31. *Answer choices:*

(see index for correct answer)

- a. Local government
- b. information systems assessment
- c. co-culture
- d. empathy

Guidance: level 1

:: ::

_____ is the field of accounting concerned with the summary, analysis and reporting of financial transactions related to a business. This involves the preparation of financial statements available for public use. Stockholders, suppliers, banks, employees, government agencies, business owners, and other stakeholders are examples of people interested in receiving such information for decision making purposes.

Exam Probability: **Low**

32. *Answer choices:*

(see index for correct answer)

- a. Financial accounting
- b. empathy
- c. deep-level diversity
- d. levels of analysis

Guidance: level 1

:: Types of accounting ::

Various _____ systems are used by various public sector entities. In the United States, for instance, there are two levels of government which follow different accounting standards set forth by independent, private sector boards. At the federal level, the Federal Accounting Standards Advisory Board sets forth the accounting standards to follow. Similarly, there is the _____ Standards Board for state and local level government.

Exam Probability: **High**

33. *Answer choices:*

(see index for correct answer)

- a. Personal environmental impact accounting
- b. Governmental accounting
- c. Product control

Guidance: level 1

:: Financial accounting ::

_____ refers to any one of several methods by which a company, for 'financial accounting' or tax purposes, depreciates a fixed asset in such a way that the amount of depreciation taken each year is higher during the earlier years of an asset's life. For financial accounting purposes, _____ is expected to be much more productive during its early years, so that depreciation expense will more accurately represent how much of an asset's usefulness is being used up each year. For tax purposes, _____ provides a way of deferring corporate income taxes by reducing taxable income in current years, in exchange for increased taxable income in future years. This is a valuable tax incentive that encourages businesses to purchase new assets.

Exam Probability: **High**

34. *Answer choices:*

(see index for correct answer)

- a. Fixed asset register
- b. Commuted cash value
- c. Accounting identity
- d. Accelerated depreciation

Guidance: level 1

:: Accounting in the United States ::

Established in 1988, the _____ is a professional organization of fraud examiners. Its activities include producing fraud information, tools and training. The ACFE grants the professional designation of Certified Fraud Examiner. The ACFE is the world's largest anti-fraud organization and is a provider of anti-fraud training and education, with more than 85,000 members.

Exam Probability: **High**

35. *Answer choices:*

(see index for correct answer)

- a. Association of Certified Fraud Examiners
- b. Uniform Certified Public Accountant Examination
- c. Federal Accounting Standards Advisory Board
- d. Certified Government Financial Manager

Guidance: level 1

:: Finance ::

The _____ of a corporation is the accumulated net income of the corporation that is retained by the corporation at a particular point of time, such as at the end of the reporting period. At the end of that period, the net income at that point is transferred from the Profit and Loss Account to the _____ account. If the balance of the _____ account is negative it may be called accumulated losses, retained losses or accumulated deficit, or similar terminology.

Exam Probability: **Medium**

36. *Answer choices:*
(see index for correct answer)

- a. Debt-snowball method
- b. Tick size
- c. Probability of default
- d. Euribor

Guidance: level 1

:: Financial accounting ::

_____ in accounting is the process of treating investments in associate companies. Equity accounting is usually applied where an investor entity holds 20–50% of the voting stock of the associate company. The investor records such investments as an asset on its balance sheet. The investor's proportional share of the associate company's net income increases the investment, and proportional payments of dividends decrease it. In the investor's income statement, the proportional share of the investor's net income or net loss is reported as a single-line item.

Exam Probability: **Low**

37. *Answer choices:*

(see index for correct answer)

- a. Equity method
- b. Hidden asset
- c. Commuted cash value
- d. Controlling interest

Guidance: level 1

:: Management ::

_____ is a style of business management that focuses on identifying and handling cases that deviate from the norm, recommended as best practice by the project management method PRINCE2.

Exam Probability: **Medium**

38. *Answer choices:*

(see index for correct answer)

- a. Management by exception
- b. Systems analysis
- c. Success-oriented management
- d. Semiconductor consolidation

Guidance: level 1

:: Accounting terminology ::

> _____ is an accounting system for recording resources whose use has been limited by the donor, grant authority, governing agency, or other individuals or organisations or by law. It emphasizes accountability rather than profitability, and is used by Nonprofit organizations and by governments. In this method, a fund consists of a self-balancing set of accounts and each are reported as either unrestricted, temporarily restricted or permanently restricted based on the provider-imposed restrictions.

Exam Probability: **High**

39. *Answer choices:*

(see index for correct answer)

- a. Fund accounting
- b. profit and loss statement
- c. Internal auditing

- d. Chart of accounts

Guidance: level 1

:: Generally Accepted Accounting Principles ::

_____, or non-current liabilities, are liabilities that are due beyond a year or the normal operation period of the company. The normal operation period is the amount of time it takes for a company to turn inventory into cash. On a classified balance sheet, liabilities are separated between current and _____ to help users assess the company's financial standing in short-term and long-term periods. _____ give users more information about the long-term prosperity of the company, while current liabilities inform the user of debt that the company owes in the current period. On a balance sheet, accounts are listed in order of liquidity, so _____ come after current liabilities. In addition, the specific long-term liability accounts are listed on the balance sheet in order of liquidity. Therefore, an account due within eighteen months would be listed before an account due within twenty-four months. Examples of _____ are bonds payable, long-term loans, capital leases, pension liabilities, post-retirement healthcare liabilities, deferred compensation, deferred revenues, deferred income taxes, and derivative liabilities.

Exam Probability: **Low**

40. *Answer choices:*
(see index for correct answer)

- a. Long-term liabilities
- b. Goodwill
- c. deferred revenue

- d. French generally accepted accounting principles

Guidance: level 1

:: Accounting journals and ledgers ::

_____ is a daybook or journal which is used to record transactions relating to adjustment entries, opening stock, accounting errors etc. The source documents of this prime entry book are journal voucher, copy of management reports and invoices.

Exam Probability: **Medium**

41. *Answer choices:*

(see index for correct answer)

- a. Subledger
- b. Subsidiary ledger
- c. Check register
- d. General journal

Guidance: level 1

:: Financial accounting ::

_____ is a financial metric which represents operating liquidity available to a business, organisation or other entity, including governmental entities. Along with fixed assets such as plant and equipment, _____ is considered a part of operating capital. Gross _____ is equal to current assets. _____ is calculated as current assets minus current liabilities. If current assets are less than current liabilities, an entity has a _____ deficiency, also called a _____ deficit.

Exam Probability: **Low**

42. *Answer choices:*

(see index for correct answer)

- a. Hidden asset
- b. Controlling interest
- c. Working capital
- d. Finance charge

Guidance: level 1

:: Commerce ::

A _____, is a document acknowledging that a person has received money or property in payment following a sale or other transfer of goods or provision of a service. All _____s must have the date of purchase on them. If the recipient of the payment is legally required to collect sales tax or VAT from the customer, the amount would be added to the _____ and the collection would be deemed to have been on behalf of the relevant tax authority. In many countries, a retailer is required to include the sales tax or VAT in the displayed price of goods sold, from which the tax amount would be calculated at point of sale and remitted to the tax authorities in due course. Similarly, amounts may be deducted from amounts payable, as in the case of wage withholding taxes. On the other hand, tips or other gratuities given by a customer, for example in a restaurant, would not form part of the payment amount or appear on the _____.

Exam Probability: **Medium**

43. *Answer choices:*

(see index for correct answer)

- a. GT Nexus
- b. Reseller
- c. Receipt
- d. Oniomania

Guidance: level 1

:: International taxation ::

_____ is the levying of tax by two or more jurisdictions on the same declared income, asset, or financial transaction. Double liability is mitigated in a number of ways, for example.

Exam Probability: **Medium**

44. *Answer choices:*

(see index for correct answer)

- a. Tax information exchange agreement
- b. Double taxation
- c. Passive foreign investment company
- d. Foreign personal holding company

Guidance: level 1

:: ::

In accounting, the _____ is a measure of the number of times inventory is sold or used in a time period such as a year. It is calculated to see if a business has an excessive inventory in comparison to its sales level. The equation for _____ equals the cost of goods sold divided by the average inventory. _____ is also known as inventory turns, merchandise turnover, stockturn, stock turns, turns, and stock turnover.

Exam Probability: **High**

45. Answer choices:

(see index for correct answer)

- a. open system
- b. process perspective
- c. surface-level diversity
- d. functional perspective

Guidance: level 1

:: Accounting terminology ::

_____ are liabilities that reflect expenses that have not yet been paid or logged under accounts payable during an accounting period; in other words, a company's obligation to pay for goods and services that have been provided for which invoices have not yet been received. Examples would include accrued wages payable, accrued sales tax payable, and accrued rent payable.

Exam Probability: **High**

46. Answer choices:

(see index for correct answer)

- a. Accounts receivable
- b. Accrued liabilities
- c. Accounts payable
- d. Fund accounting

Guidance: level 1

:: Manufacturing ::

_____ s are goods that have completed the manufacturing process but have not yet been sold or distributed to the end user.

Exam Probability: **High**

47. *Answer choices:*

(see index for correct answer)

- a. Manufacturing bill of materials
- b. Quick response
- c. Finished good
- d. Agri-Fab, Inc.

Guidance: level 1

:: Accounting software ::

_____ is any item or verifiable record that is generally accepted as payment for goods and services and repayment of debts, such as taxes, in a particular country or socio-economic context. The main functions of _____ are distinguished as: a medium of exchange, a unit of account, a store of value and sometimes, a standard of deferred payment. Any item or verifiable record that fulfils these functions can be considered as _____ .

Exam Probability: **Medium**

48. *Answer choices:*

(see index for correct answer)

- a. Money
- b. Quicken
- c. AME Accounting Software
- d. BIG4books

Guidance: level 1

:: ::

A _____ , in the word's original meaning, is a sheet of paper on which one performs work. They come in many forms, most commonly associated with children's school work assignments, tax forms, and accounting or other business environments. Software is increasingly taking over the paper-based _____ .

Exam Probability: **High**

49. *Answer choices:*

(see index for correct answer)

- a. Worksheet
- b. Sarbanes-Oxley act of 2002
- c. co-culture
- d. levels of analysis

Guidance: level 1

:: Stock market ::

A _____ , equity market or share market is the aggregation of buyers and sellers of stocks , which represent ownership claims on businesses; these may include securities listed on a public stock exchange, as well as stock that is only traded privately. Examples of the latter include shares of private companies which are sold to investors through equity crowdfunding platforms. Stock exchanges list shares of common equity as well as other security types, e.g. corporate bonds and convertible bonds.

Exam Probability: **High**

50. *Answer choices:*

(see index for correct answer)

- a. Stock Market
- b. Shareholders
- c. Microcap stock

- d. Paper valuation

Guidance: level 1

:: Generally Accepted Accounting Principles ::

> In accounting, an economic item's _____ is the original nominal monetary value of that item. _____ accounting involves reporting assets and liabilities at their _____ s, which are not updated for changes in the items' values. Consequently, the amounts reported for these balance sheet items often differ from their current economic or market values.

Exam Probability: **High**

51. *Answer choices:*
(see index for correct answer)

- a. Gross profit
- b. Profit
- c. Historical cost
- d. Petty cash

Guidance: level 1

:: Tax law ::

_____ or revenue law is an area of legal study which deals with the constitutional, common-law, statutory, tax treaty, and regulatory rules that constitute the law applicable to taxation.

Exam Probability: **Low**

52. *Answer choices:*

(see index for correct answer)

- a. Tax Court of Canada
- b. Tax Law Rewrite Project
- c. Tax law
- d. First-tier Tribunal

Guidance: level 1

:: Auditing ::

An _____ is a security-relevant chronological record, set of records, and/or destination and source of records that provide documentary evidence of the sequence of activities that have affected at any time a specific operation, procedure, or event. Audit records typically result from activities such as financial transactions, scientific research and health care data transactions, or communications by individual people, systems, accounts, or other entities.

Exam Probability: **Medium**

53. Answer choices:

(see index for correct answer)

- a. Continuous auditing
- b. Event data
- c. Audit trail
- d. Legal auditing

Guidance: level 1

:: Generally Accepted Accounting Principles ::

> In accounting, _____ , gross margin, sales profit, or credit sales is the difference between revenue and the cost of making a product or providing a service, before deducting overheads, payroll, taxation, and interest payments. This is different from operating profit . Gross margin is the term normally used in the U.S., while _____ is the more common usage in the UK and Australia.

Exam Probability: **High**

54. Answer choices:

(see index for correct answer)

- a. net realisable value
- b. Cost pool
- c. Gross profit
- d. Gross sales

Guidance: level 1

:: Credit card terminology ::

A _____ is the transfer of the balance in an account to another account, often held at another institution. It is most commonly used when describing a credit card _____ .

Exam Probability: **Low**

55. *Answer choices:*
(see index for correct answer)

- a. Merchant category code
- b. Acceptance mark
- c. Billing descriptor
- d. Balance transfer

Guidance: level 1

:: Financial ratios ::

In finance, the _____ , also known as the acid-test ratio is a type of liquidity ratio which measures the ability of a company to use its near cash or quick assets to extinguish or retire its current liabilities immediately. Quick assets include those current assets that presumably can be quickly converted to cash at close to their book values. It is the ratio between quickly available or liquid assets and current liabilities.

Exam Probability: **High**

56. *Answer choices:*

(see index for correct answer)

- a. Dividend yield
- b. Debt service ratio
- c. Quick ratio
- d. Market-to-book

Guidance: level 1

:: Shareholders ::

A _____ is a payment made by a corporation to its shareholders, usually as a distribution of profits. When a corporation earns a profit or surplus, the corporation is able to re-invest the profit in the business and pay a proportion of the profit as a _____ to shareholders. Distribution to shareholders may be in cash or, if the corporation has a _____ reinvestment plan, the amount can be paid by the issue of further shares or share repurchase. When _____ s are paid, shareholders typically must pay income taxes, and the corporation does not receive a corporate income tax deduction for the _____ payments.

Exam Probability: **Low**

57. *Answer choices:*

(see index for correct answer)

- a. Friedman doctrine
- b. Dividend
- c. Shotgun clause
- d. UK Shareholders Association

Guidance: level 1

:: Land value taxation ::

_____, sometimes referred to as dry _____, is the solid surface of Earth that is not permanently covered by water. The vast majority of human activity throughout history has occurred in _____ areas that support agriculture, habitat, and various natural resources. Some life forms have developed from predecessor species that lived in bodies of water.

Exam Probability: **Low**

58. *Answer choices:*

(see index for correct answer)

- a. Henry George
- b. Land value tax
- c. Physiocracy
- d. Land

Guidance: level 1

:: Taxation and efficiency ::

_____ is the legal usage of the tax regime in a single territory to one's own advantage to reduce the amount of tax that is payable by means that are within the law. Tax sheltering is very similar, although unlike _____ tax sheltering is not necessarily legal. Tax havens are jurisdictions which facilitate reduced taxes.

Exam Probability: **Low**

59. *Answer choices:*

(see index for correct answer)

- a. Tax avoidance
- b. supply-side

- c. Supply-side economics
- d. Fiscal illusion

Guidance: level 1

INDEX: Correct Answers

Foundations of Business

1. b: Accounts receivable

2. c: Planning

3. d: Policy

4. c: Sexual harassment

5. c: Specification

6. b: Market segmentation

7. d: Raw material

8. c: Capitalism

9. d: Social security

10. d: Currency

11. b: Performance

12. d: Entrepreneurship

13. b: Manufacturing

14. a: Commerce

15. : Supply chain

16. c: Percentage

17. d: Information systems

18. b: Retail

19. a: Venture capital

20. c: Resource

21. a: Stock market

22. : Benchmarking

23. a: Selling

24. a: Preference

25. b: Balanced scorecard

26. a: Arthur Andersen

27. d: Trade agreement

28. a: Human resources

29. d: Marketing mix

30. a: Business plan

31. b: Industry

32. c: Recession

33. d: Marketing research

34. : Quality control

35. a: Bribery

36. c: Stock exchange

37. d: Solution

38. d: Management system

39. d: Debt

40. d: Market value

41. a: Risk

42. b: Subsidiary

43. c: Property rights

44. a: Import

45. b: Small business

46. c: Career

47. a: Asset

48. a: Investment

49. a: Finance

50. d: ASEAN

51. d: Direct investment

52. c: Business model

53. a: Customs

54. c: Authority

55. c: Foreign direct investment

56. c: Payment

57. a: Office

58. a: Cooperation

59. : Frequency

Management

1. d: Social loafing

2. c: Performance measurement

3. c: Interdependence

4. c: Layoff

5. d: Environmental protection

6. d: Productivity

7. a: Career

8. d: European Union

9. d: Innovation

10. b: Vendor

11. : International trade

12. d: Performance appraisal

13. c: Intellectual property

14. d: Grievance

15. b: Knowledge management

16. b: North American Free Trade Agreement

17. c: Forecasting

18. a: Job analysis

19. a: Checklist

20. d: Discipline

21. : Coaching

22. a: Authority

23. d: Environmental scanning

24. c: Training and development

25. : Inventory control

26. d: Trade agreement

27. : Human resource management

28. c: Cost leadership

29. d: Centralization

30. d: Time management

31. : Decision tree

32. c: Interaction

33. : Risk management

34. : Initiative

35. a: Collaboration

36. : Strategic planning

37. : Distance

38. : Emotional intelligence

39. : Product design

40. a: Asset

41. d: Job rotation

42. d: Perception

43. c: Market research

44. : Ambiguity

45. d: Job enlargement

46. : Good

47. : Strategic management

48. d: SWOT analysis

49. d: Scientific management

50. c: Empowerment

51. c: Self-assessment

52. d: Variable cost

53. c: Individualism

54. c: Problem solving

55. d: Supervisor

56. : Policy

57. c: Telecommuting

58. a: Six Sigma

59. a: Business process

Business law

1. : World Trade Organization

2. c: Anticipatory repudiation

3. d: Disclaimer

4. a: Product liability

5. d: Incentive

6. a: Service mark

7. c: Puffery

8. b: Negotiation

9. : Insider trading

10. : Joint venture

11. b: Intellectual property

12. b: Bailee

13. a: Respondeat superior

14. c: Exclusionary rule

15. c: Interest

16. : Defamation

17. c: Categorical imperative

18. : Manufacturing

19. d: Security agreement

20. : Apparent authority

21. b: Constitution

22. a: Deed

23. b: Summary judgment

24. c: Wage

25. a: Impossibility

26. c: Parol evidence

27. b: Misrepresentation

28. c: Authority

29. a: Adoption

30. b: Money laundering

31. c: General partnership

32. a: Testimony

33. : Corporation

34. : Cooperative

35. b: Berne Convention

36. b: Rescind

37. d: Administrative law

38. c: Commerce Clause

39. a: Petition

40. a: Lien

41. b: Firm

42. : Hearing

43. c: Relevant market

44. : Credit

45. a: Security

46. a: Shareholder

47. : Certiorari

48. c: Appeal

49. : Offeree

50. a: Prima facie

51. b: Contributory negligence

52. b: Res ipsa

53. d: Shares

54. d: Trial

55. a: Corruption

56. a: Charter

57. : Presumption

58. a: Standing

59. : Contract

Finance

1. b: Bank

2. a: Commercial bank

3. c: Credit

4. c: Stock split

5. d: Rate of return

6. c: Absorption costing

7. d: Advertising

8. : Government bond

9. a: Journal entry

10. d: General ledger

11. a: Monetary policy

12. b: Financial market

13. b: Financial risk

14. : Market risk

15. d: Corporate governance

16. : Deferral

17. c: Capital budgeting

18. d: Arbitrage

19. b: Pension fund

20. : Going concern

21. c: Aging

22. : Retirement

23. d: Amortization

24. : Forecasting

25. b: Futures contract

26. d: Public company

27. : Vacation

28. : Partnership

29. a: Accounts payable

30. b: Asset management

31. c: Risk premium

32. : Equity method

33. a: Internal rate of return

34. d: Rate risk

35. c: Current asset

36. c: Free cash flow

37. b: Adjusting entries

38. c: Write-off

39. : Trade

40. c: Yield to maturity

41. c: Financial analysis

42. d: Operating Income

43. b: Financial accounting

44. c: Chief financial officer

45. b: Commercial paper

46. c: Future value

47. c: Shares

48. a: Cash equivalent

49. c: Presentation

50. : Strategy

51. b: Tax rate

52. d: Property

53. c: Demand

54. : Generally accepted accounting principles

55. c: Stockholder

56. c: Management

57. a: Merger

58. b: Working capital

59. d: Security

Human resource management

1. d: Compa-ratio

2. d: Unfair labor practice

3. c: Organizational socialization

4. d: Deferred compensation

5. d: Labor force

6. a: Succession planning

7. b: Card check

8. a: Job sharing

9. a: Resignation

10. d: International Brotherhood of Teamsters

11. c: Career management

12. c: Occupational Information Network

13. c: Online assessment

14. b: Nepotism

15. a: Persuasion

16. : Transformational leadership

17. d: Licensure

18. a: Seniority

19. b: Stock appreciation right

20. c: Interview

21. b: Executive compensation

22. a: Global sourcing

23. d: Concurrent validity

24. c: Prevailing wage

25. d: Closed shop

26. c: Job satisfaction

27. : Intuition

28. d: Enforcement

29. : Social loafing

30. : Pension

31. c: Case interview

32. b: McDonnell Douglas Corp. v. Green

33. c: Coaching

34. d: Collective bargaining

35. d: Construct validity

36. a: Leadership development

37. c: Graveyard shift

38. b: Tacit knowledge

39. d: Phantom stock

40. a: Equal Employment Opportunity Commission

41. c: Industrial relations

42. b: Talent management

43. : Organizational commitment

44. a: Labor union

45. a: Cost leadership

46. c: Just cause

47. b: Needs assessment

48. d: Unemployment

49. c: Rating scale

50. b: Living wage

51. : Job enlargement

52. c: Learning organization

53. b: Globalization

54. b: Test validity

55. d: Agency shop

56. c: Recession

57. : Human resource management

58. : Employment

59. a: Structured interview

Information systems

1. : Geographic information system

2. c: Galileo

3. d: Virtual world

4. : Authentication

5. : Data cleansing

6. : Mobile computing

7. b: Census

8. a: Enterprise systems

9. : Decision-making

10. c: Sustainable

11. : Google Calendar

12. : System software

13. d: Trojan horse

14. c: Consumerization

15. c: E-commerce

16. c: Business model

17. b: Data

18. a: Fraud

19. a: Network management

20. : Netscape

21. b: Intranet

22. : Government-to-government

23. c: Monopoly

24. : ICANN

25. a: Identity theft

26. : Data governance

27. d: Government-to-citizen

28. b: Sensitivity analysis

29. d: Tacit knowledge

30. a: Information management

31. c: Local Area Network

32. c: Information overload

33. : Security management

34. d: COBIT

35. a: Mass customization

36. : Web server

37. d: Mobile commerce

38. c: Mouse

39. a: Economies of scale

40. b: Database design

41. a: Botnet

42. c: Electronic data interchange

43. a: Worm

44. a: Automated teller machine

45. a: Data analysis

46. d: Query by Example

47. d: Groupware

48. a: Word

49. c: Pop-up ad

50. a: Executive information system

51. b: Change management

52. d: Payment Card Industry Data Security Standard

53. c: Fault tolerance

54. b: Affiliate marketing

55. a: Analytics

56. a: Netflix

57. : Avatar

58. d: Top-level domain

59. d: Smart card

Marketing

1. b: Preference

2. b: Consultant

3. d: Federal Trade Commission

4. d: Loyalty

5. a: Direct selling

6. d: Cooperative

7. : Negotiation

8. b: Advertising campaign

9. : Competitive intelligence

10. b: Information technology

11. c: Product differentiation

12. b: Gross domestic product

13. : Resource

14. : Appeal

15. d: Corporation

16. c: New product development

17. b: Budget

18. a: Cost

19. b: Wall Street Journal

20. c: Total cost

21. b: Respondent

22. b: Warranty

23. a: Insurance

24. : Integrated marketing

25. d: Brand awareness

26. d: Organizational structure

27. b: Strategic alliance

28. b: Household

29. c: Management

30. : Communication

31. : Credit

32. a: Product line

33. a: Argument

34. : Secondary data

35. c: Problem Solving

36. : Tangible

37. b: Distribution channel

38. d: Brand

39. d: Coupon

40. c: Quantitative research

41. b: Market segmentation

42. : Good

43. c: Blog

44. : Pricing

45. b: Copyright

46. b: Department store

47. b: Creative brief

48. d: Product placement

49. d: Loyalty program

50. b: Value proposition

51. d: Contract

52. c: Retail

53. a: Bottom line

54. c: Testimonial

55. : Manager

56. : Demand

57. b: Supply chain

58. b: Entrepreneur

59. d: Marketing

Manufacturing

1. c: Consortium

2. b: Goal

3. d: Average cost

4. a: Turbine

5. c: Total productive maintenance

6. d: Business process

7. d: Quality management

8. c: Quality by Design

9. d: Knowledge management

10. d: Supply chain

11. b: Mary Kay

12. : Aggregate planning

13. d: Inspection

14. c: EFQM

15. a: Extended enterprise

16. c: Economic order quantity

17. a: Assembly line

18. a: Supply chain risk management

19. : Solution

20. b: Process capital

21. : Clay

22. : Lead

23. d: Heat transfer

24. b: Quality assurance

25. c: Service quality

26. d: Chemical reaction

27. b: Furnace

28. b: Process engineering

29. c: New product development

30. b: Cash register

31. d: E-commerce

32. : Sony

33. b: Asset

34. c: Cost driver

35. : Technical support

36. c: Poka-yoke

37. a: Schedule

38. b: Inventory control

39. c: Reboiler

40. a: Capacity planning

41. : Steering committee

42. : Flowchart

43. b: Product differentiation

44. : Workflow

45. c: Purchasing process

46. d: Authority

47. a: Cost estimate

48. : Credit

49. c: Thomas Register

50. d: Minitab

51. b: Kaizen

52. d: Natural resource

53. : Bullwhip effect

54. d: Value engineering

55. b: Customer

56. a: Request for quotation

57. b: Process management

58. b: Total cost

59. a: Third-party logistics

Commerce

1. c: Collaborative filtering

2. b: Staff position

3. d: Tool

4. b: Pop-up ad

5. c: Compromise

6. : Merger

7. b: Policy

8. d: Cost structure

9. b: Dutch auction

10. a: Liquidation

11. c: Good

12. a: Microsoft

13. b: Freight forwarder

14. : Return on investment

15. d: Publicity

16. d: Payment card

17. a: Commerce

18. : Payment system

19. d: Productivity

20. d: Transaction cost

21. a: Marginal cost

22. d: Level of service

23. b: Empowerment

24. b: Competitor

25. b: Monopoly

26. b: Recruitment

27. c: Procurement

28. b: Semantic

29. d: Information system

30. a: Pension

31. : Value-added network

32. d: Accounting

33. d: Quality control

34. c: Product mix

35. a: Regulation

36. c: Information technology

37. b: Public policy

38. c: Free market

39. d: Consumer-to-consumer

40. c: Short run

41. b: Credit card

42. a: Interest

43. a: Jurisdiction

44. d: Market segmentation

45. : Planning

46. : Insurance

47. c: European Union

48. d: Market research

49. b: Corporation

50. : Aid

51. c: Board of directors

52. b: Import

53. d: Basket

54. : Customs

55. : Stock

56. b: Production line

57. a: Permission marketing

58. b: Social shopping

59. : Frequency

Business ethics

1. c: Better Business Bureau

2. : Socialism

3. d: Organizational structure

4. c: Habitat

5. a: Nonprofit

6. c: Electronic waste

7. b: Community development financial institution

8. b: Statutory law

9. b: Minimum wage

10. b: Insider trading

11. d: Consumer Protection

12. c: Corporate citizenship

13. a: UN Global Compact

14. b: Employee Polygraph Protection Act

15. b: Wall Street

16. a: Chamber of Commerce

17. d: Greenwashing

18. d: Communist Manifesto

19. a: Clean Water Act

20. a: Risk management

21. c: Hedonism

22. d: Natural gas

23. c: Retaliation

24. a: Cultural relativism

25. a: Utilitarianism

26. : Parental leave

27. b: Pollution

28. b: Constitutional law

29. d: Siemens

30. b: Whistleblower

31. b: Interlocking directorate

32. a: Fraud

33. c: Sustainability

34. c: Trojan horse

35. c: Sexual harassment

36. : Working poor

37. b: Collusion

38. a: Forest Stewardship Council

39. d: Ethics Resource Center

40. d: Oil spill

41. a: Capitalism

42. b: Guerrilla Marketing

43. c: Catholicism

44. d: Fannie Mae

45. : Consumer Financial Protection Bureau

46. a: Internal control

47. c: Six Sigma

48. c: Auditor independence

49. c: Biofuel

50. d: Sustainable

51. b: Model Rules of Professional Conduct

52. : Medicare fraud

53. d: Coal

54. d: Kyoto Protocol

55. a: Federal Trade Commission Act

56. : Pollution Prevention

57. a: East Germany

58. c: Edgewood College

59. : Transocean

Accounting

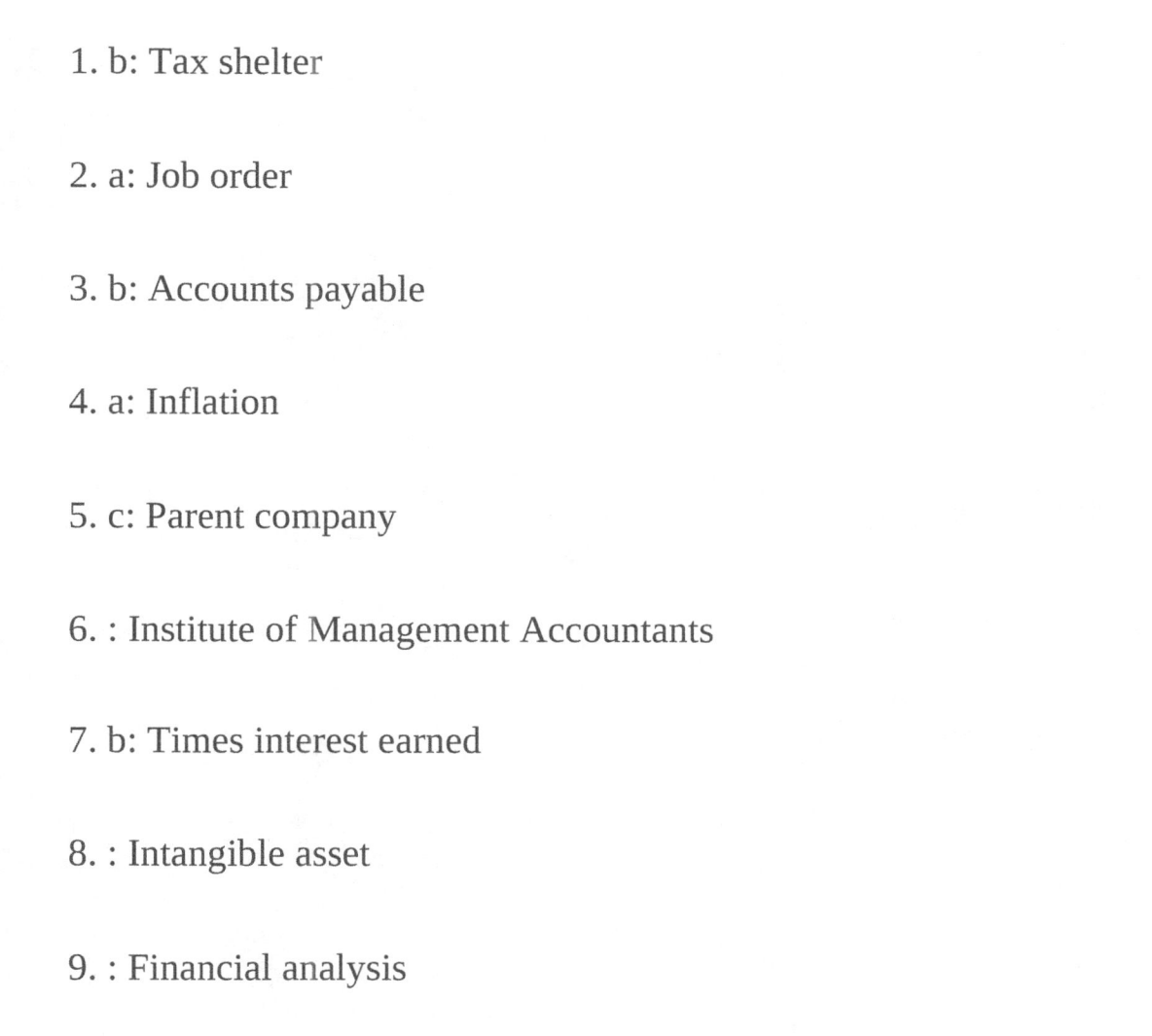

1. b: Tax shelter

2. a: Job order

3. b: Accounts payable

4. a: Inflation

5. c: Parent company

6. : Institute of Management Accountants

7. b: Times interest earned

8. : Intangible asset

9. : Financial analysis

10. a: Accounting method

11. b: Bank

12. b: Net realizable value

13. c: Inventory

14. c: Operating budget

15. c: Encumbrance

16. b: Cost driver

17. b: Corporation

18. d: Incentive

19. c: Contribution margin

20. b: Manufacturing overhead

21. c: Ending inventory

22. : Debenture

23. : Bad debt

24. : Expense account

25. b: Management accounting

26. : Preferred stock

27. a: Creditor

28. d: Adoption

29. : Regulation S-K

30. d: Balanced scorecard

31. a: Local government

32. a: Financial accounting

33. b: Governmental accounting

34. d: Accelerated depreciation

35. a: Association of Certified Fraud Examiners

36. : Retained earnings

37. a: Equity method

38. a: Management by exception

39. a: Fund accounting

40. a: Long-term liabilities

41. d: General journal

42. c: Working capital

43. c: Receipt

44. b: Double taxation

45. : Inventory turnover

46. b: Accrued liabilities

47. c: Finished good

48. a: Money

49. a: Worksheet

50. a: Stock Market

51. c: Historical cost

52. c: Tax law

53. c: Audit trail

54. c: Gross profit

55. d: Balance transfer

56. c: Quick ratio

57. b: Dividend

58. d: Land

59. a: Tax avoidance